P.ASS.
Practical Academic Support Services

The Performance Test

ISBN 978-0-9740089-1-2

Printed in the USA.

Published by:
Practical Academic Support Services, LLC.
8306 Wilshire Blvd, Ste. 1803
Beverly Hills, CA 90211
www.passlaw.com

Distributed by:
Legal Books Distributing
4247 Whiteside Street
Los Angeles, CA 90063
(323) 526-7110
www.discovery-press.com

PASS THE PERFORMANCE TEST

TABLE OF CONTENTS

Introduction

Some call the California Bar Exam a "nightmare," the biggest challenge of your life. Others say, "It's not so bad. I spent most of my summer studying at the beach." (This is, after all, the *California* Bar Exam!) The truth lies somewhere between these extremes. Expect to work hard, really hard. Then, after it's over, you too can tell your success stories. You too can think back on having *passed the Bar Exam* as yet one more of your many accomplishments.

The primary purpose of this book is to guide you to success on the Performance Test portion of the California Bar Exam. Along the way, though, you will find lots of information that will help you pass the essays and multistate portions of the Exam, and tips that will help you cope with the stress and pressure of the California Bar Exam as a whole.

Just as with any big challenge you face, the essential keys to success on the Bar Exam are: 1. PREPARATION, 2. SKILL, and 3. CONFIDENCE.

1. PREPARATION: Get *prepared* by reading this book. Learn what a performance test is and how to write passing performance test answers.

2. SKILL: The performance test requires you to be proficient in four substantive lawyering skills:

> *Legal Analysis,
> *Fact Analysis,
> *Awareness of Professional Responsibility, and
> *Problem Solving.

And success on any given performance test also requires a strong command of other, general professional skills, the most important of which are:

> *Reading comprehension,
> *Clear, effective writing, and
> *Good time management.

Read this book thoroughly, and you will understand what is meant by each of the skills listed above. You will learn how the skills are tested, what tasks you will likely have to complete, and how you can write exam answers to effectively prove to the graders that you are proficient in these required skills.

Next, practice and sharpen your skills. You will find a number of practice exams and sample answers in the Appendix portion of this book. Practice by doing these actual past performance tests, under timed conditions, and then analyzing the sample answers. Compare and contrast the sample answers with your own responses. Ask yourself, how can I make my answer better? Then rewrite your answer, and continue to practice with new exams, writing and rewriting, until you are satisfied that you are consistently writing passing quality answers.

3. CONFIDENCE: Last, but definitely not least, is *confidence*. Make this the last (and, if it is your first, the only) California Bar Exam you take. You need to walk in that California Bar Exam doorway, that "battlefield," six times (once for each of three consecutive morning sessions and again for each afternoon session). Once you pass, you have a lifetime ticket! You never have to do it again. But, in order to pass, you must go in *wanting* to pass, knowing that you *can* pass, and believing that you *will* pass the Bar Exam. The more prepared you are and the sharper your skills are, the more confident you will naturally be. You can also boost your confidence using the tools and strategies detailed in Chapter 8, "Success Strategies," to help carry you through the three long days on your road to passing.

Chapter 1: General Information on the California Bar Exam

The Bar Exam is a marathon, not a sprint. And the California Bar Exam is one of the most difficult Bar Exams in the nation. You will have to be ON, big time, for three long days. On Tuesday and Thursday, California applicants are given three one-hour essay questions in the morning and one three-hour performance test in the afternoon. On Wednesday, the Multistate Bar Examination (MBE) is administered. The MBE consists of a set of 100 multiple-choice questions for three hours in the morning, and a second set of 100 such questions in the afternoon.

Testing begins on each of the three days at approximately 9 a.m., but with pre-test administration and identification procedures, you are well advised to arrive early. The same is true after lunch and before the afternoon sessions; you will often be asked to come back to the test site early for identification procedures and other administrative matters. So, your typical Bar days look something like this:

Tuesday's and Thursday's Approximate Schedule
8:30-9:00	Identification Procedures
9:00-12:00	Three one-hour essays
12:00-1:30	Lunch Break
1:30-2:00	Identification Procedures
2:00-5:00	Performance Test

Wednesday's Approximate Schedule*
8:30-9:00	Identification Procedures
9:00-12:00	100 MBE questions
12:00-1:30	Lunch Break
1:30-2:00	Identification Procedures
2:00-5:00	100 MBE questions

*Qualifying out-of-state lawyers may take what is known as the "Attorney's Exam," which consists of only the first and third days of the Bar Exam; the essays and performance tests. If you are taking the Attorney's Exam, your exam will not include the multistate portion, so you will have the day off on Wednesday. (For more information on whether or not you qualify for the Attorney's Exam or how to register as an attorney applicant, contact the State Bar directly. Their web address is www.calbar.ca.gov.)

THE BAR EXAM LOGISTICS AND CALENDARING

The Bar Exam is administered twice annually, near the end of July and the end of February. You may register to take the Exam at either of those times and in any one of a number of different locations statewide, from San Diego to San Francisco.

Students typically register with the Committee of Bar Examiners during their first year of law school. Students attending those law schools that are not ABA- or State Bar-accredited must also take and pass the First-Year Law Students' Exam (often called "The Baby Bar") before they may take the Bar Exam. Toward the end of law school, students should take the MPRE (Multistate Professional Responsibility Exam) and complete the moral character and remaining portions of the Bar Exam application forms.

If at all possible, you should plan to take off the full two months prior to the July or February date that you plan to take the Bar Exam. You will need this time to focus on studying and preparing yourself for the Big Three Days. (More on general study tips in Chapter 8, "Success Strategies.")

THE BAR EXAM APPLICATION

By the time you are reading this book, you may be able to congratulate yourself on having completed one of the worst parts of the Bar Exam: the application. If not, you have something to look forward to! Just the moral character portion alone is enough to give most of us a headache. (And *caveat*, until the moral character portion of your application is received and approved, *you are not eligible* to practice law. The approval process can take many months, so do not delay.)

What a way to start! Get ready to search through all sorts of old documents. You may need to fish out anything from long disregarded tax returns to old letters in order to document addresses back 10 years or employers sometimes back to age 18. You must submit a photo and fingerprints. The fingerprinting process has changed and if you are a California resident, you must have your prints 'scanned'. Not all police stations have this technology, so check site availability through the Attorney General's website at www.ag.ca.gov/fingerprints/publications. And do not leave fingerprinting to the day before the application is due. Bar Exam late fees can run into hundreds of dollars depending on just how late you are.

One applicant tells her story of missing fingerprint day at her law school and having to find a nearby police station to take the authorized fingerprints: *After trying West Hollywood and Culver City and having both be unavailable for various scheduling reasons, I ended up having my fingerprints taken at the Santa Monica police station, just after a very large handcuffed prisoner!* Moral of the story, call ahead and find out the hours and availability of your local police station's fingerprinting services.

If you are already familiar with the fingerprinting process, that is to say if you have ever been convicted in a criminal proceeding, the Committee will want to know about it. All about it. In fact, they will even ask if you have ever been a party to a civil action. Do not assume that an old college drug or protest-type arrest will foreclose your moral fitness to practice law, but do be as complete, candid, and thorough as possible. Withholding essential information may be a fatal strike against your admission to the California Bar.

You will also have to give the Committee names and addresses of references who will attest to your moral fitness. These people may not be relatives or employers (present or former). Friends, colleagues, or professors may be good sources. The Committee *does* follow through and actually questions these people, so be sure to tell your prospective references to expect mail from the Bar Examiners. Correspondence from the Committee may look like junk mail, and you do not want one of your references to throw out the questionnaire by mistake. While you are at it, provide your references with postage for the envelope they will have to mail back to the Committee, and a stamped self-addressed envelope to send you a copy of the form they complete, if they do not mind sending you a copy of what they have written. *Note*: If someone does express reservations about showing you what they write to the Committee of Bar Examiners, you may want to think about whether someone else you know would make a better reference! In addition, ask people you select as references to keep you informed if their address or phone numbers change so you can report those changes to the Committee. Obviously, if your own address or phone number changes during the time your application is pending, report that immediately to the Committee as well. They have to know where to mail results when you pass!

Keep a copy of your application. In fact, open a Bar file, and keep copies of anything you send out or receive in connection with the Bar Exam. If you have a financial source reimbursing you (perhaps a law firm or even parents) or if you are applying for loans or grants to ease Bar Exam preparation and study costs, you may need receipts, canceled checks, and other documentation. You will also be prepared just in case the Committee makes any "clerical errors," for example if they inform you that they did not receive some document you have sent to them.

BAR EXAM SCORING

The California Bar Exam's scoring process can be boiled down to the following: Points are given for each portion of the Bar Exam, 2000 points in total, and these points are then scaled for each individual applicant according to a complex mathematical scaling formula. A passing scaled score is 1440, or 72% of the 2000 point total. Each of the three parts of the Bar Exam—the essays, performance and multistate—makes up a different percentage of the total scaled score an applicant receives: the six essays as a group are worth 39%, the two performance tests are worth 26%, and the MBE is worth 35%.

Do not let these percentages lull you into any false sense that the performance test is not important. Look at the math a little closer. With a zoom lens, you will see that each individual essay is worth 6.5% and each performance test is worth 13%. That means if you do very well on one performance test, you can essentially fail two essays and still pass the Bar Exam. On the flip side, however, if you do poorly on one performance test, you must do a superior job on two separate essay questions to put yourself back on the passing track. Let us illustrate this point with some actual scores.

Graders theoretically can give up to 100 points, in five-point increments, on individual essay and performance test questions. Average scores range from 60 to 80. With scaling, the passing *composite* score for the written portion as a whole may be lower than 70 (often between 66 and 68), but on any one particular essay or performance test ("PT") question a 70 (or above) is considered a passing score and a 65 (or below) a failing score. So if you were to score 60s on your contracts and real property essays (let us say, for instance, that you have a momentary lapse Tuesday about UCC rules and Thursday you miss some issues on easements and covenants), you could still pass the Bar Exam easily with just one 80 on one performance test. Remember, each performance test is worth twice what each essay is worth. If, on either Tuesday or Thursday afternoon, you were to use the preparation, skill, and confidence building techniques you learn in this book and score that one 80, you would be home free. That one 80 would wipe away any detrimental effect from the two problematic essays and, assuming you pass everything else with a 70 average, you would easily pass the Bar Exam.

Therefore, as you can see from analyzing the scoring process as a whole, it is critical to treat the performance test portion of the Bar Exam as seriously as you do the other portions of the Bar, and to prepare for the performance tests using all the tools discussed in this book.

SUBJECT MATTER TESTED ON THE BAR

Since performance tests are "open-book" exams (you are provided with the legal authorities you need to answer the question right there in the Library packet of the exam), you may be tested on *any* area of law at all—substantive or procedural, state or federal, real or test-created. (More on the various packets or booklets, the Library, the File, and other items that you will find on the performance test can be found in the next chapter, "Performance Test Approaches.")

For the MBE, you will have to learn in great detail the national majority rules and some leading minority rules in contracts, torts, real property, constitutional law, criminal law and criminal procedure, and evidence (hereinafter the "MBE subjects").

Your six combined Tuesday and Thursday morning essays could involve issues in one or more of the MBE subjects. In addition, the essays could test your substantive knowledge of national majority and some of the more important minority rules of civil procedure, corporations, wills, trusts, and professional responsibility. Community property is also a potentially testable essay subject, and it is the one subject that tests California law comprehensively (meaning case law and statutory law), though there are select California rules in wills and professional responsibility that you are also responsible for knowing. Finally, test questions in any of these substantive areas (on essay or multiple-choice questions) may involve issues about the relevant remedies that attach to the various rights you have studied, so you have to understand what is typically covered in law school remedies classes as well.

Note: _Changes as of July 2007:_

E*ffective July 2007*, the scope of testable subjects on the California Bar Exam was expanded to include California rules (in addition to the currently tested federal rules) of civil procedure and evidence. Also, what had been the tested only on the law of corporations was enlarged to include other forms of business associations including partnerships, LLCs, and general principles of agency law. For more information on these and any future changes, contact the Committee of Bar Examiners.

Chapter Review Questions for Students taking the Bar*

*Students using this text for a law school performance test course may want to skip this exercise and go directly to the next chapter.

1. I have read all the information the Committee has sent me about the Exam:
___Yes ___No.

2. I have completed all the necessary forms, paperwork and other application requirements:
___ Yes___ No.

3. I believe my main test-taking strengths are:
_____
_____
_____
_____
_____

4. Some test-taking weaknesses I must battle and overcome before the Bar are:
_____
_____
_____
_____
_____

5. The following are things I will try as a "game plan" for overcoming those weaknesses:
_____
_____
_____
_____

Chapter 2: Performance Test Approaches

The performance test (sometimes abbreviated in this book as the "PT") was launched experimentally in 1980 and became a standard part of the California Bar Exam in July 1983. The idea behind the performance test is to test those skills applicants would actually use as attorneys, to test their abilities to handle problems and concerns of clients. To do this, on a performance test applicants are asked to: 1) place themselves in the role of an attorney handling a client's case, 2) read and analyze a set of written materials, and 3) draft some document(s) based upon information from those materials.

Usually, applicants are asked to assume the role of a beginning associate in a private law firm. However, you may have to play a prosecutor, public defender, law clerk to a judge, legal advisor to a legislator, mediator, or another role. Whatever your role, approach the writing task from the perspective of that type of professional, not as a law student. Adopt the tone and vocabulary such a person would use in the particular situation; for example, use plain English and define all "legalese" (technical or jargon terms) when writing documents to lay people.

A. THE PHYSICAL PARTS OF A PERFORMANCE TEST

At the beginning of each performance test, along with a bluebook and scratch paper, you will generally be given two packets or booklets, one called "Instructions and File" and the second called "Library." The Instructions and File usually provide the factual sources and the Library provides the legal sources that you will need to perform the requested tasks.

There have been some fluke PTs that either had no Library or contained additional information packets. For example, one PT contained three packets: File, Library, and Draft Trust Instruments; another contained a File and Transcript, but no Library. In such exams, there are still sources from which you cull *the facts* and sources containing *the law* you need to write the requested documents. To complete these unusual exams successfully, you will use the same strategies and approaches you are learning here, just as you would in the more typical exams.

The most important items on any performance test are those that tell you what to do; the instructions. Performance test instructions are given in two or three parts—the general instructions, the task memo (sometimes called the "senior partner memo" or "transmittal memo"), and sometimes one or more format pages. You will find these instructional documents in the beginning of the "Instructions and File" packet.

The general instructions are largely boilerplate, meaning they are the same or very similar in every exam. However, even though the general instructions tend to be similar in most performance tests, you should get into the habit of taking a few moments out of each exam to review those instructions briefly, as they contain some unique information. The general instructions will tell you how many sets of materials you have to work with in the exam. As noted above, if yours is one of those fluke exams that either does not contain a Library or includes some additional set of material with which to work, you will see that easily from what is usually the third paragraph of the general instructions. (Why is the number of packets you are given important? So that you do not mistakenly assume that a third packet—if they give you one—is just extra scratch paper, and overlook critical information.)

The most important piece of information you will learn to look for in the general instructions, something not repeated elsewhere in the exam, is at the end of the instructions. If your assignment includes drafting more than one document, this is where they will usually state how much each document is worth. The instructions may break it down explicitly, stating "Task A is worth 70% and Task B is worth 30%," or they might simply state, "Both parts are weighted equally." If they give you a percentage split, immediately turn to the task memo (usually the very next document after the general instructions), and note in the margin next to the task memo's detailed instructions how much each one will be worth.

What is the task memo? You will usually find one sentence in the general instructions that reads, "The File contains factual information about your case in the form of [X number of documents]." The first of those documents is a memo to you containing the specific instructions for the document(s) to be drafted from the fictitious person assigning your task, typically the senior partner or your superior, though on at least one performance test the person assigning the task was described as a more junior lawyer. That instructional document will be referred to in this text as the "task memo." (Again, you may also hear that document referred to as either the "senior partner memo" or the "transmittal memo.")

The task memo is your key to success on the performance test! It must be your "Bible," your guide. The task memo should be your constant companion, so rip it out of the Instructions and File booklet, and keep it in front of you throughout the whole three-hour test. (You are free to rip apart the booklets as you wish. The only books that must remain intact are your bluebooks containing your answers.)

Following the task memo, in many performance tests you will find a document or documents that show the format you are to follow in drafting your particular assignment. If they give you such a format, follow it carefully. You will find more information on format pages and how to set up particular exams later in this book. For now, consider any format page a part of your instructions, and plan to keep the format page in front of you as you write the particular task it describes.

After reviewing all the instructional documents (just about 10 minutes into your three-hour exam), you should at least know the following:

- Whom you work for (private law firm, government, or other entity);

- Whom you represent, and some of the basic facts about your client's current problem or situation;

- Where you are located (what state and, if applicable, what federal circuit);

- How many documents the File contains, which one is the task memo, and whether or not you have format pages with which to work;

- What authorities are in the Library (cases, statutes, jury instructions) and the precedential weight of those authorities; and

- What type of document(s) you are to draft; if more than one, how much each is worth; and some basic information on format (either from a format page or from the task memo itself) for each task you are to complete.

B. HOW TO TACKLE A PERFORMANCE TEST: THE PASS APPROACH

Although each person thinks differently, and each performance test is unique, the following six-step passing approach will get you through the materials in any California Performance Test question effectively and efficiently. You do not want to sit down at the Exam and wonder what to review first or how much time to spend on any one booklet. You want a plan, an approach, an effective system. In teaching thousands of students to pass the California Bar Exam, we have determined that the following six steps work, and work well. Practice the approach as you do your practice exams, adapting the timing to complement your own strengths and weaknesses.

1. Skim the General Instructions (2 minutes)

Make sure there is nothing unusual—in other words, note whether your "universe" consists of any documents other than a Library and File. If you are to draft more than one document, note how much weight each will be given, calculate the amount of time you should spend on each task accordingly (see below), and transfer that information immediately to the margin of the task memo. (You will keep the task memo in front of you as you write, but you will likely not need to look back again at the general instructions.)

How should you calculate the time you spend on each task? The Bar Examiners suggest spending no more than 90 minutes reading and analyzing the materials, and, thus, at least 90 minutes organizing and writing your answer(s). If this 90/90 split works for you and the instructions tell you to draft two memos (one memo, a factual analysis worth 80%, and another, a legal analysis worth 20%), you would allocate approximately 72 minutes for the factual memo and 18 minutes for the legal memo.

That said, you may need to alter the 90/90 split *as your own needs dictate*. The suggested times listed for each step in this approach are just that; suggestions. In other words, if you are a slow reader but a fast writer, you may want to spend more than 90 minutes reading and outlining. Or, if you are a very fast reader but need more time to write legibly, you may want to adjust your time accordingly. Learn what works for you by doing practice exams under timed conditions, and then trust yourself on the exam. Just because everyone around you starts to write does not mean that you should if you know you need just a bit more time to read, digest, and effectively organize your answer. Do watch the time carefully, though. Three hours seems like plenty, but you could *easily* spend three days, if not three weeks, on each task. If one task is worth 20% and the other 80%, do not get bogged down on the task worth 20% to the detriment of a complete performance on the other task. Hints in the instructions, such as the fact that it is perfectly acceptable to use short cites (referring to cases by the plaintiff's name only), will also help keep you from getting bogged down in unnecessary detail.

2. Study the Task Memo and any Format Memos (10-15 minutes)

Because the Task Memo and the Format Memos are so important, both as guides for reading the rest of the File and the Library and for structuring passing answers, you should rip these documents out and keep them in front of you throughout the Exam.

Read and reread the task memo and any format pages. Highlight, underline, or in some other way mark the exact tasks you are to perform. Then, to ensure a complete answer, go back to your notes and check off each part you have completed after you finish writing that piece. This should help you to be responsive, to answer the question they ask and *only* the question they ask.

Reading and understanding the instructions may seem self-evident, but it cannot be overemphasized. A frequent criticism of lawyers is lack of responsiveness to clients, and the State Bar wants proof that *you* are attentive to detail and client needs. Also, the more clearly you understand your tasks, the easier it will be to make your way expeditiously through the lengthy File and the Library.

3. Read/Skim the File (20 minutes)

After you have absorbed the information in the instructional documents and understand what document(s) you are expected to complete in the three hours, read the File. As you read and absorb facts, float in your mind the possible legal issues or problems your client faces. Read the File with your end goal (the task or tasks you are to produce) in mind, and with those tasks in mind begin sorting relevant from irrelevant facts.

Time is of the essence; three hours go fast. Knowing your client's concerns and what type of document(s) you are asked to draft (from which you can infer the context in which those concerns have arisen) will help you see many of the legal issues before you even get to the Library (and read the Library authorities much more efficiently when you do get there). Such an analysis will also assist you in determining your client's non-legal problems and make your reading of the rest of the materials more efficient.

4. Read the Library (30 minutes)

Pull out the rules that govern your client's specific problem or concerns. Decide which authorities are good for you (i.e. support your client's position) and which are bad for you (go against your client's position). Think about how you might distinguish those authorities that do not support your client's position. Pay attention to the relative weights of the authorities you are given (know what jurisdiction you are in, and note the dates and jurisdictions of the respective authorities). Try to see how the cases, statutes, and/or other rules you are given fit together. If possible, see how the authorities can help you form a legal structure into which you will weave the facts when you ultimately write your performance test answer. (More on how facts fit into legal structures in subsequent chapters on factual and legal analysis skills.)

To do all this legal analysis and get through the Library in the short time allotted to you, you need a system to "surgically brief" the cases—in other words, to get into the case and get out of it with just the information you will need to use on your exam. The WWW.FAD system, explained below, uses an easy to remember pneumonic to point you to the essentials of the cases. You can do WWW.FAD briefs right on the Library's Table of Contents page, so all your Library notes are on one page.

What is the WWW.FAD system of case briefing? WWW.FAD stands for Who, What, Where, Facts, and Dicta. Just line up the letters underneath the case name and complete a short and simple brief for each case. (You do not have to brief the cases cited within the primary cases, just those cases listed in the Table of Contents for the Library.)

WWW.FAD

W – **WHO** (WHO IS SUING WHOM, AND WHICH PARTY IS IN THE POSITION ANALOGOUS TO OUR CLIENT)

W – **WHAT** (HOLDING —WHAT EXACTLY WAS THE COURT'S RULING)

W – **WHERE** (WHERE AND HOW TO USE CASE IN YOUR PERFORMANCE TEST ANSWER. WAS THE CASE GOOD FOR OUR CLIENT OR BAD FOR OUR CLIENT?)

F – **FACTS** (ESPECIALLY IF CASE IS BAD FOR OUR CLIENT, TRY TO FIND SOME DISTINGUISHING FACTS)

A – and

D – **DICTA** (ANY OTHER HELPFUL RULES OF LAW)

5. Reread, Think, and Outline (Read and consider additional documents, if any.) (5-30 minutes)

This is the pulling-it-together phase. Reread the Task and Format Memos, and make certain you understand what you are to produce. Go back into the File and/or the Library as necessary to review important documents and determine how you will use the legal authorities.

Think. Outline your answer. Your outline does not have to be extremely detailed but should at least include all your main headings, and should note where the main cases and/or other legal rules fit into those headings.

Visualize the final product you will soon be completing. Make sure it fits together in your own mind. Get organized before you write. The clearer you are about what you are to produce, the clearer your answer will be. Clear, organized, thoughtful writing is what makes for a passing answer.

As you think and outline, refer back to the File, the Library, and any notes you have taken (in the margins and/or on scratch paper). A word on note taking: Your grader will never see your notes. You only get credit for your final answers that appear in your bluebook, so do not overdo it. Take selective notes and organize them in a way that you will be able to read and use quickly and easily. One method that works well for many students is to take notes on the Table of Contents pages. Both the File and the Library start with a Table of Contents, and if you take notes on these, you can rip them out too and have all your notes organized on two pages.

6. Write/Type your Answer (90 minutes)

Beware, graders spend *very little* time on each exam, so give them those documents the instructions direct you to draft and in whatever order they direct you. Again, refer back to the Task Memo and Format Memos as you write to make sure your answer is complete, responsive, and well organized. Given that graders do not spend much time on your answers, make it easy for them to see your points. Use precise, short sentences; frequent paragraphs; and clearly marked or underlined headings and subheadings for different topics within a document.

Try to produce a clear and easy-to-read answer. If you write, write legibly. If they cannot read it, they will not read it. Therefore, if you plan on writing and you know that your handwriting is sloppy, either train yourself to write more legibly or use a laptop. Most of you will be drafting bar exam answers on laptops and that is generally a good thing as good typing produces the most legible answers. But do be aware the excessive typos and other errors can be distracting, so try to complete many practice essays and performance test questions so that by the time you get to the exam, you are able to quickly set out and format easy-to-read legible answers.

Chapter 3: Fact Analysis

In their quintessential document, *Information Regarding Performance Tests*, which you should receive as part of your Bar Exam enrollment packet, the Committee of Bar Examiners states, "The California performance test examines four broad categories of lawyering competency: Legal analysis, fact analysis, awareness of professional responsibility and problem solving." In this and the next several chapters, we will take each of those skills in turn, define them, and explain in plain English exactly what you need to know and do in order to pass the performance test portion of the Exam.

The Bar Examiners define the <u>fact analysis</u> competency as follows:

> *Given knowledge of legal rules and preliminary identification of legal issues, the ability to identify areas of factual inquiry, assess facts and marshal facts in support of legal arguments.*

A. FACTS IN PERFORMANCE TEST FILES

Whatever the exact nature of your performance tests, you will most likely be asked to assume the role of attorney handling a legal matter for some client. As such, you will need to learn your client's story and problem(s). In performance tests, you generally learn these and other facts by reading the File. The File may contain letters, depositions or court transcripts, articles, medical reports, photos, arrest records, notes, minutes, or any other records of events, statements, or information.

Performance test Files tend to contain much more information than you will actually need to complete your assigned task(s). In particular, PT Files tend to include many facts that are irrelevant to drafting the specific documents you are asked to prepare. This makes perfect sense when you think about the sheer size difference between performance tests and essay questions. In an essay, you will usually have one page of facts to write about in one hour. In a performance test, you may have a 15-20 page File to sort through, cull facts from, and write about for three hours.

In a law school or Bar Exam essay question, virtually every fact is stated because it is relevant. If you have 15 times as many facts to contend with in only three times the amount of time (let alone the time it takes you to read and study the law), *it has to be* that many facts in the File are simply not relevant to completing your assigned tasks.

Knowing how facts are used on the different types of tests may help you develop test-taking strategies. In essay questions, for example, it is often the case that the facts are not merely relevant but pivotal, triggering some legal rule. The presence or absence of such facts often determines a given outcome. For example, if you read in a criminal law essay exam that a "house" has a "broken window" and that "the defendant could not see" because of "dim lighting," you should ask yourself why they included those facts. Why was the window "broken?" Why was there "dim lighting?" Why did the fact pattern use a "house" rather than an office or barn as the building in question? Scan your memory. Think about the criminal law rules you know. Do these facts trigger any such rules? Of course they do. Broken window = "breaking." Dim lighting = "nighttime." House = "dwelling house of another." Maybe you have a burglary—a breaking and entering of the dwelling house of another in the nighttime with intent to commit a felony therein. Now scan the other facts to see if *all* the elements are met, and then go back and write your IRAC—Issue, Rule, Analysis, Conclusion.

STRATEGY TIP: If you are stumped on Bar essays, read through the question and ask why each fact matters. That should trigger your memory to recall applicable legal rules, which in turn should help you see what the issues are. Then you can proceed to write the IRAC—Issue, Rule, Analysis, Conclusion. Note that if you forget the precise legal rules, you should still state the issues that are raised by particular facts, since issue spotting and fact analysis will likely get you some credit.

On performance tests, invert the process discussed above. Instead of using the facts to help recall legal rules, use cues from the rules (in the Library) and the task memo to help you determine which facts are relevant. Once you set up a legal structure (some workable outline of the guiding legal elements or theories) and begin to marshal (organize) the relevant facts as they are meaningful within that structure, you will see much more clearly which facts are and which are not relevant. (More below on legal elements and organizing facts in relation to the law.)

As stated above, in a performance test File, much of what you read will be *irrelevant* to completing your assigned task(s). Therefore, a major skill on which you are being tested is your ability to distinguish relevant from irrelevant facts. As one California Bar Examiner put it, "The major distinction between an essay question and a performance test is that an essay question purposely has no irrelevant facts, while a performance test is supposed to test an applicant's ability to separate the relevant from the irrelevant." [(J. Petersen, 53 *The Bar Examiner* 16, 19 (Feb. 1984)]

Another difference between performance tests and essays is that in the former, you may be called upon to, "think outside the box." Why? In essay questions, you are limited to using only the facts they give you; your job is not to create new facts or gather additional potential evidence, but to apply those stated facts to the legal rules you have memorized. In performance tests, however, you may well encounter certain issues about which you are not given enough factual information.

You may not have enough detail to pursue a particular line of inquiry, or the File may not contain enough information to understand fully your client's underlying needs and goals. On many past exams, applicants have been asked to draft memos or plans stating how they would go about obtaining more information, and to assess what additional information would be helpful or necessary to fully understand and resolve their clients' issues. Therefore, as you work through exercises and practice tests, keep in mind that you may need to identify potential facts in addition to analyzing those facts you are given.

B. LEGAL STRUCTURES—ORGANIZING FACTS WITHIN LEGAL FRAMEWORKS

Legal structures include legal theories, causes of action, defenses, and other ways of organizing facts into legally significant frameworks. The Committee of Bar Examiners frequently uses the expression, "marshal the evidence," in performance test instructions (especially in tasks such as a closing argument to the jury). What they mean by this phrase is "grouping together under the umbrella of a single element (or factual proposition) all of the evidence which tends to prove or disprove it." (See Professor Paul Bergman's *Trial Advocacy in a Nutshell*.)

TEST YOURSELF: A fact-marshaling exercise

To illustrate how you organize or marshal facts with corresponding legal elements, let us use a hypothetical performance test-type scenario. To keep this a simple illustration, your universe will consist of only the hypothetical task memo below; there will be no Library or File.

Dear Applicant:

I am Senior Partner. Yesterday, as I was leaving the office, I got a phone call from Bill, the son of an old and important firm client. I asked him to come by tomorrow to talk in greater detail, but he briefly told me his problem. He said that he agreed to loan his friend Derek $12,000 if Derek agreed to pay him back one year later. Derek agreed, and Bill lent Derek the money. As you know, more than one year has passed and Derek still has not paid Bill. Please draft a memo for me setting forth the basics of Bill's case and outlining what further information we should get from Bill when he comes in tomorrow.

Okay, after reading this hypothetical task memo, let us analyze the applicable legal structure. What law applies here? Hopefully, your mind is saying, "This is a pretty straightforward breach of contract action" or something to that effect.

Well, what are the legal elements of a cause of action for breach of contract? In other words, what elements would Bill need to *prove* to win a lawsuit against Derek?

1. formation, 2. performance, 3. breach, and **4. damages.** ("Oh yeah, right!")

Now, what would a jury have to actually conclude *happened* in order to find for Bill?

1. To prove **formation**, the jury would have to find something akin to this: Bill agreed to lend Derek $12,000 and Derek agreed to pay Bill back one year later.

2. To prove **performance**, jurors would have to be satisfied that the evidence shows Bill actually lent Derek $12,000.

3. To prove **breach**, that Derek failed to pay Bill back one year later.

4. To prove **damages**, that Bill is out $12,000 (plus interest).

What did we just do? We first identified the applicable legal elements (formation, performance, breach, and damages). Then, we converted those legal elements into factual terms or what are sometimes called "factual propositions." Another term for factual propositions is "ultimate facts." These are, again, the facts that a judge or jury must find in order to determine that the legal elements have been proven.

What are legal rules? Legal rules are nearly always made of a bundle of legal elements. For example, the "rule" on what is a breach of contract is the "bundle" of formation, performance, breach, and damages. A legal rule is a ". . . conditional statement referring to facts. Such a rule . . . say(s), in effect 'If such and such fact exists, then this or that legal consequence should follow.' It say(s), for example, 'If a trustee, for his own purposes, uses money he holds in trust, he must repay it.'" (see Binder/Bergman's *Fact Investigation*, citing J. Frank, *Courts on Trial*.)

On most performance tests, you will find the legal rules in the Library, but you must *extract* those rules (and the element bundles of those rules) from the judicial and/or statutory sources provided. Then, you will have to look back to the File to see how the facts fit within those legal rules.

You will have to perform some variation of this meshing of facts and law whether your drafting task is a legal, investigatory, or evidence-gathering memo; a pleading (such as a trial or appellate brief); a closing argument; or other task. Even if your task is to prepare for a settlement conference or negotiation, or to counsel your own client, you will likely be obliged at some point to perform an evidence-marshaling analysis to determine the strength or weakness of your client's position.

When evidence of all the requisite legal elements (or factual propositions) is gathered, that bundle of proof forms the basis of a legal action (a prima facie case). A "cause of action" is thus a series of things that, if they all happened, grant someone a legal right to relief in a court of law.

However, counsel must prove that all the things—the factual propositions—actually did happen. "Litigators resemble historians, and litigation is largely a process of recreating historical events." (See *Fact Investigation* by Bergman and Binder.)

LAUNDRY LISTS OF LEGAL ELEMENTS

By the time you take the Bar Exam, you should have memorized a host of "laundry lists" of the elements that make up different causes of action and legal theories in each of the substantive Bar subjects.

You may want to make flash cards for each, and memorize them so that you can instantly recall them as easily as you would an important phone number (without speed dial!).

Here are two examples you should know:

Negligence = 1) duty, 2) breach, 3) causation, 4) damages.

Fraud = 1) representation, 2) falsity of representation, 3) scienter, 4) reasonable reliance, and 5) damages.

How many others do you know??

TEST YOURSELF: Obtaining Information About Your Client's Case

Litigators (and Bar applicants) have formal and informal tools to get information.

Q: What are some of the most common formal investigation tools?
A:
_____
_____
_____
_____

Q: What are some of the most common informal investigation tools?
A:
_____
_____
_____

Some answers: Important formal investigation is conducted via discovery tools such as interrogatories and depositions. Informal sources of information, often much more important than discovery, include further interviews (after the initial interview) with your own client, interviews of other people who may have relevant information, papers or things in your client's or others people's possession that you can obtain by request, and discussions with opposing counsel. More on formal and informal investigation documents in Chapter 7, Document Types: The Frequently Tested Tasks.

C. MAKING INFERENCES—GENERALIZING FROM FACTS

Triers of fact—judges and juries—listen to stories told by witnesses. However, they do not just listen; they also make decisions based upon the facts presented. To do that, they necessarily make *inferences* about the facts.

Inferences are generalizations people make, based on experience, to draw conclusions. We make inferences all the time, in law practice and in daily life. For example, when we see a person crying, we might infer that she is sad. Why? Because, based on our life experiences, people who are crying are *usually* unhappy. We do not explicitly state that generalization; we think it automatically. In place of the word *usually*, in other more or less persuasive generalizations, the words "*often,*" "*sometimes,*" or "*never*" may apply.

Looking further at this example of the person crying, if presented with other facts, we might give the evidence (the tears) a different meaning. For example, if we learned that the person crying had just chopped a dozen onions, we would not necessarily think her sad. Based on human experience, we know that people who cry are *usually* sad, *except when* they have just been cutting onions. (In that case, tears are produced as a physical reaction to the onion.) Or, to take another example, if we had evidence that the person crying had just stubbed her toe, we would not necessarily think her sad, but perhaps in pain and/or angry. Analysis: People who cry are *usually* sad, *except when* they have just stubbed their toe.

What inferences would you draw by learning the crier had just left a smoke-filled room, heard a funny joke, or won the lottery?

Additional evidence can also change an inference altogether. For example, what if the crier, Ms. Tears, got into a car accident with Mr. Krashem? Further, what if Krashem tried to prove that Tears was driving negligently based upon the evidence that she was crying? Krashem might ask the trier to conclude from the evidence of crying that Tears was upset, and then to infer that people who are upset *often* (or, at least *sometimes*) drive negligently. In what Krashem might think is an effort to bolster this reasoning, Krashem might provide additional evidence that, just prior to the accident, Tears had learned that her cat had died. Tears, however, might use this same evidence, that she had just learned about the cat's death, to support an entirely different inference. Let us say that the cat had been a gift from Tears' landlord, whom Tears felt certain she would offend if she did not accept, but that all along, Tears found the cat annoying and suffered terribly from allergies to cat fur. Accordingly, Tears might ask the trier of fact to conclude that Tears was relieved—not upset—about the cat's death, that her tears were simply the result of a routine allergic reaction, and that therefore the so-called evidence that Krashem presented to show Tears' driving proves nothing with respect to the alleged negligence.

As this Krashem v. Tears example shows, gathering additional facts can make generalizations about evidence more or less believable. If Tears had bought the cat herself and loved it very much, then the trier of fact might have reason to believe her sad. Analysis: People who cry are *usually* sad, *especially when* their pets have recently died. But this generalization does not hold when we have the additional facts that Tears herself had not bought the cat, she found it annoying, and she was allergic to it.

Keep in mind the tool discussed above for testing whether additional evidence strengthens or weakens the persuasiveness of a generalization, placing the words *"especially when"* or *"except when"* in front of the new additional item of evidence or potential evidence (to help focus a search for further evidence). For example, if you wanted to prove that Tears was not sad, you could make a mental list of "except whens" to provide alternative explanations (theories) for the tears that you can follow up on in later investigation, perhaps by interviewing Tears.

Note: If you were asked to write an interview plan for a meeting with Tears, you might ask specifically about the theories you have developed with questions like, "Did you hurt yourself before you began crying?" or "Were you doing anything that may have caused you to be teary that day, such as cutting onions or dusting the house?" or "Do you have allergies?" You might also probe for additional evidence by recreating a chronological timeline of events. For example, to help you draw plausible inferences about why Tears was crying, you would want to learn what Tears did or experienced just before crying, e.g., stubbed her toe or cat died. If you could interview Tears, one question to ask would be, "What happened just before you started crying?"

Note, too, that Tears could be crying for more than one reason, e.g., first, the cat died *and* then she stubbed her toe. Let us say Tears' response to the question, "What happened just before you started crying?" was, "I stubbed my toe." You might want to probe further and ask, "And what happened just before you stubbed your toe?" (and then ask what happened before or after that). If Tears answered, "I cut onions," and if both were true, there would be cumulative evidence of why Tears was crying—evidence that again helps negate the inference Krashem wants drawn, that Tears was negligent.

With these examples of how to investigate using chronological time lines and/or theory development, you can begin to see how the process of fact investigation and evidence marshaling are intertwined. Returning to the Bill v. Derek contracts hypothetical from earlier in this chapter, let us list the things we should look for, the factual propositions, and additional evidence, proceeding element by element. (The four elements of the breach of contract cause of action we identified above as formation, performance, breach, and damages.) Then, let us examine the generalizations we are employing to determine what such evidence helps to prove or disprove. In other words, let us marshal the evidence in Bill's case.

1. **Formation** = Bill agreed to lend Derek $12,000, and Derek agreed to pay Bill back one year

later.

Q: What possible evidence can you think of that would tend to prove that Bill agreed to loan Derek $12,000, and that Derek agreed to repay it one year later?

A: _____

_____

_____

_____

Some possible ideas of evidence follow:

- Bill's and/or Derek's testimony that Bill agreed to lend Derek $12,000, and that Derek agreed to repay Bill one year later. (*Note*: This is direct evidence, evidence that proves a factual proposition without the need of an inference. For example, to prove the existence of a contract, a party may offer into evidence the physical, written contract. One need make no further link in the chain of reasoning to prove the existence of that contract.)

- Testimony that a witness saw or heard the deal being made.

- Bill's date book or journal noting the deal.

- A written contract, agreement, or IOU. (Why is this important? What inferences are we making? People who lend a large sum of money to someone *usually* document the loan in writing.)

2. **Performance** = Bill lent Derek $12,000.

Q: What would tend to prove that Bill lent Derek the money?

A: _____

_____

Some possible ideas are as follows:

- A withdrawal in Bill's bank account at the time of the loan. Why? People who loan a large sum of money *usually* take the funds from money in their bank accounts.

- A deposit in Derek's bank account at the time of the loan.

- Evidence that Derek needed the money at the time of the loan. Why? People who need money *often* borrow it.

What other facts might help prove Derek needed money at the time? Was Derek in trouble? Did he need bail money? Why? People who are trying to make bail *usually* need to borrow a lot of money. Was he starting a new business? Why? People who start new businesses *usually* (*often?*) need to borrow a lot of money.

Can you think of any further evidence that would make these generalizations more or less believable? For example, people who start new businesses *usually* need to borrow a lot of money, *especially when* . . . they are unemployed and/or the business is a high-tech, expensive operation/other. Or, *except when* . . . they are independently wealthy and/or the business is a low-cost operation. Others?

3. Breach = Derek failed to pay Bill back one year after the loan was made.

Q: What evidence can you think of to prove breach?
A:_____
_____
_____

      - Again, bank records and testimony from both Bill and Derek, both for the same reasons as above.

4. Damages = Bill is out $12,000 (plus interest).

Q: What evidence can you think of to prove damages?
A:_____
_____
_____

What other facts might we look for to prove Bill's case? Can you articulate those generalizations and inferences you are making in order to give meaning to those events, words, or things? Note that in the analysis above, we focused exclusively on proving Bill's affirmative case. We were also asked to determine what we will need to find out when Bill comes to the office. To do this, we will need to list all the information we might potentially obtain from Bill. We might suggest calling Bill before the meeting and asking him to bring any documents relevant to the transaction, such as a contract or promissory note, bank records, or a letter acknowledging the debt.

> **LOOKING FOR DIFFERENT TYPES OF EVIDENCE: PROFESSOR BERGMAN'S *TRIAL ADVOCACY IN A NUTSHELL* HAS SOME USEFUL DEFINITIONS**
>
> **Affirmative evidence** consists of happenings that tend to prove the accuracy of a factual proposition.
>
> **Rebuttal evidence** consists of happenings that tend to undermine the other side's affirmative evidence, but are not part of your affirmative story. There are two ways of using rebuttal evidence: to deny or to admit and explain. Denial asks triers to disbelieve the other side's evidence; admit and explain admits the accuracy of the other side's evidence but asks the trier to draw a different inference from the one the other side is asking the trier to draw. Explanatory evidence, a form of affirmative evidence, tells the trier of fact why the events in a story took place the way you say they did.
>
> **Credibility evidence**, either affirmative or rebuttal, is some happening or information that affects the believability and trustworthiness of the story.

We will also need to work on anticipating Derek's potential defenses. This analysis could begin as follows: Does Derek have any defenses to formation? Stated in factual terms, Bill agreed to loan Derek $12,000 and Derek agreed to repay Bill one year later, but Derek might not be liable because:

     - One or both lacked capacity. To pursue this theory we should find out the ages of Bill and Derek, and whether either is mentally impaired.

     - The offer was invalid. To pursue this theory, let us inquire where they were when they made the deal. An office? A bar? What state were they in?

Can you think of other theories? Try to complete the analysis of Derek's potential defenses.

D. A REVIEW OF FACT ANALYSIS SKILLS

To recap, the main fact analysis skills you need to use on any given performance test are sorting relevant from irrelevant facts, identifying areas of factual inquiry, and analyzing and marshaling facts in support of legal arguments.

Chapter 4: Legal Analysis

The Committee defines the <u>legal analysis</u> skill as:

> *The ability to analyze and evaluate legal authority; identify legal issues; and generate, assess, and justify the relative merits of alternative or competing legal positions.*

What this means in essence is reading and extracting the rules from cases and statutes, sifting holdings from dicta, and determining the precedential weight of various authorities. This chapter provides a brief review of case and statutory authority, legal arguments, and precedent, and it focuses on the types of legal analysis you will need to do on performance tests.

This part of performance test preparation should seem like an old friend to most law students. Unlike factual analysis, which may be somewhat new, especially for those who did not work in firms or take clinical courses, legal analysis is the stuff that law school is made of.

On performance tests, though, you will *use* cases and statutes somewhat differently from the way in which you used them in school. You will read and analyze cases and/or statutes from the Library, not with the general purpose of avoiding embarrassment should the professor call on you, but with the explicit purpose of learning how the law has treated people whose problems were similar to those of your client, and predicting how a court (or opposing counsel for settlement purposes) will likely treat your client's matter. Depending on your performance test tasks, you may also use the authorities to argue for or against a specific treatment of your client's concerns.

A. CASES

Cases are binding and enforceable decisions made by judges, that explain, based on a particular set of facts, why a given result or outcome should be applied to the parties.

Using legal precedent involves referring to past cases to see if a court has already decided the same or an analogous issue. In our judicial system, the core idea governing the process is that like situations should be treated alike, but as Professor Hegland writes in his *Introduction to the Study and Practice of Law in a Nutshell*, "The key is knowing what's 'alike.' . . . The presence or absence of a single fact may distinguish one case from another. You must argue why, as between your client's case and the previous case(s) you cite, the facts are either similar enough so that the prior holding(s) should be followed, or different enough so that another rule should be applied to your client." (According to Professor Hegland, "<u>Holdings</u> are statements of law necessary for the decision in the case; <u>dicta</u> are statements of law which aren't necessary for that decision. . . . You can think of dicta as [the judge's] 'Oh, by the way' comments.")

To illustrate, let us say that the first case ever reported (Case A) had 3 facts in it. *Note*: By saying a case had three facts in it, this means *legally significant* or potentially significant facts, as even the first reported cases must have included many other facts, such as the parties' and judge's names, and the location and dates.

Now, assume that you are counsel in Case B. Your case has facts 1 and 3 (similar to Case A), but not fact 2. If you want the same result in Case A to apply to your clients, you will argue that the court in Case A did not *rely* on fact 2 in reaching its decision. You will argue the court relied on facts 1 and 3, the essential facts. If, of course, you seek the opposite result, you must argue that fact 2 was pivotal in the court's decision, and that the court never would have ruled as it did in Case A had fact 2 been absent. Therefore, to do justice in your case, the court must adopt a different rule.

Cases in performance test Libraries, like these fictitious "first cases ever reported," are limited in number. Your Library will probably only contain five to six cases, or fewer. You can, thus, develop the types of arguments we did above by showing which cases in your Library relied on which facts, and then comparing the presence or absence of those same facts in your File. (A note of thanks here to Professor Hegland for the idea of using the first reported case as an illustrative teaching tool.)

WHAT DOES THE TERM *COMMON LAW* REFER TO?

According to Professor Bergman, "Common law is judge-made law; the principles that result from judges writing down their decisions, and giving the reasons for those decisions. Sometimes . . . judges make sweeping statements in the course of those explanations: 'Due process of law requires that everyone get actual notice before a sanction can be imposed.' Such clarion calls often sound impressive, but they may not be worth much. You have got to remember that part of the common law heritage is that judges decide only the particular factual disputes before them. That broad principle may not be adhered to in a future case with different facts. Again, this is a reminder of why you read and discuss cases: future cases, ones you will handle, will almost always be different from those already decided, so you read cases to learn about the kinds of differences that matter. Your client has a different name? That should not matter. But what if in the case above the client didn't have actual notice because the notice was written in a foreign language, whereas your client didn't get actual notice only because he threw it down the sewer without reading it? Now we have a difference that might well matter!"

B. Statutes

Statutes, like cases, are primary authority, but they are created by legislatures, not judges. Generally, statutes provide rules to govern future matters, and are meant to apply to a category of persons (or entities), while cases resolve past disputes between specific parties.

In performance test Libraries, statutes may be included as reference materials (statutes or code sections that you are already familiar with, that you may want to refer to as you organize and write your answer) and/or as working statutes (rules or code sections that you are not responsible for knowing on the other parts of the Bar Exam, that are typically integral to the call of this particular performance test question).

You can recognize the difference between a reference and a working library in that, in the former, statutes are included for reference purposes and typically appear in a sequentially numbered block. It is also often noted that the code sections provided are identical in relevant part to a particular code with which you are already familiar, such as the Federal Rules of Evidence or the Federal Rules of Civil Procedure. By contrast, a working library may include randomly selected or isolated statute sections that may appear out of numbered sequence, and may involve statutes in any subject area, including subjects not tested on the essays and multistate exams. (Past working libraries have included statutes in such diverse areas as labor law, family law, veteran's benefits, and environmental law.) Note that, unlike statutes, cases are always working library materials; the instructions tell you to read all cases as new because even real cases may be altered for test purposes.

Where statutes in your Library are included for more than simply reference purposes—in other words, when you have a working library that includes a statute or statutes—you must read the statutory language carefully. There are no dicta in statutes; read every word and assume it is purposeful. Read statutes section by section, in order. The first sections often define terms used in the body of the law. In addition, consider legislative intent. Who did the legislature want the statute to affect and why? Does the rule even apply to your client? Consider public policy as well. Would application of the rule to your client have the effect the legislature intended? Would such application be fair and logical?

Using the exercise below, test your competency in statutory analysis. *Note*: This is also an exercise in factual analysis skills, since, as you know, facts and law are inextricably interrelated in actual cases.

TEST YOURSELF: Exercise #1—The Sam Anella Story
(with thanks to UCLA Law Professor Paul Bergman, who created this exercise)

Sam Anella has brought suit against Bo Loney's Sushi Bar, seeking general and punitive damages for food poisoning that Anella developed after eating dinner there. Anella claims that Nathan Ramirez, a chef employed by the Sushi Bar, maliciously served him contaminated fish. With regard to Anella's claim for punitive damages, assume that a pertinent statute provides as follows:

(a) In a tort action, if the plaintiff proves by clear and convincing evidence that the defendant has been guilty of malice, the plaintiff may recover punitive, in addition to actual, damages.

(b) An employer is liable for damages pursuant to subsection (a) based upon acts of an employee only if the employer had advance knowledge of the employee's unfitness and employed him or her with a conscious disregard of the rights or safety of others, or authorized or ratified the wrongful conduct for which the damages are awarded, or was personally guilty of malice.

(c) Malice is conduct that is intended by the defendant to cause injury to the plaintiff or despicable conduct that is carried on by the defendant with a willful and conscious disregard of the rights or safety of others.

Assume that you represent Anella and you seek to offer evidence that would enable Anella to recover *punitive damages* against the *employer*. Make up 3-4 items of evidence you might offer to prove that Ramirez acted maliciously, and 3-4 items that might prove Bo Loney liable for Ramirez' action.

Q: What are some items of evidence you might offer to prove that Ramirez acted maliciously?

A:_____
_____
_____
_____
_____
_____
_____

Q: What are some items of evidence you might offer to prove that Bo Loney is liable for Ramirez' action?

A:_____
_____
_____
_____

Sample Answers to Exercise #1—The Sam Anella Story

1. Possible pieces of evidence for Ramirez' malice:
   a. Ramirez (R) was in a bitter dispute with Anella (A) prior to the incident.
   b. R is not a trained sushi chef, does not know anything about fish storage and preparation except that raw fish can be dangerous and that someone trained as a chef would know how to deal with the raw fish.
   c. R lied on his employment application about his training as a chef.

d. A was picking up on R's girlfriend at the Sushi Bar that night.

2. <u>Possible evidence for Bo's liability:</u>
   a. Bo Loney (B) saw R in the bathroom, observed that he left without washing his hands, and knows that salmonella can be transmitted as a result.
   b. B found out that R lied on his employment application about his training, but did not fire him.
   c. B saw A and his friend Joe in the Bar that night and noticed A picking up on R's girlfriend and Joe flirting with B's own wife.

C. PRECEDENT: THE RELATIVE WEIGHTS OF DIFFERENT LEGAL AUTHORITY

Some authorities (*sources* of law) are binding or mandatory; a court *must* follow them. Others are permissive; if a court finds them persuasive, it *may,* but does not have to, follow them. In order to anticipate how a court will rule or argue how it should rule in your client's matter, you must know these distinctions.

Primary authorities include: **Legislative** authorities (such as the U.S. and state constitutions, statutes, some court rules, charters, or ordinances); **Judicial** authorities (typically cases and some court rules); and **Administrative** authorities (often called decisions or regulations). Primary legislative authorities are mandatory if they are decided by the legislature or a higher legislative body in the same jurisdiction. Primary judicial authorities are mandatory if they are decided by the court itself or a higher court in the same jurisdiction and are still good law, i.e. have not been overruled.

Secondary authorities include dictionaries, treatises, encyclopedias, legal periodicals, A.L.R. annotations, law review articles, restatements, legislative history. As distinguished from primary authorities, secondary authorities are never mandatory; however, they can often be quite persuasive.

To determine court hierarchies, note that in California, the highest state court is called the state Supreme Court; mid-level courts are referred to as Courts of Appeal, and the lower courts as Superior Courts. Within the federal system, the United States Supreme Court is the highest court. Mid-level courts are Circuit Courts (or Courts of Appeals [for the particular Circuit]), and the lower courts are District Courts. All must follow Supreme Court precedents, and District Courts must also follow opinions of Circuit Courts within their Circuit. Nearly all performance tests are set in the fictional State of Columbia (though some have been in the State of Franklin.) Columbia is sometimes said to be in the 9th Circuit, as is California, and sometimes in another real or fictional circuit. The Instructions will tell you where your case is located, and where your client and your own law offices are located.

TEST YOURSELF: Exercise #2—Do you Know the Precedential Value?

Assume for this exercise that your performance test is set in the State of Columbia and involves an action that takes place in state court.

Q: Name several sources of law that would be mandatory or binding on your client.

_____
_____
_____
_____
_____
_____

Q: Name several sources of law that would merely be persuasive authority in your case.

A:_____
_____
_____
_____
_____
_____

Some answers: Binding authority would include Columbia case law from higher courts than the one in which your client's matter is pending, relevant Columbia statutes, Columbia rules of court and other procedural rules, and the Columbia Constitution. Certain federal law, such as federal statutory and/or case law, and Constitutional law, would also be binding, for example, if applicable to the parties and matter being litigated. Persuasive authority would include case law from other states or from lower Columbia courts, dicta from any case law, federal case and statutory law (that is not directly relevant and binding in the particular pending action), treatises, law review articles, and other commentaries.

D. INTERACTION BETWEEN LAW AND FACTS—LEGAL ARGUMENTS

One builds a case on facts—"case" meaning a party's version of substantively critical events. These are events that occurred in the past but will, if the case goes to trial, be presented in the form of evidence to the trier of fact. In court, facts can be described by people (witnesses) as the things these people perceived with their senses—things they touched, saw, heard, felt, or smelled. Except for the limited situation of experts who may testify to their opinions in certain circumstances, most witnesses may only testify about things that are within their personal knowledge, and only as such may witnesses' factual accounts be presented as evidence to a trier of fact. The facts litigators look for to present in trial (and, therefore, the facts that you as the lawyer in a performance test role-play situation will look for to write about in your answer) are those facts that are (or may lead to) relevant and ultimately admissible evidence.

Counsel must create a story out of facts. As discussed in the previous chapter, counsel does so by linking facts with inferences in such a way as to explain what happened. Litigants do not prove the substantive law per se; they introduce evidence that proves facts that trigger legal consequences (see Bergman's *Trial Advocacy in a Nutshell*). Therefore, in addition to merely telling a story, counsel must also persuade a trier of fact why what happened should result in some legal relief for his or her client. Of course, in criminal trials, the defense counsel or defendant does not *have to* prove any part of the prima facie case, since a defendant is innocent until proven guilty. Even criminal defendants, however, often choose to present their story. And defendants do have to prove affirmative defenses (for example, insanity) should they choose to assert such defenses.

At trial, after all the evidence is presented (after the direct and cross- examinations of all witnesses, and after all documents are introduced), counsel may tell a persuasive story in the form of a closing argument. That story summarizes the evidence and explains how it should and should not be interpreted. A closing argument should tell the trier which inferences to draw and/or not to draw from explanations or generalizations about particular facts. If a closing argument persuasively explains the facts and links them to the legal elements, it should show why the client is entitled to legal relief.

Chapter 5: Professional Responsibility

The Committee of Bar Examiners defines the <u>professional responsibility</u> ("PR") skill as:

> *The ability to recognize the ethical considerations in a situation, analyze and evaluate their implications for present and future actions, and behave in a manner that facilitates timely assertion of rights.*

The Committee explicitly states that performance testing may be used to test candidates' knowledge of and sensitivity to professional responsibility concerns. Therefore, assume ethical issues *may* arise on your performance test and prepare to discuss them. (Note that not every performance test incorporates ethical issues, but be alert for them if your performance tests do.) If you see an ethical issue on a performance test, you will want to:

1. Clearly identify the issue, i.e. describe what the problem, conflict or concern is and whom it affects;

2. State the rules. (*Note*: Although normally you are wise not to cite to rules outside the Library authorities, PR rules are different. Because the Committee warns you that PR issues may arise on the PT, and because PR is a subject you are supposed to know for the essays, you may refer, from memory, to PR rules that are not included in the Library.) As with everything on the Bar Exam, try to be as precise and complete as you can, but do not worry about citing specific rule or section numbers, or using the exact language of the rules, unless those rules are explicitly given to you in the Library; and

3. Suggest any way or ways in which you and "your firm" might resolve the issues.

Keep in mind as you read through and complete practice performance tests that generally, lawyers may not:
- Counsel or assist in fraudulent or criminal conduct;
- Use false evidence;
- Reveal client confidences;
- Assist a client in committing perjury;
- Force a client to make decisions about defenses, settlements, pleas, merits of case;
- Litigate in bad faith;
- Talk directly to the represented opposing party.

And specifically during trial, lawyers may not:

- Assert personal knowledge of contested facts;
- Assert personal opinions (about the credibility of witnesses, justness of a cause, or guilt or innocence of an accused);
- Abuse the court process;
- Violate court orders;
- Secure the absence or non-cooperation of a witness;
- Pay a witness (except for travel, meals, lodging, loss of time, or expert fees);
- Suppress or tamper with evidence;
- Falsify evidence or assist in perjury.

A. SOME ETHICAL ISSUES FROM PAST PTS

PR issues can cover a broad range of actions, but knowing how ethical issues have been raised in past performance tests can help prepare you for potential ethical traps and PR issues to watch for on your exam. The more practice tests you do, the easier it will be to see them. Here are a few actions that raised PR issues on past performance tests, issues that are the kinds likely to be woven into future exams as well:

- Client pursuing or seeking to pursue unlawful or unethical objectives:

On one past PT, a client's goal was to defraud his wife, and the attorney's role in that illegal and unethical conduct was at issue. On another a client asked the lawyer to deliberately file motions to delay proceedings.

- Client confidences and potential breaches thereof:

Past PTs have involved counsel's employment of others to work on the case, including lay investigators where issues arose as to the lawyer's duties to inform such an investigator of ethical and confidentiality requirements.

- Representation of more than one client in a potentially conflicting situation:
In one exam, applicant's law firm had drafted a prenuptial agreement for both husband and wife, and was now handling a related will dispute. In another, the firm's represented a physician and the medical group who hired him against the physician's previous employer; there then arising the possibility that the group might have a claim against the physician.

- Fee arrangements:

More than one PT has had issues of client's legal fees being paid by some source other than client, testing applicant's ability to see that the person financing the representation did not interfere with the lawyer's duty to client. A recent PT also involved issues of fee splitting among lawyers.

- <u>Duty of candor vs. duty of confidentiality</u>:
One recent PT involved a client who had revealed confidential information that the government was seeking to use against him in a possible criminal prosecution.

<u>Practice Test Tip</u>: An excellent past performance test to take as a practice exam to review ethical issues is *In re Amanda Deale*, PT Feb. 1991 as *Deale* tested numerous ethical issues, with a PR-based Library.

TEST YOURSELF: Exercise—No-No List

In the spaces provided below, without looking back through this chapter, list ten things attorneys *must not* do. As you list a prohibited action, note whether it relates to generally prohibited conduct or to conduct specifically prohibited during litigation.

A lawyer **may not**:
_____
_____
_____
_____
_____
_____
_____
_____
_____

B. CLIENT CONSENT

To resolve ethical issues on performance tests, keep in mind your option to try to secure client consent. Consent does not cure every situation, but it can resolve many issues, especially those involving confidentiality and conflicts of interest. These issues are especially "good" to test because they do not "ruin" the question. Despite the apparent conflict, you can proceed to draft whatever is requested, so long as you note that someone in your firm should inform the client of the problem and secure his or her consent for whatever course of action you are recommending.

Note: If a situation on your PT requires that your firm withdraw from the case, do not let that end the writing assignment—even if it would end the representation in real life. Present all the alternatives, and then state that *if* they are not resolved, your firm should withdraw for whatever specific reasons that exist. Most likely, if withdrawal arises, it will be as a last resort should counseling the client or taking some other steps not resolve the issue.

C. WHERE TO NOTE ETHICAL ISSUES

Where a PT appears to raise an isolated ethical issue, but you do not see a place to readily weave comments regarding or analysis of that issue into the tasks you are called upon to draft, write a bracketed note to the senior partner either at the beginning or at the end of your performance test answer. This can be especially helpful if your tasks are to write to the court or opposing counsel, for example, and there is some point you want to make to the senior partner reviewing the draft before it goes out.

Some examples:

[Confidential Note to Mr. Partner: I have prepared the draft below completing the direct examination plan for Witt Ness that you requested. Because of her past criminal record and consequent credibility issues, I urge that we do everything in our power to try to put on one or more other more credible witnesses, if any will agree to testify in this matter.]

[Dear Ms. Partner: I have drafted the trial brief requested below and believe as you will see that we have a good chance of prevailing on the theories asserted. Because our client has repeatedly expressed a desire to move on, and end the fighting in her life, however, I would ask that we continue to explore any and all reasonable settlement options before we incur any further costs to the client in connection with moving forward on the present litigation.]

Chapter 6: Problem Solving

The Committee of Bar Examiners defines the term <u>problem solving</u> as:

> *The ability to identify and diagnose problems in terms of client objectives and to suggest measures to achieve those client objectives.*

Perhaps because many complaints are lodged against the practicing bar due to failure to adequately listen to or hear client concerns, or perhaps because it is just good practice, meeting the client's objectives is a theme that has been stressed on performance tests.

A. HOW PROBLEM SOLVING SKILLS HAVE BEEN TESTED

On past exams, problem solving skills have been tested in many different tasks, including in-house memoranda, client letters, and memos to investigators. Applicants have had to identify client concerns and think about ways to meet client objectives in client counseling and interviewing, negotiations of settlement, and drafting or revising contracts and estate planning documents (such as wills and trust instruments).

It may be helpful to think about problem solving tasks by breaking the definition into two parts:

　　1. Figure out what the client's "problem" is (*identify and diagnose problems in terms of client objectives)* and,

　　2. "Solve" the problem (*suggest measures to achieve those client objectives).*

To competently perform the first part of problem solving tasks, the identifying and diagnosing of problems, you must find those facts from the File that tell you what your client needs and wants. You may find details about the client's concerns, values, and/or priorities in letters to or from the client, transcripts of interviews with the client, prior documents the client signed, or through other resources. As you read, keep the following big-picture questions in mind: (1) Who is my client? and, (2) Who is suing or plans to sue whom over what (if the problem involves litigation), or who is my client dealing with over what issues (if the problem is a transactional one)?

As to the second part of problem solving, suggesting measures to help achieve the client's objectives, note that the word "measures" is plural. As it will ultimately be up to the client to decide what choices to make, the better answers often include *more than one way* for the client to achieve his or her objectives and, unless specifically instructed not to do so, a discussion of the pros and cons of each alternative, along with a suggestions as to which is the preferable choice in your view. (Keep in mind professional responsibility rules as to which decisions clients should ultimately make and which choices lawyers may make for their clients.)

B. SOLVING THE CLIENT'S PROBLEMS

In some performance tests, the types of solutions will be fairly generic; for example, you might suggest that the client settle, sue, or perhaps try mediation. In other performance tests, the solutions are more case-specific; for instance, the client may not be able to have all the goods shipped and delivered on time, but may be able to negotiate a future offer for a reduced priced shipment that will more than compensate for the current losses. As to case- or problem-specific solutions, your key is to read the File carefully. As to more general solutions, let us illustrate some of what you might want to keep in mind using a simple breach of contract action, a hypothetical first introduced in the earlier chapter on Fact Analysis. The problem, you may recall, involved two parties, Bill and Derek. Derek allegedly breached the agreement the two had made to repay a $12,000 loan from Bill.

Bill is our client, and he has one main problem: Derek owes Bill $12,000. What are Bill's objectives? Bill wants the money back. From the sparse facts given, think about how Bill's problem could be solved. Then, determine whether, if you had additional information, you could think of any other potential solutions for Bill. For example, you might want to know whether Bill needs the money immediately. And, if so, does he need all of it immediately, or can he wait for some of it? Is Bill on speaking terms with Derek? Does he know where Derek is? How might these facts help you fashion solutions?

That you are allowed to think of additional facts on performance tests, to think "outside the box" if you will, is one of the key differences between essays and performance test questions. On essays, you are like a historian. You look at those facts you are given as having already occurred. They are frozen; like in an appellate record, facts on essay questions are not subject to review. No matter how far-fetched they may seem, your job is not to assess their credibility, nor to go outside the record. You are simply to use the facts they give you on essay questions (*all* the facts they give you) and apply them to the rules you know. However, in order to effectively problem solve on performance tests, you may have to think of facts as "hot," as more malleable; you may need to question some of them (perhaps because their source is of doubtful credibility) and you may need to gather additional facts about certain issues. You are often permitted, even required, to go outside the four corners of the pages in order to write a complete answer.

TEST YOURSELF: Problem Solving Exercise #1

Take the previously discussed Bill vs. Derek hypothetical, and try listing potential alternative solutions to Bill's problem. Write down as many possible solutions as you can think of in the following spaces and try to write the pros and cons of each solution you propose. Then review the list of possible solutions outlined below and compare it to your own.

Bill may be able to solve his problem with Derek by:

1. _____

*Pros:*_____
_____

*Cons:*_____
_____

2. _____
*Pros:*_____
_____

*Cons:*_____
_____

3. _____
*Pros:*_____
_____

*Cons:*_____
_____

Here are some suggestions for potential solutions to resolving Bill's dispute with Derek. Bill may solve his problem by:

Request: Bill could ask Derek for the money. (We must ask Bill if he has asked Derek yet.)

Demand: Bill could write Derek a formal letter of demand, or have his attorney write one. He could plan on a series of letters, progressing from nice to nasty, first written by Bill himself, then later by counsel.

Proposing a payment plan, or settling for a smaller sum: Bill could propose a payment plan for Derek to repay $1,000 per month, or some other mutually agreeable sum, i.e. they could renegotiate the original contract. If Bill knows Derek has a job and can pay something each month, but has not paid Bill because he does not have the entire sum, this method may work beautifully. In addition, if Derek is judgment proof (has no other assets of value on which Bill could collect even if he were to prevail in a suit) or if Derek is likely to declare bankruptcy (in which case any sum Derek gave Bill just prior to bankruptcy might be considered a preference and might then have to be given back), then renegotiating the deal or settling for a smaller sum total may be worthwhile.

Lawsuit: Bill could sue Derek.

Pros: If Bill has a good case and will likely win, then Derek may be "persuaded" to pay Bill back when he is served with a complaint (Bill will show Derek he means business). Bill could get revenge and possibly feel a sense of justice.

Cons: Cost (attorneys' fees and costs could eat up much of the $12,000); possibility of losing; time (Bill might have to wait years to have his day in court); difficult/costly if, for example, Derek's whereabouts are unknown or if Derek now resides out of state. (Query: Did their agreement contemplate a provision for attorneys' fees in case of breach? We need more information.)

In addition, even if Bill sues, he may have a choice of courts in which to sue. If the limit in small claims court is $10,000, then Bill may want to forego $2,000 and file there. It would be faster and less costly, and he could do so without counsel.

Force or fear: Bill could send a thug to Derek's house to rough him up a bit and coerce the money out of him. **NO!!** We put this one in here to make you laugh (and see if you were reading carefully and are still awake), but on your Bar Exam, **do not even joke about anything close to unethical or illegal.** If you do, the grader may well determine, even if you know the law and reason well, that you are morally unfit to practice law.

Caveat: Avoid joking on the Bar Exam generally. It is a time to show you have the dignity of a lawyer, first of all, and second you never know if the person reading your exam shares your sense of humor.

Mediation: Bill could try to persuade Derek to go together to a neutral third party to resolve their dispute.

Arbitration: Bill and Derek could select someone to arbitrate their dispute.

Using a guarantor: Could Derek find someone else to guaranty the obligation?

Putting up some security: Could Derek provide Bill with any collateral or security for the obligation?

Performing services in lieu of payment: Could Derek paint Bill's house or perform some other service for Bill?

From the Bill/Derek hypothetical above, you can see that even in a "simple" breach of contract action, there may be a variety of possible solutions to your client's problems, depending on the individual facts of the case. On performance tests, because time is so severely limited, usually thinking of even one or two alternatives is enough to answer the question adequately.

Problem solving is one of the most creative and fun skills tested on the Exam. The more you practice, the easier it will become.

TEST YOURSELF: Problem Solving Exercise #2

Your client, Dr. Kutz, M.D., comes to you. Dr. Kutz claims that one of her patients, a man named Yves Dropper, told her that he (Dropper) overheard a woman named Ms. Speek telling someone how badly Dr. Kutz had treated Speek.

Yves said he heard Speek say, "Ever since Dr. Kutz 'fixed' my ankle, I have been in constant pain. She fixed me all right. She is a butcher, that Dr. Kutz! I am going to sue her. Have you ever had any problems with Dr. Kutz? Maybe you would like to join in my suit against her?"

In your interview with Dr. Kutz, Dr. Kutz tells you she is afraid of a lawsuit. She feels she has not done anything wrong, but fears her malpractice insurance might be increased. She knows that litigation is time-consuming and stressful, and suspects that if other patients find out, her reputation could be damaged—even if she ultimately prevailed. Dr. Kutz is also angry. She feels she has been slandered by Ms. Speek, and Dr. Kutz suspects that Speek may be out telling other patients (and potential patients) these vicious lies.

Q: You have a meeting scheduled tomorrow morning with Dr. Kutz. What more do you want to ask Dr. Kutz, if anything?

A:

_____
_____
_____
_____
_____
_____

Q: What alternative courses of action are available to Dr. Kutz, at this point? Consider both informal and formal action that may be taken.

A:

_____
_____
_____
_____
_____
_____

Q: How would *you* advise Dr. Kutz to proceed now? Consider both the short and long term.

A: _____
_____
_____

C. LAWYERING SKILLS REVIEW

In this and previous chapters, you have read and studied the main lawyering skills or competencies that are tested on the California Bar's Performance Test. Take a moment now and do the following exercise, to review those essential lawyering skills and to make sure you understand what is meant by each.

TEST YOURSELF: The Essential Lawyering Skills

Q: In what areas of lawyering skill must you demonstrate competency in order to write a passing performance test answer?

A:

_____
_____
_____
_____

Q: What do you think the Committee of Bar Examiners means by the term "legal analysis"?

A:

_____
_____

Q: What do you think the Committee of Bar Examiners means by the term "fact analysis"?

A:

_____
_____

Q: What do you think the Committee of Bar Examiners means by the term "awareness of professional responsibility"?

A:

_____
_____

Q: What do you think the Committee of Bar Examiners means by the term "problem solving"?

A:

_____
_____

Chapter 7: Document Types–the Frequently Tested Tasks

On each performance test, the applicant is asked to draft one or more documents that the Bar Examiners expect a beginning lawyer would be able to draft in practice. (In the Appendix portion of this book, you will find a list of all the tasks applicants have been asked to draft to date, and a short summary of the context in which they were tested.)

The expectation is that you will *complete* any and all tasks assigned, in the most organized and thorough manner possible, in the three allotted hours. Emphasis on the word "complete." You are expected to finish. That may mean rushing through certain parts in order to complete everything assigned rather than risk leaving any task or part of a task incomplete.

Caveat: Do not ever write something like, "Oops, I ran out of time." If you have not finished, conclude anyway. Do not call attention to your not having completed one or more tasks.

There are a number of strategies to help you get through the tasks in the three hours. Early in this book, you learned the importance of having an approach—an efficient method for proceeding through the packets of materials the proctors hand out to you. You also learned about the different skills in which you must demonstrate proficiency: fact analysis, legal analysis, professional responsibility, and problem solving. You are also undoubtedly aware by now that though three hours is a long time, any time spent "daydreaming" is time away from your ultimate goal: the passing answer. (Most of us know only too well that after-lunch glazed look that often appears about 3:00 p.m. where we find ourselves reading the same sentence several times and still do not understand it. Tips on how to combat the afternoon lull and develop other general test-taking success strategies follow in the chapter on Success Strategies.)

The purpose of this chapter is to provide yet another concrete tool for success: familiarity with the frequently tested tasks. While the trend is to give you more and more specific instructions and formats to follow to complete your tasks, the more familiar you are with the types of documents you may be asked to draft, the more likely you are to be able to get into the exam—and out of it in three hours—with a complete, thoughtful, and well-organized answer.

By being familiar with documents, we mean seeing what they look like but also understanding how and in what context lawyers use these documents to help clients achieve their goals. Performance tests are like lawyering role plays, with you, usually, playing the role of lawyer.

Recall that you are most often asked to pretend you are a beginning lawyer in a fictional scenario; your client is either involved in or contemplating litigation, or is seeking your counsel in a transactional matter. Occasionally, you will play another role, for example that of law clerk to a judge or legislative body.

As with dramatic role plays, the more you understand about the scenario, the more likely you are to convincingly play your part. The same is true in performance tests. The more you understand about what lawyers do in practice, the more naturally you will adopt an appropriate tone in your writing, spot and intelligently comment on any ethical issues, and help solve your client's problems. Also, if you can view your PT as a role play, this will help you get *into* the problem, so you can move quickly enough through the materials to accomplish your end goal—producing a passing answer in three hours.

In past performance tests, some of the tasks applicants have regularly been asked to complete include:

- A persuasive brief to a court,
- A memorandum of law to a senior partner,
- An opening statement or closing argument in a judge or jury trial,
- A letter to the client,
- A witness declaration or affidavit,
- An internal discovery plan, or
- A proposal of settlement to the opposing counsel.

In addition, a number of times applicants have been asked to complete less typical tasks, such as:

- Drafting jury instructions,
- Revising a will or trust, or
- Planning a witness interview.

In this chapter, you will find a discussion and general form suggestions for drafting each of the document types that are likely to be tested, along with approaches for more unusual tasks. No matter how much you prepare, though, you may be hit with some task that is unfamiliar to you. But this is no cause for panic. Good performance test answers do not require that you *memorize* a specific format. When the Examiners want applicants to set up their answers in a specific manner, they give specific format instructions. Typically, they insert an additional format page just after the task memo. And, if they do include such format instructions, follow them as precisely as possible. You can see examples of such format pages from past performance tests in the Appendix portion of this book. (People v. Wils, Estate of Keefe, and Marriage of Eiffel each included format pages immediately following the task transmittal memos.).

Other exams do not contain separate format pages, so there may be a bit more leeway in set-up. In these types of performance tests, applicants will find the clues you need about set-up and what to include in the task memos themselves. But, most often and most important, so long as your organization turns on a logical application of the law and facts given and is responsive to the call or calls of the question, the answer format you choose (if no specific format is requested) will likely be well received.

> **Caveat**: Whatever task you are assigned, if they do give a format, follow it. Even if you wrote hundreds of memos as a law clerk using a different format, write this memo using the format provided. Not only will it likely help your score to show that you can follow directions, but the graders' score sheets are likely to be set up in the manner the instructions direct so that the person grading your exam will expect to see your answer presented that way.

In addition to following directions such as whatever format tips they give you, what really helps in writing a passing answer is to have a clear understanding of the ends you are trying to achieve by drafting a particular document and how that document fits into the context of the legal problems or issues you are analyzing. Let us take for example, a most fundamental concept in litigation—why cases ever go to trial in the first place—and see how an understanding of that concept might help you tackle a performance test.

Why *do* cases go to trial? Often, the parties either disagree about something that happened in the past, and/or, they agree about what occurred but disagree as to what should be the legal result of those occurrences. Now think about this basic aspect of litigation and how it relates to the performance test. When you are reading the File, and you see that the parties have conflicting versions of the past, you will need to pay particular attention to fact analysis skills. Be on the lookout for discrepancies in different peoples' accounts of what happened, scan the File for information you can use to discredit the opposing side's version of events. If, however, the parties in your performance test essentially agree about past events but dispute their legal consequences, the focus of what you are being tested may be more your legal analysis skills. One consequence for you here is that such a PT may require more time and attention to case law and/or statutes in the Library.

If your task is to draft a trial brief, you will know that you must write a persuasive argument stating why, given the law and facts, your client should prevail. You will know this, not because you memorized a "trial brief form" that says a trial brief is a persuasive document, but because you understand the lawyering process at trial. You know that, as counsel, you appear before a trier of fact (judge or jury) to argue the law and facts on behalf of your client, and to persuade the trier that your client's position should prevail. (More information on trial briefs below.)

The tone you adopt when writing a performance test is often an essential element to passing the exam. Where you want to convince a trier of fact or opposing party that your client's position is correct, you want to sound persuasive. However, where you are asked to give all the options or evaluate the pros and cons of something, you will want to sound as objective as possible.

Adapt the tone and vocabulary in each document to your audience. When you are writing to an audience of lay people, your own client or perhaps a jury, you may use a less formal tone than when addressing the court or a legislature. But rather than memorizing lists of documents that are formal, which are persuasive or analytical, try to learn why and when attorneys draft particular documents and understand how the document you are to prepare fits into what you are trying to accomplish for your client. Your tone may well come naturally once you understand these goals. Also, sometimes they will try to fool you by calling a document you know to be a persuasive document by an analytical name —a memorandum (really a brief by another name). So long as you calmly read the directions and see who you are writing to an why, you will be able to formulate an appropriate response.

Tip: When writing to lay people, define legal terms in plain English.

What if your performance test task were to draft a discovery plan and not only have you never written one but you do not know even what a discovery plan is let alone what it should look like. How should you proceed? (*Note*: You will find more information on discovery and the various discovery devices below, but here, just consider how you might reason through and successfully handle the task if you were not familiar with the document.) Begin as usual: study the Instructions. Even before you learn the facts from the File and the law from the Library, you can likely get a pretty good idea of what you will need to write by thinking things through. Ask yourself, "What am I being asked to write and why? Well, what is discovery? What is a plan?" Your thinking might proceed as follows:

I am being asked to do a "discovery plan." I am supposed to be an associate in a law firm. The senior partner told me, in the task memo, that the client is contemplating filing a lawsuit after suffering severe physical injury while trespassing on the defendant's property. I know that "discovery" is the process that allows our client, as a party (i.e. once we file a complaint), to obtain information, documents or things that are now exclusively in the other side's possession, and which will either help us understand the strengths and weaknesses of their case, our case, or both. The partner wants me to plan or strategize about how we are going to get that information, i.e. which tools of discovery will we use (deposition, interrogatories, requests for admission, other), when we will want to use them and why, and what we are looking for.

You can begin to see already that in asking you to draft a discovery plan, what you are really being tested on, is your ability to analyze the strengths and weaknesses of your client's and the opposing party's cases, and find out more information about them. You can handle that! You do not need a form book.

Now let us take this discovery plan example one step further. In considering *when* to use which discovery tools, context and some logic will help your analysis. Your internal thought process might go something like this:

> *If we send interrogatories <u>first</u>, we will learn how to proceed with the rest of our discovery, i.e. we might find out who has further information, whom we need to depose, and where any potential deponents are located. We could learn about documents we will want to review, and more. In addition, interrogatories will be much less expensive than depositions (as they do not involve court reporters and all that attorney time—for preparing and for sitting through the sessions). We should start with less expensive discovery tools and proceed to more costly ones if we need them. We should consult our client before spending more money than we need to.*

Whether your task is determining *how* to draft some document, or strategizing about *when* to do or perform various acts, think and reason through the issues, and you will likely see a way to formulate a responsive answer. Whatever you do, do not panic if you find you are not personally familiar with the tasks you are to perform.

THE TASKS APPLICANTS WILL HAVE TO COMPLETE IN A THREE-HOUR PERFORMANCE TEST

In the rest of this chapter, you will find descriptions and, where applicable, format suggestions for the types of tasks you may be asked to complete on your performance test. These documents, in the order presented below are:

A. LEGAL MEMORANDUM,
B. PERSUASIVE BRIEF
C. DECLARATION OR AFFIDAVIT
D. CLOSING ARGUMENT
E. OPENING STATEMENT
F. JURY INSTRUCTIONS
G. WITNESS CROSS OR DIRECT EXAMINATION
H. DISCOVERY/INVESTIGATION PLAN
I. CLIENT LETTER
J. CLIENT OR WITNESS INTERVIEW

K. CLIENT COUNSELING PLAN
L. NEGOTIATION/SETTLEMENT PROPOSAL OR AGREEMENT
M. OTHER NON-LITIGATION TASKS
N. ANALYSIS OF A CONTRACT, WILL, TRUST, OR STATUTE
O. ALTERNATIVE DISPUTE RESOLUTION TASKS
P. LEGISLATION
Q. UNUSUAL OR UNFAMILIAR TASKS

A. LEGAL MEMORANDUM (This may also be called Memorandum of Law, Memo or Memorandum, Analytical Memorandum.)

Most students have drafted at least one legal memorandum in their law school legal research course, and thus most applicants are familiar with this type of document. The memorandum of law is probably one of the most, if not the most, frequently tested document type on the performance test. Applicants may be asked to draft one long memo, or a shorter memo in conjunction with another task or tasks.

When an applicant is asked to draft a legal memorandum on a performance test typically this means the applicant must identify a cause of action or legal theory, or potential defense thereto. You may be asked to analyze whether a particular law affects one or more of the parties; whether and under what theories certain evidence may be admitted; whether settlement is advantageous and, if so, under what circumstances; or you may have to address an infinite variety of legal (and possibly factual) questions. You may also be asked specifically to evaluate the likely success of a particular course of action and/or propose alternative solutions to handling your client's problems.

When drafting a legal memorandum, adopt a balanced tone; tell the person to whom you are writing (most often someone in your own office, usually a senior partner) both about the strengths and about the weaknesses of your client's positions.

<u>FORM NOTES</u>

A typical Bar Exam memorandum of law includes an introductory header, sometimes a statement of facts, and body of text analyzing the relevant issues. Many people like to begin a memorandum with some sort of introductory heading, such as in the box below:

```
┌─────────────────────────────────────────────────────────────────┐
│  M E M O R A N D U M                                            │
│                                                                 │
│  To:  [Whomever assigned the task to you in the task memo.]     │
│                                                                 │
│  From:  [You:  Remember your name is "Applicant" on the Bar Exam.] │
│                                                                 │
│  Re:  [Identify the topic briefly with either the main issue and/or your client's name] │
│                                                                 │
│       [Body of Analysis]                                        │
└─────────────────────────────────────────────────────────────────┘
```

Following that introduction, the body of your analysis will typically be organized around each main legal theory, or each element of one or more causes of action or defenses. To make it easy for your grader to see your main points, you should try to give each one an appropriate heading or sub-heading.

If they give you a more specific, particularized format, follow it. For example, be alert for directions that tell you to omit a Statement of Facts and proceed directly to your analysis. Follow these instructions. You will not "wow" the grader with a superb Statement of Facts if the directions have specifically instructed that you not include one, and you will waste precious time.

If they do not give you a format, go with the typical: Header (To, From, and Re), Fact Statement (short, about 100 words), Analysis of Issues (separated into sections, by issue, if you are addressing more than one question), and Conclusion (again, short, no more than one paragraph.)

In your Statement of Facts, if you are asked to write one, select the facts that are relevant to those issues you are analyzing. Since this is an in-house document, you will want to expose facts that support and facts that negate your client's positions. Contrast this with the Statement of Facts portion of a persuasive brief (see below), where your goal is to select those facts that, though stated accurately, paint a picture that helps persuade the reader of your client's position and does not reveal your client's weaknesses. Remember, in a legal memo, you may well end up concluding that your client's position is not supportable, that you do not expect to win with a particular course of action, and that therefore you recommend settling or even withdrawing a complaint if necessary. *Note*: As always, abide by applicable rules of professional responsibility and ethics that you know. For example, *do not* counsel or suggest pursuing a claim that you determine is not well grounded in law and fact.

CAVEAT: *Just Because a Task is called a "Memorandum" does not make it an Analytical Memorandum of Law.* In one past performance test, applicants were asked to draft a "memorandum in support of a motion" directed to the judge. (Note it was not called a "Memorandum of Points and Authorities" which is often used interchangeably with the term "brief" but rather a "memorandum in support of a motion." In that exam, while the task was called a "memorandum," it was in fact a persuasive assignment. But the term confused some applicants. The lesson here is that you must think about your audience and the goal of your assignment. If the task memo is directed toward someone on your side, in-house, and if it tells you that you are "analyzing" or "thinking through" an issue, that suggests it is an analytical memorandum of law. Whereas if the task memo suggests that your document is in support of or in opposition to some argument, and is directed to someone who is not already on your side whom you must convince of your position, it is more likely a persuasive document—regardless of the name they give the task.

B. PERSUASIVE BRIEF (Related tasks may be: a brief in support of motion, memorandum of points and authorities, trial brief, and/or appellate brief.)

In this type of task, you are typically writing a legal argument to a judge in order to persuade the judge to make a particular decision or ruling. The problem may be set in state or federal court, or some other quasi-judicial body such as an administrative agency. And you may be asked to draft a brief covering any area of substantive or procedural law.

Applicants will want to use respectful, formal language when addressing a court, just as one would in practice. For example, write out terms in full that you might abbreviate in an informal, in-house memorandum. You may use bullet points where appropriate (for example, in listing reasons for supporting a position that you intend to develop in a later part of your brief), but do not write your full brief in outline style. Rather, write in basic prose style, with complete sentences and paragraphs. (By contrast, an outline might be the perfect format to use in an in-house investigation or discovery plan task.)

FORM NOTES

You will not be expected to prepare tables or indices. However, you may be asked to start the task with a Statement of Jurisdictional Basis. If your case is set in federal court, for example, in this section you will need to briefly state how your client has satisfied the requirements of either federal question or diversity subject matter jurisdiction.

The next part of a persuasive brief-type task is typically a Statement of Facts. In this section, you must summarize those facts relevant to supporting your client's legal arguments—usually in about 100 words. Do not distort or fabricate facts, but do be selective in both the facts you choose and the order in which you present them, in order to maximize support for your client.

Following the Statement of Facts is the Body of your argument. The most important part of the body of your argument, and the key to success on this type of assignment, are your **persuasive headings**. In the Examiners' words, selected from a representative set of performance test instructions, "This office follows the practice of writing carefully crafted subject headings that illustrate the arguments they cover. The argument heading should succinctly summarize the reasons the tribunal should take the position you are advocating. A heading should be a specific application of a rule of law to the facts of the case and not a bare legal or factual conclusion or a statement of an abstract principle."

Below are some examples, from actual performance test format pages, of what would be proper and improper persuasive headings. Review these (you may even want to read them aloud several times) so you can make certain you understand how to draft a proper heading if you are assigned to write a persuasive brief on one of your performance tests.

> *Improper: Defendant had sufficient minimum contacts to establish personal jurisdiction.*
> *Proper: A radio station located in the State of Franklin that broadcasts into the State of Columbia, receives revenue from advertisers located in the State of Columbia, and holds its annual meeting in the State of Columbia, has sufficient minimum contacts to allow Columbia courts to assert personal jurisdiction.*
>
> *Improper: The evidence is sufficient to convict the defendant.*
> *Proper: Evidence of entry through an open window is sufficient to satisfy the "breaking" element of burglary.*
>
> *Improper: The Plaintiff is not entitled to back pay.*
> *Proper: Because Plaintiff refused to accept defendant's offer to place her on administrative leave, she is not entitled to back pay.*
>
> *Improper: The Prisoner's rights were violated.*
> *Proper: Requiring the Petitioner to take psychotropic medication in the absence of a hearing establishing violent behavior constitutes cruel and unusual punishment under the 8th Amendment.*
>
> *Improper: The underlying facts establish Plaintiff's claim of right.*
> *Proper: By placing a chain across the driveway, by refusing access to others, and by posting a "No Trespassing" sign, Plaintiff has established a claim of right.*

Format Page Example. An example of a recent performance test where applicants were to set up part of their answers in a very specific format was *Estate of Keefe* (February 2002). Accordingly, the Exam set out very detailed format directions. The relevant portion of the instruction/format page for the very particular type of Memorandum of Points and Authorities applicants were to draft in that question stated that:

Section I. Introduction: This consists of a concise one-paragraph summary of the nature of the underlying case, the basis for the summary judgment motion, and the basis for the opposition.

Section II. Response to Moving Party's Statement of Undisputed Facts: This is in two-column format. In the first column we restate the alleged Undisputed Facts. In the second column, we respond with "Agree" or "Disagree," indicating whether we agree or disagree that the fact alleged to be undisputed is in fact undisputed.

Section III. Responsive Party's Statement of Disputed Facts: This is a two-column section identical in format to the Moving Party's Statement of Undisputed Facts (Section II of their Memorandum). In the first column, we state those facts we believe are disputed. The second column lists citations to evidence that establish these facts.

Section IV. Response to Moving Party's Arguments: In this section, we draft arguments that respond point by point to the arguments made in the moving party's Memorandum of Points and Authorities in Support of Motion for Summary Judgment. In support of our arguments, we cite to our Disputed Facts by the number assigned in Section III, and to relevant cases to support our legal assertions. We also make any additional arguments that support the position that there are triable issues of fact or that there are legal issues precluding entry of judgment as a matter of law.

Section V. Conclusion: This is a brief statement asking the court to find in our favor.

End of format page excerpt from *Estate of Keefe* (February 2002).

C. DECLARATION (OR AFFIDAVIT)

In a declaration (also called an affidavit), you are presenting facts in the name of a witness (called the "declarant" or "affiant"), facts that person could testify to if he or she were called to the witness stand in court. In other words, you are writing facts that are personally known to the declarant, and are truthful, logical, and relevant. Declarations often provide the supporting documentation that go along with persuasive briefs, and though they are recitations of facts, they are persuasive in nature in that you are selecting those facts that are necessary to and help support your client's legal position.

FORM NOTES

You will typically be given a format, but for purposes of a performance test, a declaration may be presented quite simply, as the example below indicates.

Declaration of X

I, X, declare as follows:

1.

2.

3.

The above-mentioned facts are all true and correct to the best of my personal knowledge,

_____
X, Declarant

Note that the first numbered paragraph often contains background information on who the declarant is, for example stating if that person is a party to the action or what that person's connection to the case is. Each of the remaining numbered paragraphs recites an important relevant fact that is truthful and is within the declarant's personal knowledge.

Format Page Example. This example below of format language for affidavits or declarations, language that has been repeated with various minor changes over the years, comes from

Centerville Housing Authority v. Richardson (February 1993) where applicants were told:

> Affidavits should meet the following requirements:
>
> > -Affidavits are to contain facts necessary to support the legal position asserted in the motion or other request;
> >
> > -Only truthful, logically relevant, and material facts shall be included;
> >
> > -Only facts which are personally known to the affiant shall be included;
> >
> > -Facts should be presented in numbered paragraphs;
> >
> > -Each numbered paragraph, to the extent possible, should contain only one factual allegation;
> >
> > -Captions, signature lines, and sworn acknowledgment will be added by support staff.

End of format page excerpt from *Centerville Housing Authority v. Richardson* (February 1993).

D. CLOSING ARGUMENT TO JURY (Related assignment: closing argument to a judge, concluding statement in an administrative hearing, or position paper to a legislative body.)

In this task, you are expected to write out what you would say at the close of a trial to convince jurors that, given the evidence presented in court and the relevant legal rules, they should find in favor of your client. You will be including points about your evidence and the evidence presented by your adversary, credibility (or lack thereof) of particular witnesses, and ultimately convincing jurors that your client has met its burden of proof and/or that the opposing side has failed to meet its burden of proof. You should also be sure to anticipate and rebut any arguments that you anticipate your adversary will make in his or her closing argument, since most often applicants are asked to give the argument for the party that must first address the jury.

CAVEAT: If you are drafting a closing argument as the prosecutor in a criminal case, be sure not to overstep ethical rules. For example, be keenly aware that the entire burden of proof is on your client (the government); the accused (who is innocent until proven guilty) does not have to prove anything in the case-in-chief.

FORM NOTES

On TV, trial lawyers often give dramatic closing arguments that either tell a story or revolve around some catchy theme. On performance tests, the Instructions will often prompt you to "marshal" or organize the evidence around what they refer to as the "ultimate facts." As is discussed at length in the earlier chapter on Fact Analysis, what is typically meant by an ultimate fact is a factual statement of an essential legal element. For example, in a simple negligence action, where the elements are duty, breach, causation, and damages, the fact that the plaintiff suffered medical injuries for which she had to pay doctors $100,000 to treat, is an ultimate fact; that fact is the restatement in factual terms of the legal element "damages."

If the PT Library or File (as part of the trial transcript) includes jury instructions, let these be your guide as to which legal elements must be proven. Then, using facts that were established as evidence in trial, lay out explicitly for the jurors those inferences you want them to draw from the evidence.

Cite specifically to those elements of law that must be proven, perhaps quoting from the jury instructions themselves, rather than necessarily citing to specific cases or statutes. Remember that your audience is composed of lay people so avoid jargon and define any legal terms you use. You can be less formal than you would be if you were addressing a judge, but be sure to be as organized as possible so the jurors (and grader) can easily follow your points. Even though in real life you would be talking and one does not speak "headings," you will want to insert "headings" (perhaps in brackets) for the grader to see your main points, just as you would in presenting any written document.

Format Page Example. An example of format language for closing arguments states:

> You should begin with an understand of the legal principles that will be applied to
> the facts in the case. In some cases, you will be provided with jury instructions.
> In other cases, the instructions will not yet be drafted and you will have to rely
> upon an analysis of legal authority. The instructions or legal authority will give
> you the framework for your closing argument. However, the closing argument
> should not discuss or make reference to these authorities; a closing argument is not
> a legal brief or an essay. The argument must show how the evidence presented
> meets the legal standards which are or will be set forth in the jury instructions.
> The argument is based on the evidence presented, not histrionics or personal

opinion. Write out your argument exactly as you plan to give it. [PASS Editorial Note: This means greet the trial of fact, for example, start with "Good morning, Ladies and Gentlemen of the Jury," and write as if you are speaking directly to the jury, with language appropriate to lay people, or to the court in a bench trial.]

It's important that the argument be in your own words, but remember that you're communicating with a group of lay people. Your job is to help them understand how the law relates to the facts presented, and to persuade them that they have no choice but to find for your client. In doing that, you should consider the following:

-State explicitly the ultimate facts that the jurors must find in order for your client to prevail.
-Organize the evidence in support of the ultimate facts.
-Incorporate relevant legal principles or jury instructions into your argument.
-Discuss the sufficiency of the evidence and the credibility of witnesses.
-Draw reasonable inferences from the evidence to support positions you have taken.
-Anticipate opposing counsel's arguments and point out weaknesses in his case.
-Refer to equities or policy considerations that merit a finding for our client.

The most important factors are organization and persuasiveness; if you immerse the jury in a sea of unconnected details, they won't have a coherent point of view to discuss in the jury room. Never hold back any argument assuming that you will have a second opportunity to make it on rebuttal.

End of format page excerpt from *Xenophanes* (July 1993).

E. OPENING STATEMENT

This document is a sort of road map or preview that you are giving to jurors at the beginning of a trial, to let them know what evidence you intend to present at trial. You can only discuss evidence that you believe, in good faith, will be presented at trial—in other words, you may not discuss evidence you know will be found inadmissible.

FORM NOTES

The task memo and/or format memos will likely give you a sense of how you are to set up the opening statement, but often you will begin by introducing yourself, then proceed witness by witness to discuss the evidence. An example of the type of language that may be used follows below:

> *Ladies and Gentlemen, my name is Applicant. I represent _____, the Plaintiff in this case, and will be talking to you today about some of the evidence you are going to hear in the coming days. First you will hear from Mr. _____. Mr _____ will testify about _____. Next, you will hear from Ms. _____, who will tell you about_____. Last, you will see documentation of _____ (and you may discuss any exhibits or documentary evidence that will be presented at trial.)*

F. Jury Instructions

It is possible that you could be asked to draft or edit jury instructions. In this document, you are to present the law or ultimate facts jurors must find in order to decide the case. Often these instructions are presented in paragraphs or bullets, each discussing one legal element or ultimate fact.

FORM NOTES

According to the format memo in the February 1996 California Performance Test, which asked applicants to draft jury instructions, "The objective [of jury instructions] is to fairly state the law while emphasizing factors that support a favorable result for our client." That same 1996 performance test format memo gave several examples of jury instructions for cases in tort involving issues of negligent infliction of emotional distress, two of which follow below.

> *If you find that Harry Jones, as an adjacent landowner to the Chesterfield airport, suffered emotional distress as a result of the noise from aircraft landing, taking off and in-flight, you may award damages to the plaintiff.*

> *If you find that the employee of the defendant, Speedy Process Service, made an invalid service of the writ on Mary Williams and thereafter knowingly filed a false affidavit of valid service, you may award damages to the plaintiff for negligent infliction of emotional distress.*

G. WITNESS CROSS- (OR DIRECT) EXAMINATION

Like the closing argument to a jury, in this task applicants are asked to write out what they would be saying in court—here, however, in either the direct or cross-examination of witnesses. Direct examination is where counsel elicits (in question and answer form) relevant admissible evidence from his or her own witnesses. In cross-examination, counsel questions the opposing party's witnesses with the goal of getting those witnesses to make statements or admit to facts that support his or her own client's version of events, or in order to cast doubt on the credibility of those witnesses.

A cross- or direct examination-type task is a backdoor way of also testing you on evidence. Because relevance is one of the most fundamental concepts in evidence, it may be helpful to keep in mind (and, where appropriate, to write out explicitly) why a question is relevant. For instance, assume that you are counsel for the plaintiff in a personal injury action based on alleged domestic violence. You are questioning the witness, a police officer, whose version of events contradicts that of your client. If, in questioning the officer, you were to be able to elicit the fact that the officer was once employed as a personal security guard for the defendant, this would be helpful evidence in impeaching the witness' credibility.

FORM NOTES

You may be asked to draft an examination (cross or direct) that you or another lawyer in your law firm would conduct, or you may be asked to draft questions you think opposing counsel is likely to ask of your witnesses. In either case, the Instructions will typically give you a very precise format to follow, one that helps you lay out both the questions and anticipated responses. For each witness, you may be asked to list the subject that the questions address, and then write out the questions and anticipated answers in full. After that, you will likely be asked to note any evidentiary objections that you or opposing counsel might make, give responses to those objections, and finish with the judge's likely ruling as to whether or not the witness will have to answer each question.

Format Page Example. An example of format language for witness cross-examination plan states:

> When preparing a witness cross-examination plan, you should (1) state the topic of
> each series of questions; (2) under each topic, list the precise questions you
> propose be asked of the witness; (3) identify any objections you anticipate will be
> lodged by opposing counsel; (4) state the best response(s) to the objection; and (5)
> state the likely ruling. For example, the following was taken from the cross-

examination plan in <u>Smith v. Jones</u>:

Topic: Witness' prior inconsistent statement concerning who had the right of way.

Questions:
        Q. On direct, you testified that the light was green for Defendant, is that correct?
        A. Yes.
        Q. Immediately after the accident, you spoke to a police officer, is that correct?
        A. Yes.
        Q. You told the police officer that the light was green for Plaintiff, didn't you?
        A. Yes.

Objections Anticipated: Hearsay.

Response: Prior inconsistent statement offered to show two stories, not for truth of either version.

Likely ruling: Admitted with limiting instruction.

End of format page excerpt from *Dodson v. Canadian Equipment Company* (July 1993).

Tip re: Direct Examination: If your task were to draft a direct examination plan you would likely use a similar format to that set forth in connection with cross examination above, with topics, questions, objections, responses and likely rulings.

H. DISCOVERY PLAN AND/OR INVESTIGATION MEMO

Applicants have been tested in the past on both informal fact investigation and formal fact gathering (called "discovery"). Informal fact gathering includes everything from talking to anyone who may have relevant information to reviewing public records or documents obtained via the Freedom of Information Act. You may suggest examining scientific data (with or without the assistance of an expert), taking pictures or measurements, or doing other sorts of physical testing. Some of the main discovery devices that you may suggest using in your discovery plan are depositions, interrogatories, requests for admission, requests for production of documents, and subpoenas (all of which are explained in more detail below.)

<u>FORM NOTES</u>

If there is a format memo telling you how to set up your answer, as always, follow the instructions as closely as possible. If not, usually the most logical way to organize these investigation plans is element by element. Set out each of the elements to be proven; then, under each one, list the evidence you currently have and the evidence you wish to locate and why. Here, you will succinctly say why the evidence is relevant and/or what it would help to establish. Next, list the possible sources you would look to or tools you might use to obtain each particular item of evidence.

CAVEAT: Do not suggest any unethical or illegal methods to get information you want.

The instructions may also ask you to point out any evidentiary concerns with regard to getting a statement or physical evidence admitted into evidence. For instance, you may get credit for noting, in conjunction with the listing of a certain letter that you wish to obtain, that it must be authenticated before it will be received into evidence by the court.

Test Yourself: What are the main discovery devices you are likely to include in a discovery plan?

Q: List the discovery tools you are likely to suggest to obtain evidence in a discovery plan.
A:_____
_____
_____
_____
_____
_____

Some Answers:

<u>Depositions:</u> You may depose parties and/or non-party witnesses. This is live questioning, under oath, with a court reporter making a transcript. You are typically seeking information from the deponent about what happened, when, why, and how—i.e. information within the deponent's personal knowledge. Note that you may also ask the deponent about documentary or physical evidence.

Interrogatories: You may only send interrogatories to parties. These are written questions, again about facts within the party's knowledge (what happened, when, why, and how), and/or about documentary or physical evidence to which the party may have access. Note that it is much less expensive to send interrogatories than to take depositions because you do not need to hire a court reporter.

Requests for admission: Written questions that ask a party to admit or deny certain facts.

Requests for production of documents: Written request for a party to produce documents.

Subpoena: Written request to anyone with custody of certain documents to produce those documents.

I. LETTER TO CLIENT

In order to write a good letter to a client in the PT context, decide first what the specific purpose of the letter is. Why does whoever is assigning you this task (usually a senior partner in your law firm) want you to write to the client?

It may be that your goal is to render some legal opinion to the client (tell the client, for instance, how likely he or she is to succeed with a particular course of action). You may be writing to update your client on what has happened in his or her case, or you may be helping to prepare the client for an upcoming court hearing, deposition, or interview. Your client will almost always be a lay person, too, so use simple language and explain any legal jargon you use.

You also must be keenly aware of your client's needs and desires. If you can, think of different ways to help the client achieve his or her goals, and explain the benefits and risks of any proposed course of action in simple, plain English. Take into account the psychological and financial implications, in addition to the legal aspects, of anything you propose. In addition, realize that your client may be expressly or impliedly suggesting some course of action that is illegal or unethical; if so, you must counsel the client as to why that action may not be pursued.

J. CLIENT OR WITNESS INTERVIEW

You may be asked to write out a plan for interviewing your own client or another person who was involved in, observed, or knew about your client and/or his story. (One past PT where applicants were asked to critique an interview plan that a more junior lawyer had drafted is an excellent practice test for those wanting to try their hand at this type of task, *see In re: Cook* 7/86).

FORM NOTES

If you are asked to write or critique an interview plan, you will likely be given a format or guidelines to follow. If you are not given more specific guidance, consider the goals of an interview, and set up your answer in a way that logically meets those goals.

In the first part of an interview plan, you want to include language that puts the witness at ease as much as possible. For example, tell the witness how long you intend to meet and the topics you expect to cover, i.e. tell the person what to expect in the interview. If you are meeting for the first time with your own client, this initial interview should also include discussions of fee arrangement—in other words, tell the client how much and on what basis (hourly, contingency, or other) your firm charges.

Next, it may be helpful to try to establish a chronology of events for the witness' story—what this witness observed and when. After that, you may probe one or more areas of questioning further to develop a particular legal or factual theory that is helpful to your client (and/or to find out more about something that may be potentially damaging to your client).

Last, before the witness leaves, it may be important to conclude by confirming any particularly important information that came out during the interview and to thank the witness. You may also need to have the witness sign something or provide the witness with documents to review, sign, and return. You may also want to arrange for the witness to meet with you again and/or provide you with physical or documentary evidence that the witness may have.

K. CLIENT COUNSELING

Lawyers counsel clients in litigation and non-litigation contexts. In each, the lawyer tries to help the client make an informed decision about a particular problem, issue, choice, or path. You could be asked to counsel your client in a performance test by writing a letter to the client, writing an internal memo about counseling the client or in the context of some plan for meeting with the client.

FORM NOTES

Follow whatever specific guidelines you are given about how to set up the document by keeping in mind the following basics for client counseling. If they do not give you a format, start by identifying the client's problems and clarifying the client's goals. (This you may do with the client, or by reading information from the File, for example the transcript of a previous interview with the client or a letter from the client.)

Next, articulate, in light of the client's goals, alternative courses of action or competing solutions to the client's problems, and identify the legal consequences of each of these alternatives. You will also want to consider and likely write about any important non-legal consequences to the client, such as the possible effects of these alternatives on the client's business and social life.

Last, you will want to give the client any guidance you can to help the client choose among the various solutions, making certain that you abide by relevant rules of professional responsibility, and, if necessary, request relevant additional information from the client.

L. NEGOTIATION, SETTLEMENT PROPOSAL OR AGREEMENT

This task usually asks you to develop a compromise or settlement offer that helps resolve a number of different areas of conflict that exist between your client and an adversary. If a format is not given, the basics of this type of task involve setting out the factual context for the settlement, what both parties agree about or, if necessary, the parties' differing views of the facts at hand, followed by the specific proposed agreement you are presenting. You may also need to be persuasive in an effort to urge the opposing party to agree to your proposal.

Keep in mind some of the generally positive aspects to settling a case, including:

- Cost savings (as compared with litigation),

- Increased privacy (court documents are public record, unless sealed, but you may agree to keep settlement-related documents private), and

- Speed (settling often speeds up the sometimes very lengthy litigation process).

Before you can negotiate a successful deal, you must first learn your client's goals and needs. This involves the same first steps as counseling. Then, however, you will move on and try to persuade the other side either to accept your client's terms or to come to some agreement acceptable to both parties (or all, if there are more than two parties).

In practice, you often learn about clients by talking with them. Your client is often your first and most helpful source of information. You may also need to talk with others and/or review documents. PT Files usually contain notes from meetings with your client, documents the client produced, or notes the client wrote. Often, you will need more information than what is given in the File, and you will be asked to detail such potential, additional evidence or information in a memo to the senior partner or to an investigator you have hired, or in a letter to your client.

Generally, when you negotiate on behalf of a client, your primary job as counsel is to present his or her claims, concerns, and proposals to the other side, and try to get them to accept your own client's terms. Although your client must consent to any final agreement or bargain reached in the process, you may negotiate on your own.

As with interviewing and counseling, lawyers negotiate for their clients in both the litigation and non-litigation contexts. When a dispute is resolved in the litigation context, the standard legal remedies for a prevailing party come in the form of money damages. In negotiating solutions to clients' problems (both in litigation settlements and in alternate forms of dispute resolution), you may be able to fashion agreements that involve non-monetary terms or deals, either in addition to or instead of money damages. Often, such terms will suit your client's needs better than money damages. For example, if your client is involved in a contract dispute for the sale of goods, in addition to negotiating about damages, consider shaping an agreement with the opposing party by bargaining about other terms, such as delivery time or place issues, payment, amount of product delivery, exchange for related products or services, or anything else that may be mutually workable to meet the financial as well as the legal and psychological needs of all the parties.

In addition to knowing what *your* client wants, you should know how a court would likely decide the dispute, i.e. what are the legal rights and remedies of each party. Even if you fashion a "creative agreement," such as those described above, knowing the law is vital. It may give you leverage in the negotiation process. If your research shows that your client is not entitled to any legal relief, make sure that you do not file a complaint, and if one is already filed, that you withdraw it, as filing a frivolous lawsuit is sanctionable conduct.

You should also consider the amount of time and money it will take for the dispute to be resolved, and how important time, money, and other considerations are to the respective parties. Try to learn as much as you can about the opposing party's wants and needs—this will help you know what to press for and what to concede.

Consider the following problem solving example: Your wealthy client has been slandered by some tabloid press. Given your client's finances, negotiating with the paper's counsel for a public apology and retraction of its statements, perhaps in a *New York Times* advertisement, might be a perfectly acceptable solution to both parties. Your client's reputation could be restored, at least in the eyes of those who read *The New York Times*. And the paper, while it may have paid a lot for the ad, probably paid less than it would have paid in legal fees and costs (and possibly a hefty judgment), had the case gone to trial.

As to tactics and strategies, when you finally sit down to negotiate with the other side after counseling your own client and conducting necessary legal research (on your performance test, after reading and analyzing the File, Library, and any other documents), you can take several approaches. One is to start with an assertive, but realistic, position and make only a few concessions. When you concede on a small point, you may lose little and in turn get the other side to give on some terms that really matter to your client. Another strategy is to start with an aggressive stance, expecting to give in on many terms. A third strategy is to ask for something reasonable that you know the other side will accept, then forcefully state that yours is a "take it or leave it" offer from the outset and you will not bend. Further, show them why the offer is reasonable and why they should accept it.

What is essential on a performance test is not to adopt one or another strategy, but if you have this type of assignment, to make explicit the reasoning for whatever strategy you choose. As you read performance test materials, note the terms and conditions your client seems adamant about and those the client seems willing and able to compromise on, and show the graders how your efforts meet and fulfill your client's needs and goals. (As far back as *Klare v. Journal of Human Experience* from July 1984, where tasks were to draft one memo outlining a negotiation strategy and a second presenting an opening offer of settlement to opposing counsel, and on many subsequent exams, applicants were asked to draft one or more documents involving settlement issues.)

Tip: Ethical Advocacy. In arguing for a proposed settlement as in other contexts, it is vital to demonstrate to the bar grader your ability to act in a *zealous yet ethical manner* on behalf of your clients.

M. OTHER NON-LITIGATION, TRANSACTIONAL TASKS

While the litigation context is a more common setting for performance tests, there have been tests involving other areas as well. Also, given the recent movement away from litigation and toward both alternative methods of dispute resolution and preventive law (education and planning to prevent legal problems from ever arising), it is quite likely that performance tests of the future will be set more frequently in these areas.

You may be asked to draft documents that cover a broad range of planning, counseling, or deal making, in either a business or personal context. Business clients may seek advice concerning proposed agreements with other persons or entities, compliance with government regulations, and applications to various government agencies and offices for licenses. For individuals, these areas of law include the purchase and sale of property, pre- and post-nuptial agreements, and estate planning.

On past performance tests, applicants have been asked to draft estate plans, evaluate business related proposals, and more. In order to begin such a task, you would use the same sorts of approaches discussed above with respect to counseling, interviewing, and negotiation. In particular, you would start by developing a clear understanding of your client's objectives and concerns. You should begin this process by gathering information from the File—locate any information from the client or about the client's situation from other sources (interview transcripts, letters, contracts, property descriptions, photographs—whatever they put in the File may be relevant.) Then, identify the legal and non-legal issues actually and/or potentially raised by the proposed transaction(s). Look at the task memo, and study the Library for clues as to the main legal problems or issues you are expected to discuss. Information about the client's goals and desires, which often appears in the File, will help steer you toward the non-legal problems you should mention.

The next part of an analysis of a typical transactional performance test will likely involve drafting or editing some proposed agreement or statement of your client's position. You may have to present this to other parties, for example in negotiating with them, or you may be asked simply to counsel your own client about his or her options. As with litigation-related performance tests, doing practice tests will help make clear the types of tasks you must do to complete a transactional performance test.

N. ANALYSIS OF A CONTRACT, WILL, TRUST, OR STATUTE

Applicants asked to handle such tasks have typically been asked to review a document that someone else drafted, looking provision by provision to determine whether the agreement is valid, enforceable, and most advantageously worded for your client. From the File, you can determine your client's specific goals, what terms are essential to your client and what terms your client is willing to give on, and the strength of your client's bargaining power.

FORM NOTES

As always, if they give you a format, follow it. If not, you should proceed through the document, paragraph by paragraph, and suggest what language should be deleted, added, and modified. You may also edit the document for ambiguities and see that it fits the law provided by legal authorities from the Library.

O. ALTERNATIVE DISPUTE RESOLUTION ("ADD") TASKS

In a performance test, if you were asked to prepare a client for a mediation and/or arbitration, would you be thrown? What are arbitration and mediation?

In an arbitration, the parties agree to let a neutral third party (often someone knowledgeable in the subject matter of the dispute) make a final and binding decision. Arbitration resembles courtroom litigation but is less formal; for example, rules of evidence may not be adhered to as strictly as in a court.

In mediation, parties also go voluntarily before a neutral third party, the mediator. Unlike arbitrators or judges, however, mediators do not impose a binding decision on the parties; rather, mediators try to facilitate dialogue between the disputing participants and allow them to come to their own, mutually agreeable solution, instead of rendering a judgment for one of them. A mediator may also help them draft a written memorandum of the agreement reached, which usually takes the form of a binding contract. The benefits of mediation over litigation include:

- Less cost to the client,

- Informality, as parties are not bound by evidence rules,

- More control since the parties themselves, not a judge, make the ultimate decisions;

- Convenience, such that parties also may be able to schedule ADD sessions at times that are more convenient to them rather than simply when the court clerk places the matter on the judge's calendar, and

- Privacy is enhanced in mediation, as there are no court-filed documents that become public record.

In summary, while in practice there may be great differences, for purposes of completing performance tests, think about preparing for a mediation as you would for a settlement conference, and for an arbitration as you would for a trial, paying close attention to any additional procedural rules you are given in the Exam itself.

P. Legislation

Since lawyers also act as legislators, some past performance test tasks have included redrafting statutes and advocating amendments to legislation. As with lawyering tasks, if you are asked to draft or revise legislation on a performance test, focus on content and follow any form given to you. Your tone should be more formal than in a client letter, for instance, but you need not adhere to a format unless the instructions so specify. If you are instructed to advocate the endorsement or passage of certain legislation, your tone should be partisan and persuasive. However, if you are instructed to evaluate the pros and cons of certain legislation, adopt an objective, neutral tone.

Q. Unusual or Unfamiliar Tasks

The material above should help you familiarize yourself with the commonly tested documents. Occasionally, however, the Examiners will include, as one of your tasks, a document that you have never heard of. If this happens to you, stay calm, read the instructions carefully, and follow them as closely as possible. It may well be, once you get into the instructions and assignment, that you will see that they have simply called the task by a document name with which you are unfamiliar. (As mentioned above, legal briefs in support of motions are often called Memoranda of Points and Authorities. But this is not true in every jurisdiction so some applicants are unfamiliar with the term "Points and Authorities." Reading through the instructions, it would become clear, however, to such an out-of-state applicant that the task is really the old, familiar "brief" called by a different name.) Or it may be that you will have to review the task instructions a number of times to understand fully what they want from you. Bottom line: Remember, if the task is unfamiliar to you, it is likely unfamiliar to everyone else around you, and the key to success will be—as always—in reading and carefully following whatever instructions they give you.

TEST YOURSELF: Document type exercises

Below you will find two exercises to test yourself in order to determine if you are familiar with the different types of documents that may be tested on your performance test. There are instructions for each.

EXERCISE #1—DEFINE THE DOCUMENTS

The following are examples of the types of documents you might be asked to draft on the actual Bar Exam. All of them have appeared on actual past performance tests. Do you know what each one is? Take a moment to think, and in the space next to each term, try to define the document, in your own words. Write the document's function or purpose, state any specific rules you know about limitations of its form or usage, and, if possible, note the context in which such a document would be used.

NEGOTIATION LETTER/SETTLEMENT PROPOSAL:

_____

_____

MEMORANDUM OF POINTS AND AUTHORITIES:

_____

_____

POSITION PAPER:

_____

_____

CLIENT COUNSELING PLAN:

_____

_____

APPELLATE BRIEF:

_____

_____

DEMAND LETTER:

_____
_____

MEMORANDUM OF LAW:

_____
_____

DISCOVERY PLAN:

_____
_____

JURY INSTRUCTIONS:

_____
_____

CLOSING ARGUMENT:

_____
_____

CLIENT/WITNESS INTERVIEW:

_____
_____

TRIAL BRIEF:

_____
_____

CLIENT LETTER:

_____
_____

WITNESS DIRECT EXAMINATION:

_____
_____

INTERROGATORIES:

_____
_____

WITNESS CROSS EXAMINATION:

_____
_____

DECLARATION:

_____
_____

AFFIDAVIT:

_____
_____

CONTRACT:

_____
_____

WILL:

_____
_____

TRUST:

_____
_____

STATUTE:

_____
_____

OPENING STATEMENT:

_____
_____

EXERCISE #2—DOCUMENT MATCHING

This exercise reviews the documents employed at the various stages of litigation. These stages appear in chronological order below. In each, you will find a numbered list of events that happen or that lawyers do. Next to each item is a blank line. Below each numbered list is a lettered list. These items are documents that might be drafted in connection with those events or things on the numbered list above.

The lettered lists are not in order. Place the letters corresponding to those documents you might draft at each event in the spaces provided on the numbered lists. *Note*: Some documents can be matched to more than one numbered entry.

As you work, make sure you know: 1) what each event is and why it happens, 2) what each document is and why it is written, and 3) whether or not any other documents might come into play at each event.

STAGE 1. PRE-TRIAL
COUNSEL IDENTIFIES AND SHAPES BOTH THE FACTS AND THE LAW

1. Initial client interview   _____
2. Factual investigation   _____
3. Legal research   _____
4. Discovery   _____
5. Settlement conferences   _____
6. Pre-trial motions   _____
7. Plea bargaining   _____

a) Memo of law
b) Motion for summary judgment
c) Post-interview notes
d) Memo summarizing interview
e) Stipulation re: evidence
f) Outline of negotiation strategies
g) Memo re: future investigation
h) Memo of law objectively stating strengths and weaknesses of client's legal case
I) Pleading asking court to exclude evidence
j) Memo re: research plan or strategy
k) Discovery plan
l) Settlement offer
m) Outline of questions for deposition
n) Summaries of transcripts
o) Summary of applicable case law
p) Memo re: info to be gathered
q) Memo planning what to ask client
r) Memo re: client objectives and concerns
s) Memo re: pros and cons of settlement
t) Demand letter
u) Interrogatories

STAGE 2. TRIAL
FACTS AND LAW ARE BOTH ESTABLISHED AND ARGUED AT THIS STAGE

1. Voir dire   _____
2. Plaintiff/Prosecution (P) case-in-chief   _____
3. Opening statements   _____
4. Direct examination of P witnesses by P   _____
5. Cross-examination of P witnesses by D   _____
6. Motion for judgment   _____
7. Defense case-in-chief   _____
8. Direct examination of D witnesses by D   _____
9. Cross-examination of D witnesses by P   _____
10. Rebuttal   _____
11. Surrebuttal   _____

12. Jury instructions   _____
13. Closing arguments   _____

a) Defense motion stating that, after hearing P's case-in-chief, sufficient evidence was not presented to prove a claim of right
b) Questions to be propounded to one's witnesses in order to establish certain evidence
c) Persuasive argument marshaling all the facts, showing how they prove the elements in the client's case, and presenting the burden of proof and jury instructions in such a way as to convince the trier your client should prevail
d) Outline of questions to be asked of potential jurors to determine if they could fairly and impartially judge the case
e) Questions to be propounded to an opposing witness to test or diminish his credibility or refute or contradict his statements
f) Memo of oral presentation that resembles a "road map" summarizing evidence to be presented at trial

STAGE 3. APPEALS
LEGAL ARGUMENTS PROCEED BASED ON THE FACTS AS SET AT TRIAL

1. Assembling record of lower court   _____
2. Forming and agreeing to issues on appeal   _____
3. Appellate briefs   _____
4. Appellate arguments (oral)   _____

a) Organizing and marking excerpts of record
b) Statement or letter to opposing counsel that attempts to coordinate and agree upon issues on appeal
c) Memo or statement that selects facts from trial court transcript that are necessary and relevant to issues on appeal
d) Like trial brief, except using agreed facts from lower court record, this is persuasive and more formal legal argument—using points and authorities—to persuade a court (judge) that your client should prevail
e) Statement of which issues are on appeal (those not resolved to the parties' satisfaction in the lower court)

Chapter 8: Success Strategies

Success should be in view; there is a light at the end of this tunnel. But know that the road is not an easy one. The first tough pill to swallow is how anti-climactic law school graduation is. Congratulations! You have your J.D., but not much time to party because your biggest test is yet to come. Be proud of your achievement. Now move on.

A. PREPARE YOURSELF AND PREPARE YOUR FRIENDS AND FAMILY

Get used to the idea that your biggest test is yet to come, and start getting others used to it, too. Let family and friends know that you appreciate their participation in the congratulatory stuff, but you will not have time to sightsee (if they are from out of town) or to play (if they are locals).

If you are lucky, you will graduate before your Bar review course starts. This will give you a day or two to relax and enjoy the festivities. If you are unlucky, graduation may come smack in the middle of Bar review. You might even have to skip a lecture to go through ceremonies. So be it. Toss your mortarboard in the air, have a glass or two of good champagne, take the one day off, and then go back to work. (Party when the Bar Exam is over —and plan to whoop it up when you find out that you have passed!)

Preparing the folks around you is important, but it is not easy. Every *little* thing you are asked to do (or want to do) will be just that: one little thing. But many little things add up, and can easily distract from your preparation and training, from *your Bar Exam*. If you must do things for or with certain people (like go to work or get your kids to school), or for yourself (like laundry and dishes), do them at your least productive time—if at all possible.

Say "No." Say, "The Bar Exam comes first." Say, "This is my Bar Exam summer or winter." Say these things and mean them. People who truly love you will not want you to repeat the Bar Exam. They will not want to live through It more than once themselves. If they have already, they undoubtedly would not mind if this were the last time!

Doing this may mean asking for time off from work or arranging extensive childcare during your prep period. To the extent you can, make these arrangements ahead of time. You do not want to be busy making logistical arrangements when you should be studying. It is sometimes tough for others to do without you, or you without them, but you may not be able to do it any other way.

There really are few Supermen and Superwomen. Only you know your limits.

You may have noticed "Bar Exam" capitalized throughout this text. Why? Because It is important. It is your Main Event. Give It capital letters, and a red flag. Bold and underline It. The Bar Exam *is* important; treat it as such.

Continually, the stories from candidates who failed prior Bar Exams show that they did not make the Test important enough.

There is no substitute for hard work and preparation. The more you do, the better you will feel. Be honest with yourself, and assess what *you* need to do to pass. You, not anyone else. If your grades were not superior in law school, work harder. You must, and you must face up to that fact. Prove you can win now. But do not be fooled. No one, no Bar review or individual, can guarantee your Bar Exam passage; you must earn it. Fight for it. Be strong.

TEST YOURSELF: Are you Prepared?

1. The following are the biggest responsibilities and distractions I face during my Bar Exam preparation period:_____
_____
_____
_____

2. Which of the above can I eliminate, put off, or delegate to others? Can I hire someone to help (or arrange for family help) with certain ongoing responsibilities, such as childcare? Have I warned my employer that I may need time off for Bar Exam study?
_____
_____
_____
_____
_____

3. I have explained to my family and close friends how much time and effort studying for the Bar Exam takes. Yes _____ No _____

4. What have I told my family/friends/significant other about how they can be of the most help to me during this time?
_____
_____
_____
_____

5. Write a detailed plan (starting here with an outline) showing how you will reduce your non-Bar Exam studying obligations to free up time to study during the two months prior to the exam. (Consider how you will finance taking time off from work and paying for extra help if you need it. Remember, all of these exercises are for your eyes only, so be honest with yourself!)

———
———
———
———
———
———
———
———
———
———
———
———
———
———
———
———
———
———
———
———
———

B. PREPARE YOURSELF PHYSICALLY

As stated in the Introduction to this book, Bar Exam success depends on skill, preparation, and confidence. The first chapters focused on the skills you need to write passing performance test answers. Complete and effective preparation involves physical, mental, and spiritual components, as well as mastering the requisite skills. In this part of the book, we will discuss some of those other aspects of preparation that will give you the confidence to pass your Bar Exam.

Do not underestimate the physical part. Even holding a pen and writing three days straight may be a physical challenge. (Some applicants swear by finding just the right smooth-gliding pens to help ease tension that develops in the hands.)

Choose an exercise routine, and get started on a frequent and regular basis—as soon as possible before your Bar Exam preparation begins. If you are already into some sport or exercise and enjoy it, do that. If not, try vigorous walks! They do not feel as much like "work" as some exercise does, but they provide good workouts and, literally, a breath of fresh air and change of pace!

There are many reasons for exercising during stressful periods such as Bar Exam preparation, many of which are the same reasons for routine exercise throughout your life. You will likely:

- Feel better,

- Be more alert,

- Help dissipate and rid yourself of much of the stress this period brings,

- Enjoy a pleasant change from all the sitting and studying, and help avoid burnout, and

- Sleep better.

TEST YOURSELF: Exercise

Q: The following are types of physical exercise that I enjoy:
A:_____
_____

Q: I (check one) _____have started ___will start*
doing _____
for _____ minutes per day.

   *If you checked "will start," come back to this page each day and make a check mark in the space below until you actually begin some routine—even walking!

C. PREPARE YOURSELF MENTALLY

The Bar Exam is as much a mental as a physical game. Make sure you are a winner from the outset.

1. Choose your Study Spot

Find one spot to do between 80 and 90% of your "hard-core" studying. This will be your place. You will love it, and you will hate it, but you will spend a lot of time in it. There is research that suggests that studying in different locations best prepares one for performing in a strange spot on the day of a test, as a person may become dependent on cues from his or her study environment. Sticking to one place for Bar Exam study does have its advantages, though. It helps you stay disciplined, and you do not have to take precious time away from your work to decide where to study each day and figure out how to get there, where to park, etc. It is also good, if you can, to find a place where you can store your books so you do not have to carry all those outlines from place to place.

Choose a place that is quiet, has a comfortable temperature, and preferably, is close to either your home, office, or review classes. Unnecessary driving time will deprive you of study and relaxation time. If you do have to drive a lot, buy or make cassette tapes so you can review rules of law in the car.

Choose a place where you will not feel self-conscious in grubby clothes. If you are disciplined, you can be productive at home.

Note from one successful applicant: "I studied at home and passed the first time. I set a routine and varied little from it. By 9:00 a.m., I had to be at my desk or at the kitchen table. (I had two "spots," for variety!) That meant that if I woke at 7:30 a.m., I could sit, drink coffee, and relax for an hour and a half. But, if I woke at 8:45 a.m., it was a quick rush through the headlines and on to the outlines! Every morning. Every single morning. No excuses."

If you know that at home you will be more apt to study the fine distinctions between talk show hosts than those of burglary, robbery, and theft, then try studying at a library, office, or someplace without a TV.

You do not need to go to your law school library, where you will likely run into competitive, nosy Bar Exam candidates. Your colleagues, however dear they are to you, may disturb you. Some of your "friends" may tell you that they were at the beach swimming and have not read a single outline. That may make you feel jealous or that you can "kick back" too. Others will say they studied for 14 hours straight, without food or bathroom breaks. That may make you feel you are not doing enough. Either way, only you can decide what is right for you. Do not fall for the peer pressure traps!

If you want a library atmosphere, try another law school where you do not know anyone, a college, or the public library. Any place where you can concentrate is fine.

Another successful applicant said this: "My apartment was small and crowded, so I rented office space in a law firm for two months. The other lawyers in the suite were supportive, it was close by, and my roommate/husband could watch all the TV he wanted without bothering me."

Ideally, the search for your Bar Exam study spot should begin during finals and MPRE study, so that you have found a good spot by graduation. (Be honest with yourself; pick a place that is good for you.) Note, too, that locations can differ during the day and evening. You may find that your apartment is fairly quiet during evenings and weekends, but learn when you begin Bar study there of the endless and uniquely daytime noises—lawnmowers, children crying, dogs barking. So make sure you try out your spot during the times you intend to study for the Bar.

Two more comments on study spots. One, be flexible. Change if your spot is not working for you. Two, a bit of noise is not all bad. Your actual Bar Exam will be taken in a room full of many hundreds of people, not all of whom will be completely silent, especially if you type!

Another success story: This applicant attacked the noise factor challenge with a sort of "If you can't beat them, join them" approach, doing all of his practice essay writing in the middle of a crowded shopping mall. He figured if he could concentrate there, he could concentrate anywhere. And, yes, he passed the Bar Exam the first time!

2. Get into a Study Routine

Ideally, by the Bar Exam, your internal body clock should be on "Bar Exam Standard Time." In other words, your peak concentration periods should be from approximately 9:00 a.m. to noon, and 2:00 p.m. to 5:00 p.m. There are two ways to get into that routine: Either a) make it your schedule from the beginning of your Bar preparation period forward or b) study at the times of day you do best at first, and then gradually switch to Bar time a few weeks before the Exam.

To decide how to get on Bar time, consider your least productive time ("LPT") and most productive time ("MPT"). If your natural MPT is during Bar times, stay on that schedule from the outset; if your MPT is in the evening, switch over a few weeks before the Exam.

Once you have assessed your MPT and LPT, now what? Do active independent study during your MPT—meaning your study outside of review courses. The active work you will do includes the following:

- Reviewing outlines,
- Taking practice tests and analyzing model answers,
- Making and studying flashcards,
- Reading outside resources if necessary to learn rules you do not understand,
- Reviewing and centralizing notes.

If possible, take classes during your LPT. Especially those review courses that involve passive learning—listening only to lectures—as opposed to active learning, such as doing practice tests and analyzing problems. Visit your significant other, family, and friends, and do your chores during your LPT.

Another note on timing: For the Bar Exam, you need to be *on* and extremely productive for three-hour blocks, twice per day. If you train, therefore, in approximately four-hour time blocks, you can build up your stamina and concentration (attention span) so that, by the time of the Bar Exam, three-hour blocks will be no problem. No need to do four-hour blocks during your entire preparation period, but try to build up to them gradually by the time of the Bar Exam.

3. Centralize your Sources

Centralize your sources (class notes, notes from rules, lecture notes from Bar review, and one summarized outline). The easiest way to centralize is to *begin* by picking one source where you will take and keep all notes. If you use a printed text, use either the most comprehensive resource to begin with or the easiest to handle physically. Carry your central source everywhere, and only take notes in that one place. Or, take notes on three-hole punched paper so you can centralize them in a binder.

Note: If you have already begun studying when you read this book, start centralizing from today forward. Start taking all your notes from now on in the one source you have annotated most thoroughly to date. Let us say you have several study sources: a commercial outline, a casebook, law school class notes, and Bar review lecture notes. The first time you read the cases, you may have taken notes directly in the casebook. At the review lecture, you took notes on a legal pad. When you read the commercial outline, you highlighted in yellow pen. As soon as possible before the test, however, you will want to have transferred all pertinent points from the various sources into one notebook or outline. Remember: Time spent centralizing is not wasted; it provides a great review.

However you do it, centralizing is critical. Centralizing enables you to end up with a complete and definitive source to review before the test. Reviewing from a centralized source is much more efficient than having to have to flip pages from one book to another. Also, if you do your final review from a single source, such as one of your commercial outlines, you risk leaving out important points, tips, jokes, anecdotes, mnemonics, or examples from your notes. You might miss *the one explanation that really made sense to you.* The more you personalize your outlines, the more likely you are to remember the rules.

TEST YOURSELF: The One Page Exercise

Once you have centralized all your material on a particular subject into one definitive source, you can then try to summarize that subject in a one- to three-page outline. By the time of the Bar Exam, it is a good idea to have a one-page approach, perhaps a checklist or a flow chart, for each subject tested. *Pretend* you were going to cheat on the Bar. *Do not cheat*—obviously—just do this as a mental exercise. If you could only fit one page on each subject in your pocket, what would you write down on each page?

Get these one-page "crib sheets" ready by the last week before the Bar. At that point, one sheet per subject is about all your mind can really focus on. And, if you want to review anything on the Tuesday or Wednesday evenings or Wednesday or Thursday mornings of the Bar, that is even more true.

If you do your one-pager for PR while studying for the MPRE, that is one subject less that you will have to do before the Bar Exam.

In addition to using the MPRE to find effective ways of learning the law and centralizing a wide variety of study resources, use the MPRE to evaluate your test-taking strengths and weaknesses, and your personal needs. Pay close attention during this trial run to what works for you and what does not. This way, you can remedy any potential problems before the REAL THING. For example, did you have trouble sleeping the night before the MPRE. Why? Did you have a drink? Did you read your notes just before bedtime? Did you spend the evening before the test with someone who was not very supportive? Do you have noisy neighbors? Do what it takes to ameliorate any such problems *before* the Bar Exam!

If reviewing at bedtime caused insomnia before the MPRE, you will know not to do it before the REAL THING.

More notes on sleepless nights from successful applicants: *"I would lie awake, and no matter how hard I tried, I could not escape the fact patterns of contracts, torts, and property questions running through my head. I eventually found that reading a few pages of a novel, before trying to sleep, took me into another world—far, far away from law—and enabled me to relax. Non-fiction, like the newspaper, did not do it, nor did TV. Only a novel really took me away."*

Another student said that he read World War II naval battle plans and imagined ships and war tactics to take his mind off the Bar Exam and get some sleep.

Whatever it takes; you need your sleep. So figure it out before the week of the Bar Exam.

If you did not eat breakfast on the morning of the MPRE, were you comfortable, lightheaded, or tired? Did you have a headache during the test? *Use* such information to maximize your comfort level during the Bar Exam. If you spent the evening before the MPRE with law school buddies who were also taking the test and you found that stressed you out, spend Bar Exam evenings with a non-law friend, or at least make certain it is someone supportive. Or spend that time alone with funny movies. (*Reflecting on one Bar Exam veteran who repeated the Bar several times, the failed Bar Exams seemed to coincide with turmoil and stress in the examinee's personal life, and the passed Bar Exam, with a relatively calm phase of that applicant's personal life. While this may not have been the only or even the primary cause for the failed tests, it surely was significant.*)

Bottom line: The better you feel during the Bar Exam, the better your chances for succes.

D. PLAN THE EVENT

Learn what the Bar is all about. Plan your transportation. Plan out your Bar days; plan the time before and in-between test sessions. Know what will happen when; what you will bring, wear, and eat; and every other detail you possibly can. Make the whole Event totally expected and routine. Eliminate surprises and decisions—as much as possible.

1. Should I stay at the Hotel? As you may know, the Bar Exam is often administered at costly hotels. Though you may not have an option of staying at home instead of a hotel, if you can take the Bar Exam at a location close to your home, weigh the pros and cons of staying on site carefully before you hand over your credit card.

Some of the *Pros* of staying on site:

No traffic. You are there. You do not need to fight or worry about traffic or your car breaking down. You do not need to drive in your nervous state, potentially endangering your own life and the lives of those around you. You do not need to wait for, pay for, or deal with a cab. *(One examinee who took a cab to the test in Oakland from her home in San Francisco was apparently "entertained" on the fairly long ride by the driver who told her all about Test. The cab driver had allegedly passed the previous Bar Exam but had still not been able to land a decent law-related job!)*

Someone will come clean your room (and make the bed). Especially if clutter or a messy house makes you feel scattered, disorganized, and/or annoyed, and if your home is messy, the hotel may be for you. You may get accustomed to the feel of the hotel, get comfortable there, and be generally more relaxed. And if you travel much and/or are used to hotels, you may feel right at home.

Room service. You can order prepared foods, and won't have to spend time or energy cooking or getting take-out foods.

Your friends or classmates may stay at the hotel. This can be both a *pro* and a *con*. On the one hand, you may feel strength in numbers, and feel like you are not alone, if you are with your classmates. On the other hand, law students are generally competitive and self-centered. Staying in a hotel full of them (especially at such a stressful time) may not be ideal. You may find a more supportive, nurturing network from family and non-law school friends. Remember the cardinal rule—it is *your Test*. Only you know how your classmates make you feel. Plan accordingly.

The *Cons*:

　　You are in an unfamiliar surrounding. Presumably, you have spent some time making the room you sleep in at home suit your own needs. You are used to the surroundings in your bedroom, and you probably feel comfortable, and perhaps more secure, there than elsewhere.

　　Sharing a room. You may end up sharing a room with a law school friend with whom you are not used to sharing sleeping quarters, or who may give off nervous vibes.

One colleague told of two law school friends and classmates, who shared a hotel room before the Bar Exam, and their negative experience. In that case, one could not sleep, while the other had taken a sleeping pill and fallen right to sleep. The sleepless one tossed and turned for some time, only to discover she was still wide awake. She decided to "borrow" one of her friend's sleeping pills. However, in reaching for the pill bottle, which had been left out on the sleeping friend's side of the room, the sleepless friend tripped, and a book belonging to the sleeping friend fell right on top of that once-sleeping applicant. The latter had been so suddenly awakened that she could no longer fall back to sleep, while the former, now intoxicated from the effect of the pill, slept soundly. The one who had been awakened was angry, to say the least, and warned her "friend" that if she failed, there would be no forgiveness.

To make the final choice of where to stay, weigh the *pros* and *cons* and reserve a hotel room only if you believe it will be best for you. If you opt for the hotel, though, reserve a room early; some test sites have thousands of applicants. Also, consider asking for a late checkout on the Thursday of the Bar Exam so that you do not have to worry about checking out before you have finished the Exam.

2.　Should I use a laptop?　Your Bar Exam is not the place to learn to type or become familiar with word processing. A good rule of thumb is, type the Bar Exam only if you typed law school exams.

If you decide to use a laptop, register early and make sure you understand all the rules about word processing. From the Committee website, download a copy of the rules applicable to laptop users and study them. On applicable exam days, you will be required to arrive in advance to prep your laptop.

3.　Should I Visit the Test Site?　Whether or not you ultimately stay on site, if you are able to visit the Test site before the Bar Exam do so.

Successful Applicant's Note: "*I took two trips to the hotel where my Bar Exam would be administered before I sat for the Bar Exam. The first time, I asked to see the room where the Bar Exam would be given. I went in and sat there for some time. I observed and tried to remember the surroundings so they would be somewhat familiar on the day of the Test. Though my Bar Exam ended up being given in a different room from the one I had been shown, the hotel and its conference rooms had become sufficiently familiar that I was undoubtedly more comfortable than I would have been had I not visited the test site. Also on that first visit, I lunched at the hotel restaurant, for two reasons: 1) to combine the trip with a meal so the study break could be "justified" and 2) to decide whether I would eat at the hotel or brown bag it on Bar Exam days. I chose the bag. My second visit to the site was a traffic test. I went at the same time I would go that fateful July morn, on a weekday. Since I had planned to stay at home and drive to the Test each morning, I wanted to know how long it would take (during weekday rush hour), how early I would have to leave, and, minor detail, exactly how to get there so I would not get lost. I also found out how much the hotel charged for parking so I would be sure to have the exact change.*"

For the Bar Exam, you might want to bring a sack lunch even if the hotel food is good. With so many test takers, you may have to wait in a very long line to get a seat in any hotel or local restaurant. You will also have to listen to other applicants while you stand in line, and probably while you eat—bad news! You do not want to hear what people thought of the test. Your lunch break should be to relax and gear up for the afternoon, not to rehash and freak out about the morning session. If you are staying at the hotel, consider eating in your room. You could order the food in the morning so it will be waiting for you when you return, and you will not even have to think at all during the break.

Test Yourself Exercise

1. My concerns/fears about the Bar Exam are (be as specific as possible):

_____
_____
_____
_____
_____
_____

2. These are the confidence building steps I am taking to overcome each of the concerns listed above:

_____
_____
_____
_____
_____

E. BUILD YOUR CONFIDENCE

Emotional preparation or "confidence building" is important for the Bar Exam—both because the Bar Exam is such a grueling experience and because so much rides on it (not just pride but often the means to support oneself and family).

Many people feel confidence (like lawyering) is a gift; one either has it or does not. That is simply not true. Confidence (and lawyering) can be learned. People can practice and train, just as people train for baseball or tennis. Preparation in and of itself, "working out" your legal and test-taking skills, helps enormously to increase your confidence. So, too, can the confidence-building suggestions below.

1. Building Confidence through a Sports Analogy

If you are a "sports person," pretend you are training for the Big Game. You get the idea; psych up for challenge and victory. You can do it. You can win! You must get that part into your head, your heart, and your soul. Try a chant during your exercise routine. To the beat of a daily walk/jog, chant, "I can do it; I will pass. I will pass; the Cal-i-for-nia Bar Exam. I can do it; I will pass." Or, make a sign that reads, "I will pass," and put it above your bed or on the fridge.

2. Building Confidence through a War Analogy

It might help to visualize the Bar Exam as a war. In planning for war, generals prepare for each battle. In the "Bar War," *you* are the general. However, unlike a real war general, you have the distinct advantage of knowing exactly how many battles there will be and what each battle will be like.

You will face three battles: the multistate, the essays, and the performance tests. By taking practice tests, you can learn a lot about each. What an opportunity for planning!

In a war, generals use different soldiers, weaponry, and strategies (plans of attack) for different battles. So should you! In order to plan your attacks, analyze your strengths and weaknesses, and those of your enemy(ies). Learn to identify, confront, and overcome them during your training period ("Bar boot camp").

What are your enemies' strengths and weaknesses? Let us personify each part of the exam as an "enemy," and expose strategies to beat him. The Multistate? He is fast. The multistate will get you running so quickly you will not have time to catch your breath. The better prepared you are, the easier your counterattack. His weakness is his armor. It is not thick enough to cover him completely. He is left partially exposed; one of every four answers is his naked spot. Aim, knock off wrong answers by crossing them out, fire (fill in a choice), and *move on*. If you are not sure you hit the right one, star and come back to it *if* you have extra time *after* you are all finished. Develop a strategy for guessing, for inevitably you will have to guess here or there. If you do not know the answer, rule out as many wrong answers as you can, and then aim, fire, and move on. If you run out of time completely, mark in all one letter for the remainder of the questions—before they call time. You are not docked for guessing.

In contrast to the multistate, the Performance Test is slow. But beware, he endures three long hours and can be tricky. Read carefully. The PT can try to psych you out. Psych it back; call it performance tease! It can fool you by taunting, "Here I am, no tricks. I am giving you all the law, showing you all my cards." Do not believe it! Sure he is giving you the sources of law, but *you* have to pull the rules out of cases and statutes, and very quickly at that! He also will throw totally irrelevant information at you, which you must cast aside. And he can, and usually does, throw you ethical issues as surprise attacks, curve balls that are not in the instructions. Fight back. Stay calm. Know what to expect, and proceed. Take your time, but move steadily. He will just stay there looking scary while you sweat. Stick it out, keep up your concentration, and victory is yours.

Last, but not least, are the Essays. These are like a firing squad, shooting you with issue after issue. Know and memorize the elements of all the rules, theories, and causes of action. By the Bar Exam, be able to make a quick telephone call into your brain (pretend it is the "411" of legal rules), and ask for the rule you need. Have confidence; the brain has terrific capacity to store information. Can you remember a host of details, such as phone number, birthdate, favorite flavor ice cream or musician, about someone you once had a crush on? Can you quote football or baseball scores and statistics from years gone by? Whatever your passion, think for a minute how much you can remember about it. Make the law your passion! To attack each essay:

    a. Go through the test and pick out issues.

    b. As you see an issue, write out the problem or concern it raises. While writing, ask yourself why it is there; why did they include particular facts?

    c. Dial "411" and ask the legal rules operator (your memory) what the rule is. It is there; trust yourself.

    d. Stay calm and wait for the response.

    e. Then, write the rule and an analysis, and a conclusion if you have one, and then move on.

If the legal rules operator disconnects you in step c. above, i.e. in case you do not know the answer, *guess*. But again, plan your guessing strategy. Some possible guessing strategies, if you see an issue but do not know the rule, are:

> a. Analogize the problem to a rule or an area of law you do know. Think about what the rule would likely be, given what the law is in an area of law you do know, and then write something based on that analogy. For example, the crime is armed robbery and you do not know the rule. You know that simple robbery is the taking and carrying away of the property of another by the use of force or fear. Armed robbery must include, on top of those elements, another one, such as [force or fear], which is produced or caused by the presence of some arm or weapon.

> b. Try making a policy argument. For example, if you do not know the rule but can see that the issue presents a situation that would be manifestly unjust unless *x* or *y* result occurs, argue based on fairness for that result.

> c. State the issue, conclude, and move on to the next issue.

Whatever happens, if you do not know the answer, do not panic. If you freeze up, you will likely waste time you could be spending writing about things you *do* know. Be creative. Use common sense. Know that this happens to everybody at some time or another. Think hard and keep writing. Say something about an issue—better to identify it even if you do not know the exact rule than to ignore it. Never give up.

Remember, your pen or laptop is your sword; wield it mightily. Once you are sitting in that cold Bar Exam battlefield, close your eyes and feel the power go from your brain, through your body, to your fingers, into your sword. Then fight! With each sentence, cut the enemy down to size. Be angry. Anger is much more powerful than fear. Do not let the Bar Exam intimidate you. You have the ability. You would not be taking It if you had not already proven that by leaping so many tremendous hurdles to get this far. You are here, you are prepared, and you can leap this hurdle too. You can pass the California Bar Exam.

OPEN THE DOOR TO SUCCESS

You might try to visualize the Bar Exam as a door. All you have to do is push to open It. But it is a very heavy door, so you have to push hard. Once inside, though, you do not ever have to push again. It is a lifetime license. If this is not your first Bar Exam, resolve to make it your last!

Unlike law school finals, Bar Exam questions test basic knowledge. For the most part, the Bar Examiners do not test dissenting opinions, obscure rules, or minutia. Whether or not you did superbly in law school does not matter now. You now have another chance, the chance to win. Winning the Bar Exam just means passing, not getting an "A." You are not writing the definitive law review article or "Brandeis brief," and trying to do so on the Bar Exam might hurt more than help you.

Work hard, but do not break under the pressure. Do not burn out. Be honest, and assess the amount of work *you* need to do—*you,* not anyone else. The work you have to do just to pass may be what the person next to you would have to do to get an "A," or vice versa. Only you really know. Trust yourself. Believe you will pass. Say it, sing it, feel it, and *do it.* You *can* pass the California Bar Exam. Now just do it!

Conclusion

To PASS the Performance Test portion of the California Bar Exam you must do three things:

1. PREPARE THOROUGHLY, 2. MASTER THE REQUIRED SKILLS, and 3. HAVE CONFIDENCE IN YOURSELF.

You have it all now.

Study this text;

Do the Test Yourself questions in each chapter; and

Complete (write and rewrite under timed conditions) the past performance tests in the Appendix, and study the sample answers to those questions. If you need or want to do additional practice tests, do those under timed conditions as well.

Tip: Practice, Practice, Practice. Practice tests as we have emphasized are perhaps the single most important key to success on the PT, essays, and MBE portions of the Bar Exam.

By taking these steps, you can get yourself fully prepared, master the requisite skills, and develop the confidence to believe that you can write effective, passing answers to any and every performance test question you face.

So now just do it:

Prepare to PASS;

Believe you *will* PASS; and

Go out and PASS the California Bar Exam!

APPENDIX A

SELECTED PERFORMANCE TEST QUESTIONS

Table of Contents

Thursday Afternoon
JULY 26, 2001

California
Bar
Examination

Performance Test B
INSTRUCTIONS AND FILE

PEOPLE v. WILS

INSTRUCTIONS

FILE

Memorandum from Susan Sola to Applicant

Office Memorandum re Drafting of Opening Appellate Briefs

Excerpts From Arno Pir's Direct Examination at Trial

Excerpts From Vivian Pir's Direct Examination at Trial

Excerpts From Thomas Wils' Direct Examination at Trial

Jury Instructions: Given

Jury Instructions: Refused

PEOPLE v. WILS

INSTRUCTIONS

1. You will have three hours to complete this session of the examination. This performance test is designed to evaluate your ability to handle a select number of legal authorities in the context of a factual problem involving a client.

2. The problem is set in the fictional State of Columbia, one of the United States.

3. You will have two sets of materials with which to work: a **File** and a **Library**. The **File** contains factual materials about your case. The first document is a memorandum containing the instructions for the tasks you are to complete.

4. The **Library** contains the legal authorities needed to complete the tasks. The case reports may be real, modified, or written solely for the purpose of this examination. If the cases appear familiar to you, do not assume that they are precisely the same as you have read before. Read them thoroughly, as if all were new to you. You should assume that cases were decided in the jurisdictions and on the dates shown. In citing cases from the **Library**, you may use abbreviations and omit page citations.

5. Your response must be written in the answer book provided. In answering this performance test, you should concentrate on the materials provided, but you should also bring to bear on the problem your general knowledge of the law. What you have learned in law school and elsewhere provides the general background for analyzing the problem; the **File** and **Library** provide the specific materials with which you must work.

6. Although there are no restrictions on how you apportion your time, you should probably allocate at least 90 minutes to organizing and writing.

7. This performance test will be graded on your responsiveness to instructions and on the content, thoroughness, and organization of your response. Grading of the two tasks will be weighted as follows:

    Task A — 40%
    Task B — 60%

OFFICE OF THE STATE PUBLIC DEFENDER
STATE OF COLUMBIA

MEMORANDUM

To: **Applicant**

From: **Susan Sola, Supervising Deputy State Public Defender**

Date: **July 26, 2001**

Subject: People v. Wils, Columbia Court of Appeal No. 1610201

Our office has recently been appointed by the Columbia Court of Appeal to represent Thomas Wils, an indigent Ruritanian émigré, on his appeal from a judgment of the Columbia Superior Court convicting him on a jury's verdict of burglary and robbery.

I believe that Wils' only potentially meritorious claims of error on appeal are that the trial court: (1) refused to instruct the jury on a *bona fide* belief in a claim or right to another's personal property relating to burglary; (2) refused to instruct the jury on a *bona fide* belief in a claim or right to another's personal property relating to robbery; and (3) failed to instruct the jury *sua sponte* on trespass as a lesser included offense of burglary.

Please draft for my approval the following two sections of an opening appellate brief *only*:

    1. A statement of facts. 40

    2. An argument demonstrating, for each of the three claims of error identified above, that the trial court erred and that its error requires reversal of the judgment.

I shall draft the remaining sections of the brief in due course.

In performing each of these tasks, please follow the guidelines set out in the memorandum on the drafting of opening appellate briefs.

OFFICE OF THE STATE PUBLIC DEFENDER
STATE OF COLUMBIA

MEMORANDUM

To: **Deputy State Public Defenders**

From: **Beth Jay, State Public Defender**

Date: **April 5, 2000**

Subject: The Drafting of Opening Appellate Briefs

All opening appellate briefs must conform to the following guidelines.

- All opening appellate briefs must include the following sections: a table of contents; a table of cases; a summary of argument; a statement of the jurisdictional basis of the appeal; a procedural history; a statement of facts; an argument comprising one or more claims of error; and a conclusion.

- The *statement of facts* must contain the facts that support our client's claims of error and must also take account of the facts that may be used to support the People's opposition. It must deal with all such facts in a persuasive manner, reasonably and fairly attempting to show the greater importance of the ones that weigh in our client's favor and the lesser importance of the ones that weigh in the People's favor. Above all, it must tell a compelling story in narrative form and not merely recapitulate each witness's testimony.

- The *argument* must analyze the applicable law and bring it to bear on the facts in each claim of error, urging that the law and facts support our client's position. It need not attempt to foreclose each and every response that the People may put forth in their brief, but must anticipate their strongest attacks on our client's weakest points, both legal and factual. It must display a subject heading summarizing each claim of error and the outcome that it requires. The subject heading must express the application of the law to the facts, and not a statement of an abstract principle or a bare conclusion. For example, do *not* write: "The Trial Court Erroneously Instructed the Jury on Defense of Others." *Do* write: "By Failing to State That Defendant Was Entitled to Defend Strangers as Well as Members of His Family, the Trial Court Erroneously Instructed the Jury on Defense of Others."

***

```
1   BY DEPUTY DISTRICT ATTORNEY JAMES LEIBSON

2       Q      Your name, sir?

3       A      Arno Pir.

4       Q      Where were you born?

5       A      Ruritania.

6       Q      When did you come to this country?

7       A      More than 50 years ago, as a child.  My parents fled as refugees.

8       Q      Where do you live?

9       A      I live with my wife at 2211 Blake Street in New Hope.

10      Q      What do you do for a living?

11      A      I'm a wine merchant.

12      Q      Do you know the defendant, Thomas Wils?

13      A      Yes, I did, I do.

14      Q      Can you identify him?

15      A      Yes, he's the young man at the far table, in the dark suit and tie.

16  THE COURT

17      Let the record reflect that the witness has identified the defendant.  Proceed.

18  BY MR. LEIBSON

19      Q      When did you meet him?

20      A      I welcomed him to New Hope two or three years ago; I was the Secretary of

21             the Ruritanian-American Freedom League.

22      Q      What is the Ruritanian-American Freedom League?

23      A      It is an organization dedicated to obtaining freedom for our homeland, which

24             has long been dominated by its neighbor Caledon.

25      Q      You said you met him two or three years ago?

26      A      Yes, he had fled from Ruritania and had just received political asylum.
```

1	Q	Did he come to live with you?
2	A	Yes, with my wife Vivian and me.
3	Q	How was that?
4	A	He was alone in a new country, and Vivian and I had never had any children.
5	Q	You invited him to live with you?
6	A	Yes.
7	Q	Did you have an arrangement?
8	A	What do you mean?
9	Q	For instance, did he have to pay you rent?
10	A	No, no, no, of course not. We provided him with room and board, and I think my wife would give him some spending money.
12	Q	Did he have to repay you?
13	A	Not at all. All he had to do were some odd jobs around the house, jobs Vivian wanted me to do but I didn't get around to.
15	Q	Did you agree to pay him for any of his work?
16	A	No, absolutely not. I provided him with room and board.
17	Q	Did you agree to give him anything for his work?
18	A	No, I didn't, but I think Vivian did.
19	Q	If you know, what?
20	A	I think Vivian promised him an old car that I no longer used, a Triumph Spitfire, if he finished some work in the garage.
22	Q	How much was it worth?
23	A	Maybe $2,000.
24	Q	Did you end up giving it to him?
25	A	No.

1	Q	Why?
2	A	I believe he wanted it before he finished the work, Vivian refused, they got
3		into an argument, and she threw him out.
4	Q	Did she consult you?
5	A	Consult? Vivian is not a person who consults.
6	Q	When did she throw him out?
7	A	I think in April of 1999, or maybe May.
8	Q	Did you hear from him afterwards?
9		hanging up on him before long.
10	Q	If you would, please go back in thought to July 3, 1999.
11	A	OK.
12	Q	Do you remember what happened that day?
13	A	Yes, Thomas came by my shop.
14	Q	Did he look like he looks today?
15	A	No, he was very thin and dirty and smelly.
16	Q	Did he say anything to you?
17	A	Yes, he said he wanted the Triumph. He demanded it.
18	Q	What did you do?
19	A	I tried to get rid of him as quickly and quietly as I could. I had lots of regular
20		customers in the shop, getting ready for the Fourth of July.
21	Q	What did you do?
22	A	I told him I didn't have the car; it was at home. I also told him I didn't have
23		the title documents; Vivian probably kept them in her purse.
24	Q	Did he leave?
25	A	No, he kept demanding the car.

1	Q	What happened next?
2	A	I told him I was leaving on a business trip later that day, and I would return
3		on July 20th or 21st, and I would give him the car and the papers at that time.
4	Q	Did he leave then?
5	A	Yes, he did.
6	Q	Did you go off on your business trip later that day?
7	A	I did.
8	Q	And you returned —
9	A	On July 5th, right after the incident.
10	Q	Subsequently, did you receive any bills for credit cards issued to you and your
11		wife?
12	A	Yes, I did.
13	Q	Did you notice any charges that were not made by you or your wife?
14	A	Yes, I did.
15	Q	What were they?
16	A	An airline ticket to New York on our Bank of Columbia card, and motel bills,
17		restaurant bills, clothing, I think, jewelry, and such things on our Columbia
18		Federal Savings and Loan card.
19	Q	Do you remember the amounts?
20	A	Roughly, I believe, $1,200 for the ticket, almost $2,000 for jewelry, maybe
21		about $800 for the rest.
22	Q	What was the first date for these charges?
23	A	July 5th.
24	Q	And the last?
25	A	July 31st.

1   Q   You didn't notify the issuers of these credit cards of their loss before the 31st?

2   A   No, I'm embarrassed. Vivian and I had so many credit cards I didn't realize

3   these were missing until the bills arrived.

4   *   *   *

5

1 BY DEPUTY DISTRICT ATTORNEY JAMES LEIBSON

2 Q Ma'am, what is your name?

3 A Vivian Pir.

4 Q Where were you born?

5 A Ruritania.

6 Q When did you come to this country?

7 A Almost 50 years ago.

8 Q Did you come with your parents?

9 A Yes, we escaped; I was 8.

10 Q Where do you live?

11 A In New Hope.

12 Q What do you do for a living?

13 A I'm a certified public accountant.

14 Q Are you married?

15 A Yes, to Arno Pir.

16 Q Do you know Thomas Wils, the defendant here?

17 A I do.

18 Q Can you identify him?

19 A Yes, he's at that table, in the navy blue suit and cobalt tie.

20 THE COURT

21 Let the record reflect that Mrs. Pir has identified the defendant. Proceed.

22 BY MR. LEIBSON

23 Q When did you meet him?

24 A About two or three years ago, when I was President of the Ruritanian-

25 American Freedom League.

26 Q Did you meet him here in New Hope?

27 A Yes, I did. He had recently escaped from Ruritania.

1	Q	At some point, did he come to live with you and your husband?
2	A	Yes, he did.
3	Q	Did you and your husband invite him?
4	A	Arno did; I was hesitant.
5	Q	Why?
6	A	Well, we never had any children, and Thomas was an adolescent.
7	Q	Did you and your husband have an arrangement with the defendant?
8	A	We agreed to provide him with room and board, and he agreed to do
9		construction work, including remodeling the garage.
10	Q	Did you pay him any money?
11	A	No; I think he got some from other Ruritanian-Americans; he would do odd j
12		jobs.
13	Q	Why didn't you pay him?
14	A	We provided all that he needed. And I wanted him to get on his own two feet,
15		go to college, or at least get a real job.
16	Q	Did he want to do that?
17	A	No.
18	Q	How did you know?
19	A	He would say, again and again, that he wanted to enjoy life, and that he didn't
20		want to be a "working stiff."
21	Q	Did you agree to give him anything for his work?
22	A	I agreed to give him an old car that Arno no longer used, but not in exchange
23		for work.
24	Q	For what?
25	A	I told him I would give it to him for transportation if he went to college.
26	Q	Did he ever go to college?
27	A	No.

1	Q	Did he ever ask you for the car?
2	A	Yes, he demanded it. He said he needed to sell it for money; his odd jobs
3		were drying up. I could understand why, with his attitude.
4	Q	Did you have an argument with him in April or May of 1999?
5	A	Late in April.
6	Q	Can you describe it?
7	A	Yes, it was heated but short. He demanded the car and I refused and threw
8		him out.
9	Q	Did you hear from him afterwards?
10	A	I didn't; Arno did.
11	Q	Do you remember what happened on July 5, 1999?
12	A	Yes.
13	Q	Was Arno in town?
14	A	No, he was away on a business trip.
15	Q	What did you do on that morning?
16	A	About 9 or 9:30, I went to the dentist.
17	Q	When did you return home?
18	A	Sometime before noon.
19	Q	Did you see anything unusual when you entered your house?
20	A	No, not when I entered, but when I got near the kitchen.
21	Q	What did you see?
22	A	The kitchen was in disarray. Then I saw Thomas stuffing food into his mouth.
23	Q	Were you startled?
24	A	Yes, I screamed and demanded that he get out immediately or I'd call the
25		police.
26	Q	Did he go?
27	A	No, he demanded the car, and started at me.

1	Q	What did you do?
2	A	I grabbed for a broom or mop to protect myself.
3	Q	What did he do then?
4	A	He punched me hard in my shoulder, pulled my purse from my arm, and
5		started rummaging through it.
6	Q	Did he say anything?
7	A	Yes, he hollered, "If you won't give me the papers for the car, then I'll take
8		what I can get."
9	Q	What did you do?
10	A	I was stunned that he would actually punch me; when I came to my senses,
11		he had turned to run out of the house; I tried to chase him, but he got away.
12		* * *

1   BY DEPUTY PUBLIC DEFENDER THEODORE STROLL

2   Q   What is your name, please?

3   A   Thomas Wils.

4   Q   How old are you?

5   A   Almost 21.

6   Q   Where were you born?

7   A   Ruritania.

8   Q   You learned English there?

9   A   Yes, I started studying it in elementary school.

10   Q   When did you leave?

11   A   I didn't leave; I escaped, about three years ago. Ruritania is a police state.

12   Q   When did you arrive in this country?

13   A   The same year. I landed in New York, and then came to New Hope. I

14   received political asylum.

15   Q   Were you welcomed by the Ruritanian-American community?

16   A   Yes, at first.

17   Q   And by Arno and Vivian Pir?

18   A   Yes, Arno was the President of the Ruritanian-American Freedom League, and

19   Vivian was the Secretary. They invited me to live with them — in a way.

20   Q   What do you mean?

21   A   They offered me room and board if I helped around the house.

22   Q   You accepted?

23   A   Yes, but I didn't know —

24   Q   Let me interrupt, what was your arrangement?

25   A   I was supposed to do handyman work, but Vivian made me turn the garage

26   into a guest house with a bathroom and kitchen.

1	Q	Did they pay you anything?
2	A	No, just room and board; Vivian bought me cigarettes and things like that, and
3		sometimes she gave me a few dollars to rent a video.
4	Q	How old were you?
5	A	About 19.
6	Q	Did you try to change your arrangement?
7	A	Yes, I told Vivian I would not finish the work in the garage unless she paid me.
8	Q	Did she agree?
9	A	She promised to give me an old car that Arno didn't use anymore, a Triumph,
10		so that I could sell it.
11	Q	How much was it worth?
12	A	I don't know, maybe $4,000.
13	Q	You didn't want it to drive?
14	A	No, I'm afraid to drive; I black out sometimes. The Secret Police in Ruritania
15		beat me.
16	Q	Did you finish the work?
17	A	Yes, I did.
18	Q	What happened then?
19	A	I asked for the Triumph. She said no, told me to leave, and threw me out.
20	Q	Did you go?
21	A	Yes.
22	Q	When was that?
23	A	In April of 1999.
24	Q	Where did you go?
25	A	To stay with Ruritanian friends in New Hope.
26	Q	Did you settle with anyone in particular?
27	A	No, I went from one to another, until they all turned me away.

1	Q	Do you know why they did that?
2	A	Vivian told them all I was a bum, used drugs, got drunk; I overheard her saying
3		that once.
4	Q	What happened then?
5	A	I had to live on the streets and beg for food; it was worse than Ruritania.
6	Q	How long did you do that?
7	A	More than two months.
8	Q	Do you remember what you did on July 3, 1999?
9	A	Yes, I went to Arno's store — he has a liquor store — and I asked for the
10		Triumph.
11	Q	What happened?
12	A	He said he didn't have the ownership papers, Vivian did, and she had them
13		either in her purse or somewhere in the house. He said that he was going
14		away on a business trip later that day, and would give them to me when he
15		got back in two weeks.
16	Q	Do you remember what you did on July 5, 1999?
17	A	Yes, I went to Arno and Vivian's house to get the Triumph and the ownership
18		papers.
19	Q	You got into the house?
20	A	Yes.
21	Q	How?
22	A	When I lived there, I put in a new lock in the kitchen door. I knew how to take
23		it out.
24	Q	Was Vivian home?
25	A	No. I had waited for her to leave.

1	Q	Did she return?
2	A	Yes, about 45 minutes after I got there. I sat in the kitchen and waited for her.
3		After a while, I made myself a sandwich out of some liverwurst I found in the
4		refrigerator. I was starving. I hadn't eaten for days.
5	Q	What happened?
6	A	She came in the front door, walked into the kitchen, and when she saw me
7		she started to scream and then to curse, and she told me to get out before
8		she called the police.
9	Q	Did you leave?
10	A	No, I asked for the Triumph.
11	Q	Did she give it to you?
12	A	No, she threatened to hit me with a broom.
13	Q	What did you do?
14	A	I pushed her shoulder and took her purse from her arm; I opened the purse
15		and looked for the ownership papers.
16	Q	Did you punch her in the shoulder?
17	A	No, that's a lie, I just pushed her shoulder.
18	Q	Did you find the ownership papers?
19	A	No, I saw some credit cards and a silver mirror and a cellular phone, and just
20		took them instead. I figured if they wouldn't give me the car I had worked for
21		and earned, I'd take what I could get.
22	Q	What happened next?
23	A	I ran away. She chased me, but I was faster.
24	Q	What did you do with the mirror and the phone?
25	A	I pawned them.
26	Q	For how much?
27	A	Maybe $5 for the mirror and $10 for the phone.

1	Q	What about the credit cards?

1   Q   What about the credit cards?

2   A   I used them to go to New York and live there awhile. I ran up about $4,000

3   worth of credit card debt. That's what the Triumph was worth, and so I guess

4   I got even with them.

5   Q   Did you stay with any Ruritanian-American friends in New York?

6   A   I thought they were friends, but Vivian poisoned their minds, and they turned

7   me in to the police.

8   Q   You were arrested?

9   A   Yes, on July 31st.

10   *   *   *

11

IN THE SUPERIOR COURT OF THE STATE OF COLUMBIA
COUNTY OF LAKEPORT

THE PEOPLE,	)	No. 1020161
	)	
Plaintiff,	)	JURY INSTRUCTIONS
	)	
v.	)	GIVEN
	)	
THOMAS WILS,	)	
	)	
Defendant.	)	
_____	)	

       *   *   *

Defendant is accused in Count 1 of the Indictment with having committed the crime of burglary.

In order to prove such crime, the People must prove each of the following elements, and must do so beyond a reasonable doubt:

    1. Defendant entered a house, apartment, or other building;

    2. Defendant entered such house, apartment, or other building without consent; and

    3. Defendant entered such house, apartment, or other building with the intent to commit larceny.

       *   *   *

Defendant is accused in Count 2 of the Indictment with having committed the crime of robbery.

In order to prove such crime, the People must prove each of the following elements, and must do so beyond a reasonable doubt:

1. Defendant took personal property;

2. The personal property belonged to another;

3. Defendant took such personal property from the person or immediate presence of the other;

4. Defendant took such personal property without the consent of the other;

5. Defendant took such personal property by using force against the other or by causing the other to fear; and

6. Defendant took such personal property with the intent to commit larceny.

       *   *   *

Larceny is the taking of the personal property of another, without his consent, with the intent to steal.

       *   *   *

Dated: October 30, 2000.   /s/ Patricia C. Sheehan

                                            Judge of the Superior Court

IN THE SUPERIOR COURT OF THE STATE OF COLUMBIA

COUNTY OF LAKEPORT

THE PEOPLE,	)	No. 1020161
	)	
Plaintiff,	)	JURY INSTRUCTIONS
	)	
v.	)	REFUSED
	)	
THOMAS WILS,	)	
	)	
Defendant.	)	
_____	)	

*   *   *

A *bona fide* belief on the part of the taker of personal property in his right or claim to the property taken negates the intent to steal.

Requested by: Defendant

*   *   *

Dated: October 30, 2000.   /s/ Patricia C. Sheehan

Judge of the Superior Court

California
Bar
Examination

Performance Test B
LIBRARY

PEOPLE v. WILS

LIBRARY

Selected Constitutional and Statutory Provisions

People v. Brown (Colum. Ct. App. 1957)

People v. Cutler (Colum. Ct. App. 1967)

People v. Alvarado (Colum. Ct. App. 1982)

SELECTED CONSTITUTIONAL AND STATUTORY PROVISIONS

Section 13 of Article VI of the Columbia Constitution. Harmless Error.

No judgment shall be reversed, in any case, on the ground of any error of any kind, unless, after an examination of the entire case, including the evidence, the court shall be of the opinion that the error complained of has resulted in a miscarriage of justice.

*

Section 211 of the Columbia Penal Code. The Crime of Robbery.

Robbery is the larcenous taking of the personal property of another, from his person or immediate presence, and without his consent, accomplished by means of force or fear.

*

Section 459 of the Columbia Penal Code. The Crime of Burglary.

Every person who, without consent, enters any house, apartment, or other building, with intent to commit larceny, is guilty of burglary.

*

Section *484 of the Columbia Penal Code.* The Crime of Larceny.

Larceny is the taking of the personal property of another, without his consent, with the intent to steal.

*

Section 602 of the Columbia Penal Code. The Crime of Trespass.

Every person who, without consent, enters any house, apartment, or other building is guilty of trespass.

People v. Brown

Columbia Court of Appeal (1957)

Defendant was convicted in the superior court of the crime of burglary, which had been alleged in the indictment to have been committed by entering a certain house with intent to commit larceny involving a certain bicycle. The entry was conceded, as was the taking. Defendant now appeals.

Defendant was a youth of 18 years of age, and, for a few days immediately prior to the taking of the bicycle, was staying at the home of one Ralph Yount, working for his room and board. He took the stand as a witness, and testified: "I took the bicycle to get even with George, and of course I didn't intend to keep it. I just wanted to get even with him. He was throwing oranges at me in the evening, and he would not stop when I told him to, and it made me mad, and I left Yount's house Saturday morning. I thought I would go back and take George's bike. Instead of getting hold of his, I got Frank's, but I intended to take it back Sunday night; but before I got back they caught me. I took it down by the grove, and put it on the ground, and covered it with brush, and crawled in, and Frank came and hauled off the brush and said: 'What are you doing here?' Then I told him that I covered myself up in the brush so that they could not find me until evening, until I could take it back. I did not want them to find me. I expected to remain there during the day, and not go back until evening."

Upon the foregoing state of facts, the superior court gave the jury the following instruction: "I think it is not necessary to say very much to you in this case. I may say, generally, that I think counsel for the defense here stated to you in this argument very fairly the principles of law governing this case, *except in one particular*. In defining to you the crime of larceny, he says it is essential that the taking must be 'larcenous'. That is true: The taking must be with the intent to deprive the owner. But counsel adds the conclusion that you must find that the taker intended to deprive him *permanently*. I do not think that is the law. I think in this case, for example, if the defendant took this bicycle, we will say for the purpose of enabling him to get away, and then left it, and intended to do nothing else except to help himself get away, it would be larceny, just as much as though he intended to keep it forever."

This instruction is erroneous, and demands a reversal of the judgment as a miscarriage of justice under section 13 of Article VI of the Columbia Constitution. Section 459 of the Columbia Penal Code states: "Every person who, without consent, enters any house, apartment, or other building, with intent to commit larceny, is guilty of burglary." If defendant's story is true, he is not guilty of larceny in taking the bicycle and hence is not guilty of burglary; yet, under the instruction, the words from his own mouth convicted him. The court told the jury that larceny might have been committed, even though it was only the intent of the party taking the property to deprive the owner of it *temporarily*. We think the authorities form an unbroken line to the effect that the larcenous intent must be to deprive the owner of the property *permanently*. While the larcenous intent of the party taking need not necessarily be an intent to convert the property to his own use, still it must in all cases be an intent to permanently deprive the owner thereof.

For the foregoing reasons, it is ordered that the judgment be reversed.

People v. Cutler
Columbia Court of Appeal (1967)

Defendant was charged with the robbery of Joseph H. Anderson. A jury convicted him of the offense. The superior court sentenced him to a term of imprisonment of six years. We reverse.

At trial, Anderson testified as follows. He operated a catering service in Lakeport. On the evening of May 18, 1965, the doorbell of his home rang shortly before midnight. He stepped out onto the porch. Defendant approached with his hand in his coat pocket. After some conversation, he pulled out a gun. Anderson attempted to seize the weapon and succeeded in knocking it out of defendant's hand. Defendant then snatched Anderson's wallet from his back pocket and fled.

Defendant testified that he met Anderson several weeks before the incident and that Anderson employed him on one occasion to do some catering work. Anderson did not pay him for the work and, when defendant requested payment, Anderson asked him to wait a few days. On the evening of May 18th, he went to Anderson's home to obtain payment. While the two were discussing the debt on the porch, Anderson proposed giving him some marijuana instead, and defendant said no; Anderson offered to pay him double the money he owed him if he waited a month; defendant again said no, telling Anderson he needed his money and wished only to be paid. At this point, Anderson agreed to pay him. He started to remove his wallet from his back pocket to get the money. He apparently changed his mind and returned to discuss his earlier marijuana proposal. Defendant persisted in his refusal, and Anderson again started to remove his wallet. Stopping suddenly, Anderson moved his hand to his waistband and pulled out a knife. Defendant had armed himself before going to Anderson's home because he had heard stories about Anderson's brutality; when he saw a knife in Anderson's hand, he brought out his gun to defend himself. Anderson then knocked the weapon out of defendant's hand. Taking advantage of the opportunity that presented itself in the struggle, defendant snatched Anderson's wallet and fled. Defendant did not intend to rob Anderson when he went to the house, but intended only to recover money owed to him.

Over defendant's objection, the prosecutor argued to the jury, "If you think a man owes you a hundred dollars, or fifty dollars, or five dollars, or a dollar, and you go over with a gun to try to get his money, it's robbery." And, "If you go to a man's home, and merely because he's supposed to owe you some money, take money from him at gunpoint, you have robbed him." Again objecting to further argument by the prosecutor that a robbery was committed even if defendant believed Anderson owed him money, defendant suggested that a necessary element of larceny, the intent to steal, was requisite to robbery, but was overruled by the court.

Defendant's objection was well taken. Under Section 211 of the Columbia Penal Code, "[r]obbery is the larcenous taking of the personal property of another, from his person or immediate presence, and without his consent, accomplished by means of force or fear." An essential element of robbery is the larcenous intent that accompanies the taking. Since robbery is but larceny aggravated by the use of force or fear to accomplish the taking of personal property from the person or immediate presence of the other, the larcenous intent requisite to robbery is the intent requisite to larceny. The taking of property is not larceny in the absence of an intent to steal, i.e., an intent to deprive its owner of it permanently.

Although an intent to steal may ordinarily be inferred when one person takes the property of another, particularly if he takes it by force, proof of the existence of a state of mind incompatible with an intent to steal precludes a finding of either larceny or robbery. It has long been the rule in this state, and generally throughout the country, that a bona fide belief, even though mistakenly held, one has a right or claim to the property negates larcenous intent. A belief that the property taken belongs to the taker, or that he has a right or claim thereto, is sufficient to preclude larcenous intent. Larcenous intent exists only if the actor intends to take the property of another without believing in good faith that he has a right or claim to it.

Defendant testified that, in going to Anderson's home, "my sole intention was to try to get my money, and that was all." The jury was properly instructed that if the intent to take the money from Anderson did not arise until after defendant brought out his gun, there was no robbery. Since the jury returned a verdict of robbery, it believed defendant intended to take money from Anderson by force before he went for his gun. Accordingly, defendant's only defense to robbery was the existence of an honest belief that he was entitled to the money. The trial court's approval of the prosecutor's argument that no such defense exists was erroneous. It removed completely from the consideration of the jury a material issue raised by substantial evidence. It precluded any finding that intent to steal was absent. It thereby caused a miscarriage of justice within the meaning of Article VI, Section 13 of the Columbia Constitution, and requires reversal.

Defendant Rita Ann Alvarado was charged with burglary. Following a jury trial in the superior court, she was convicted and sentenced to four years in prison. She appeals.

This case arises from a dispute between defendant, a user of heroin, and Julian Habecker, a dealer in the substance. On the morning of May 6, 1979, defendant gained entry into Habecker's house. No one was present. Defendant claimed to have bought from Habecker a day or two earlier some fake heroin. Rummaging about, defendant proceeded from room to room, taking several hundred dollars, some heroin, several phonograph records, and a few posters that had been tacked to the walls. She then left. She boasted of her exploit to fellow heroin users, who subsequently informed on her and caused her arrest.

This was primarily a case that featured recalcitrant prosecution witnesses. The defense essentially relied on the absence of direct proof and on the untrustworthiness of the prosecution's witnesses. But there was evidence, albeit self-serving and ambiguous, that defendant was motivated by a desire to have retribution for Habecker's sale of bogus heroin. Defendant used this evidence as a basis for arguing the theory that she was not guilty because she took only the property she had given Habecker for the "drugs."

The first of defendant's two contentions is that the evidence is not sufficient to support her conviction for burglary. Under Columbia law, evidence is sufficient to support a conviction for a particular crime if a rational trier of fact, viewing such evidence in the light most favorable to the People, could find the defendant guilty of all of that crime's elements beyond a reasonable doubt.

Section 459 of the Columbia Penal Code states: "Every person who, without consent, enters any house, apartment, or other building, with intent to commit larceny, is guilty of burglary." It effectively defines "intent to commit larceny" as an element.

Defendant's claim focuses on the asserted insufficiency of the evidence for the element of intent to commit larceny. Her theory rests upon the observation there was no proof the property she took was not previously hers, which she recovered because Habecker cheated her. Under *People v. Cutler* (Colum. Ct. App. 1967), it is an established principle that a bona fide belief in a right or claim to the property taken, even if mistaken, negates the element of intent to commit larceny because it negates the intent to steal.

With specific reference to this case, we can identify three rational inferences from the evidence. One is that defendant intended to, and did, retrieve *only* the property she had given for the bogus heroin. Another is that she intended to, and did, merely take items for the general purpose of economic gain. But by far the most reasonable inference is that she intended to, and did, take what she took to "settle the score," and was not especially concerned with obtaining the *exact* amount of money and *exact* property she had given; rather, she meant to obtain whatever money and property were conveniently available, in retribution for the fraudulent drug deal. We note, for example, that she took some *heroin*. Reason does not suggest she had given Habecker heroin as some or the entire purchase price for other heroin.

The inference of intent to commit larceny is reasonable and credible. Any rational trier of fact could surely have drawn it and concluded beyond a reasonable doubt that defendant intended to steal. The other elements of the crime are essentially conceded and are well supported by the evidence. There was sufficient evidence to support the burglary conviction.

The second of defendant's two contentions is that the superior court erred by failing to instruct the jury *sua sponte* on trespass as a lesser included offense of burglary. Her trial counsel did not request any such instruction.

A trial court must instruct the jury *sua sponte* on a lesser included offense only if there is substantial evidence that, if accepted, would absolve the defendant from guilt of the greater offense but not the lesser — in other words, only if there were substantial evidence showing the absence of the element distinguishing the greater from the lesser. Evidence is substantial only if capable of inspiring belief on the part of the jury.

We agree with defendant that trespass is indeed a lesser included offense of burglary. The test is whether the greater included offense contains all the elements of the lesser included offense and others in addition. It is satisfied here. Like trespass, burglary contains the (1) unconsented (2) entry (3) into a building. But, unlike trespass, burglary contains as well (4) intent to commit larceny, which entails intent to steal.

We do not agree, however, there was substantial evidence that, if accepted, would absolve defendant from guilt of burglary but not trespass. Defendant argues there was indeed such evidence: When she entered Habecker's house, she did not intend to commit larceny, but intended *only* to take items as to which, to quote *People v. Cutler, supra*, she had a "right or claim" under a "bona fide belief," a state of mind that would have "negate[d]" any intent to steal. We cannot deny that *some* evidence existed, but it was hardly *substantial*. The only evidence on the point was a completely ambiguous statement by defendant's mother to the effect that defendant had once said she had intended to recover some property Habecker had stolen from her. Yet the evidence disclosed that defendant conducted a general ransacking of the house, indiscriminately taking items never specifically related to any right or claim.

It follows that the superior court did not err in failing to instruct *sua sponte* on trespass as a lesser included offense of burglary. But even if the superior court had in fact erred, we could not reverse the judgment. Article VI, Section 13 of the Columbia Constitution declares: "No judgment shall be reversed, in any case, on the ground of any error of any kind, unless, after an examination of the entire case, including the evidence, the court shall be of the opinion that the error complained of has resulted in a miscarriage of justice." In *People v. Watson* (Colum. Supreme Ct. 1956), the Supreme Court held that a court may form such an opinion only "if it is reasonably probable that a result more favorable to the complaining party would have been reached in the absence of the error." In light of the altogether insubstantial evidence supporting trespass rather than burglary, no reasonable probability of this kind shows itself here.

The judgment is affirmed.

ANSWER 1 TO PERFORMANCE TEST B

I. STATEMENT OF THE FACTS

Nature of the relationship between the alleged victims and Defendant

Arno and Vivian Pir, a Ruritanian couple in their late fifties, welcomed defendant, Thomas Wils, into their home several years before the events giving rise to this action. The Pirs had emigrated from Ruritania many years ago and both were officers in the Ruritanian-American Freedom League.

Through their activities in the league, the Pirs became aware of Thomas Wils, who had recently escaped from a dictatorship in Ruritania. The Pirs had never had any children, and Thomas was a young man, approximately 19 years old. Thomas had been granted political asylum in the United States because of the abusive treatment he had received at the hands of the Ruritanian government.

It is undisputed that Thomas came to live with the couple under an informal relationship, something between an adoptive family relationship and an employer-employee relationship. The agreement was that the couple would provide Thomas with room and board and Thomas agreed to do "odd jobs" around the house. Vivian would sometimes give Thomas spending money. At times, Thomas was asked to do assorted routine maintenance jobs for the couple. Thomas described his duties as those of a "handyman" around the house.

The couple had an admitted interest in seeing Thomas get on his own two feet, and either go to college or get a "real job."

This arrangement lasted until some time in April or May of 1999.

Promise to give defendant the Triumph Spitfire

At some point during the relationship between Thomas and the Pirs, Vivian Pir agreed to give Thomas an automobile, a Triumph Spitfire. There is some dispute on the record with respect to whether the car was given in exchange for work Thomas had agreed to do on the garage. Mr. Pir stated during his direct examination that Vivian had agreed to give the car in exchange for work. Vivian stated that she "agreed to give" the car to Thomas, not in exchange for work, but so that Thomas could use it for transportation if he went to college.

The testimony of Thomas is more in line with the belief of Arno. Thomas testified that Vivian agreed to give him the car after Thomas had requested payment for his assigned task of "turn[ing] the garage into a guest house with a bathroom and kitchen." At some point during the work, Thomas, apparently concerned about the amount of time and effort involved, believed he should be paid for this work. Thomas testified that Vivian offered him the automobile as payment because, though Thomas could not drive, Thomas could sell the auto and use the cash from the sale as payment for services rendered. Thomas was not capable of driving because of his blackouts as a result of having been beaten by the police in Ruritania.

Events of April 1999

In [or] around April of 1999, Thomas completed the task of turning the garage into a guest house -- though Arno's recollection was that he had not completed "the work" in the garage. Upon completion, Thomas demanded the payment of the car from Vivian. She refused to pay him -- though the precise facts vary according to the testimony. The two apparently exchanged heated words and Vivian "threw Thomas out."

Following that incident, Thomas made a handful of attempts to request that the couple give him the car, which Thomas clearly believed was rightfully his.

He also sought shelter and support from fellow Ruritanians, and also sought employment as a handyman, but was turned down at every juncture.

Events of July 3, 1999

On July 3, 1999, after being essentially without a home for three months, Thomas approached Arno at his place of business, and requested, once again, that the car be delivered to Thomas.

Arno told Thomas that Arno did not have the car with him, but that Vivian probably had the title documents in her purse. He also told Thomas that the car was at home.

After repeated requests for the automobile, Arno informed Thomas that the car would be delivered to Thomas when Arno returned from his vacation on July 20th or July 21st.

Thomas left peacefully.

Events of July 5, 1999

Though there is some disagreement in the testimony regarding the particulars, the essential facts are that Thomas entered the house of the Pirs while both were away, in order "to get the Triumph and the ownership papers." Thomas' understanding from the conversation with Arno was that the title papers were somewhere in the house or in Vivian's purse. Thomas waited for Vivian to leave before attempting to get the car. Thomas also testified that he waited for Vivian to return before asking her about the car. After waiting for a while, he made himself a sandwich because he had not eaten in days.

When Vivian returned, she saw Thomas, and reacted in an aggressive manner, shouting at Thomas and telling him to leave. She also grabbed a broomstick and threatened to hit Thomas with it, though Vivian's testimony was that Thomas demanded the car and "started at her" before she grabbed the broom. Thomas then pushed Vivian aside -- though Vivian testified that Thomas punched her in the shoulder -- and pulled the purse from Vivian's arm. After rummaging through the purse, Vivian claims that Thomas yelled, "If you won't give me the papers for the car, then I'll take what I can get."

After rummaging through the purse looking for the title papers, unable to find the papers, Thomas instead took some credit cards, a silver mirror and a cellular phone.

As Thomas began to leave, Vivian chased after him, but he ran away from her.

<u>Defendant's subsequent actions</u>

Thomas testified that he believed that the value of the car was $4,000. Although Arno testified that the value was, in his opinion, about $2,000, there is nothing in the record to show that Thomas knew that this was or may have been the actual value of the car.

Seeking to exact payment for his services, Thomas pawned the mirror and the phone for $15. Thomas ran up about $4,000 worth of credit card debt (what he believed the Triumph was worth), and therefore believed that he had "got[ten] even with them."

Thomas was arrested on July 31st.

II.   ARGUMENT

A.   BY FAILING TO INSTRUCT THE JURY THAT A BONA FIDE BELIEF OF CLAIM TO PROPERTY NEGATES THE INTENT TO STEAL IN A BURGLARY CASE, THE JURY WAS UNABLE TO CONSIDER OVERWHELMING EVIDENCE THAT WOULD HAVE NEGATED DEFENDANT'S INTENT TO COMMIT LARCENY, THE TRIAL COURT COMMITTED ERROR RESULTING IN CAUSING A MISCARRIAGE OF JUSTICE

The elements for a claim of burglary in the State of Columbia require that the defendant enter a house, without consent, with the intent to commit larceny. Section 459 of the Columbia Penal Code; <u>People v. Alvarado</u> (Ct. App. Columbia, 1982); <u>People v. Brown</u> (Ct. App. Columbia, 1957). The issue here is whether the trial court's failure to give an instruction that would have negated an element of larceny is manifest injustice requiring the defendant's conviction to be overturned.

In <u>Brown</u>, the Court of Appeals overturned a jury verdict on the grounds of an erroneous instruction on the elements of burglary. The court found that the jury instruction failed to properly set forth an element of the claim of larceny. In that case, the necessary element required to convict defendant missing from the jury instruction was the intent to deprive the defendant of his or her property permanently. Since the crime of burglary requires there to [sic] be a larceny, the judge was required to instruct the jury on the elements of larceny as well. The appellate court ruled that the trial court was in error in refusing the defendant to introduce this particular instruction and, accordingly, vacated the verdict of the trial court.

Although the element of larceny missing in the present case is not the intent to deprive permanently, the principle stated in that case holds completely true in the case at bar.

Here, the jury was instructed only that defendant enter a house, without consent with the intent to commit larceny. The Superior Court refused defendant's proffered instruction, that a bona fide belief on the part of the taker of a right or claim to the property negates the intent to steal.

The law is settled that "a bona fide belief in a right or claim to the property taken, even if mistaken, negates the element of intent to commit larceny because it negates the intent to steal." <u>People v. Cutler</u> (Columbia Ct. App. 1967); cited in <u>People v. Alvarado</u> (Columbia

Ct. App. 1982). In other words, showing a bona fide belief in the ownership or right to the property negates a necessary element of larceny, intent.

It should be pointed out that although the court in Alvarado held that the defendant's actions in that particular case did not demonstrate a bona fide belief in the right to the property under a burglary conviction, the facts are easily distinguishable from the case at bar. In the Alvarado decision, the defendant entered the residence of an individual she did a drug deal with, allegedly in order to exact payment because the drugs she bought were "fake." Defendant rummaged through the house, taking more heroin, some money, posters, and other items. The trial court found the defendant's evidence of a claim of bona fide right completely implausible, because the defendant would not have paid someone heroin in order to obtain heroin.

Here, by contrast, at the time Thomas entered the house of the Pirs, he had the intent merely to collect on the car that had actually been promised to him and that he actually believed was his. Vivian, the witness who most contradicts Thomas' testimony, admitted herself that she had "agreed to give" the car to Thomas. Whether consideration was paid for the car or not is irrelevant with respect to whether Thomas had a bona fide belief in his entitlement. None of the parties has disputed his bona fide belief in his entitlement to the car, and the record is replete with evidence that he believed that the car was his as a matter of right.

Under the holding Brown, because the trial court failed (in fact, refused) to instruct the jury on a necessary element of larceny in a burglary case that a bona fide belief of entitlement would negate intent, the court committed error and a miscarriage of justice occurred.

Under Section 13 of Article VI of the Columbia Constitution, where the error complained of has resulted in a miscarriage of justice, the appellate court should overturn the judgment. Here, but for the failure to include the jury instruction, the jury would have been free to consider the bona fides of defendant's belief in his entitlement to the car. Since the record is so replete with evidence of the bona fides of his belief, the error was clearly a miscarriage of justice and the conviction should be reversed.

B.   BY FAILING TO INSTRUCT THE JURY THAT A BONA FIDE BELIEF OF CLAIM TO PROPERTY NEGATES THE INTENT TO STEAL IN A ROBBERY CASE, THE JURY WAS UNABLE TO CONSIDER OVERWHELMING EVIDENCE THAT WOULD HAVE NEGATED DEFENDANT'S INTENT TO COMMIT LARCENY, THE TRIAL COURT COMMITTED ERROR RESULTING IN CAUSING A MISCARRIAGE OF JUSTICE

The State of Columbia defines robbery, in relevant part, as a "larcenous taking of the personal property of another." Columbia Penal Code Section 211. The courts have construed this to require that in order to convict someone of robbery, that person must have the necessary intent to steal at the time of the robbery. Cutler, at 5.

The facts of Cutler are controlling here. Cutler involved a defendant who went to another's house, claiming that he only went there to collect a debt which he believed was owed to him. On facts which were hotly disputed, a scuffle ensued, pursuant to which the defendant obtained possession of the victim's wallet, which the defendant then claimed was sufficient to extinguish the debt. The defendant ended the encounter by running away with the wallet of the victim.

The trial court excluded an instruction to the jury proffered by defendant that "a necessary element of larceny, the intent to steal, was requisite to robbery." Cutler, at 5. This court overruled the trial court's exclusion of that instruction, finding that "[a]n essential element of robbery is the larcenous intent that accompanies the taking." Id. Refusing to allow the jury to consider evidence of defendant's bona fide belief that the debt was owed to him was prejudicial error, said the court, since such a finding would have negated intent, and therefore defeated a robbery charge.

In the present case, the defendant's bona fide belief that the property was his is even stronger than it was in Cutler. In Cutler, the defendant and the victim completely denied that the debt was even due. Here, one of the defendants has, in fact, admitted that the car was going to be given to defendant. In addition, defendant was looking in victim's purse, exactly the place he was told he could find the title to the car. Therefore, regardless of whether defendant's taking of property other than the title to the car, it is manifestly evident, not even disputed, in fact, that defendant lacked the intent to steal when he allegedly committed the burglary and when he allegedly committed the robbery.

The fact that defendant allegedly punched the victim is also immaterial, since it does not help to show felonious intent. Whomever's story you believe, the victim was clearly either defending himself or at least responding to hostility of the victim.

Therefore, for the same reasons that it was manifest injustice to exclude the jury instruction with respect to the burglary charge, it was manifest injustice with respect to the robbery charge, and the conviction should be overruled.

C.   THE TRIAL COURT ERRED IN NOT INSTRUCTING THE JURY SUA SPONTE ON TRESPASS AS A LESSER INCLUDED OFFENSE OF BURGLARY BECAUSE THERE IS SUBSTANTIAL EVIDENCE DISTINGUISHING THE LESSER INCLUDED OFFENSE OF TRESPASS FROM BURGLARY, CAUSING A MISCARRIAGE OF JUSTICE AND REQUIRING THAT THE TRIAL COURT'S JUDGMENT BE OVERTURNED

There is yet another ground for overturning the burglary conviction. A trial court is required to instruct the jury sua sponte on a lesser included offense where there is substantial evidence that distinguishes the lesser offense from the greater one. Alvarado, at 9. Trespass has been held unequivocally to be a lesser included offense of burglary. Id. Trespass involves unconsented entry into a building. Id. Burglary requires the additional element of an intent to commit larceny. Accordingly, if there were substantial evidence that the defendant did not commit larceny, then the burglary charge would have been distinguishable from the trespass offense and the court would have been required to instruct the jury on trespass, rather than burglary. Id.

As discussed above, there is more than substantial, there is overwhelming, indeed uncontroverted, evidence that the defendant lacked the intent to steal at the time he entered the home of the victims. Not only did the defendant so testify, one victim outright [sic] admitted defendant's entitlement to the car; the other admitted that she had agreed to give defendant the car. In addition, the defendant searched through plaintiff's purse, where he was told the papers would be. Although there could have been a mischievous reason for going into plaintiff's purse, this is rendered doubtful by the fact that the victim admitted that defendant yelled that if he could not get the papers to the car, then he would take what he could get. He even waited around for Vivian to return home so he could ask her about the car.

This establishes that defendant did not have the intent to steal when he entered the premises.

The court in Alvarado held differently, as discussed above. The court reasoned that although the defendant came forward with some evidence that she did not have the intent to steal, that evidence was only a comment made to her mother that she was going to the victim's house to get back property the victim had stolen from her. In addition, the court ruled that defendant's actions, once inside the house, did not comport with the defendant's story. Cutler.

Here, the facts show overwhelmingly that the defendant's actions, once inside the house, only ratified his belief that he was entitled to ownership of the car.

It should be pointed out that the fact that defendant took property other than the title to the car is immaterial as to whether he had the intent to steal at the time of the trespass. It is evident, even from the words of the victim's mouth, that defendant only took the property because he could not find the title to the vehicle.

Also, the fact that it was possible that defendant could have charged more on the credit card but for the coincidence of his arrest upon having spent about $4,000 is likewise immaterial. It does not help the prosecution establish a case against defendant for burglary, his intent at the time of the trespass having been otherwise established.

Because the court improperly failed to instruct the jury sua sponte on trespass, manifest injustice occurred. Manifest injustice can be seen from the fact that the jury would almost certainly have preferred to convict defendant of trespass, rather than burglary, given the facts. The exclusion of the trespass instruction gave the jury no choice but to convict defendant of burglary, causing a miscarriage of justice.

For the foregoing reasons, the judgment of the trial court should be overturned to prevent a miscarriage of justice.

Statement of Facts

Thomas Wils is a Ruritanian emigre who fled his home country approximately three years ago at the age of nineteen. He landed in New York, where he was granted political asylum. Arno Pir and his wife, Vivian Pir, who were members of the Ruritanian - American Freedom League, offered to give Wils free room and board in exchange for certain work around the Pir household.

The Pirs insist there was never any agreement to pay Wils for his work around the house; they simply provided room and board and some occasional spending money. Wils also agrees that this was the initial arrangement between them.

However, the parties' accounts differ when it comes to certain work in the garage that Wils was to do. Wils stated in his testimony that he told Vivian he would not complete the work in the garage unless she paid him. According to Wils, Vivian then promised to give Wils an old Triumph in return for his work. When Wils finished his work and asked for the promised car, Vivian refused to give it to him and threw him out.

Vivian, on the other hand, insists that she never promised Wils the car in exchange for work, but only for transportation if he were to go to college. Arno Pir testified that he believed that Vivian had promised Wils the car if he finished the work in the garage, but that he also believed Vivian threw him out because he demanded the car before the work was done.

All parties agree that there was an argument [in] April or May 1999 when Wils demanded the car, Vivian refused, and threw Wils out of the house. Wils then went to live with other Ruritanian friends. After he ran out of money and places to live, he started to live on the street and beg for food.

Finally, Wils went to Arno's liquor store on July 3, 1999, when he asked Arno for the car. Arno told him he didn't have the car, that it was at home, and that Vivian had the title documents in her purse. Arno further promised that he would give Wils the car and the ownership papers when he returned from his business trip on July 20th or 21st.

On July 5, 1999, Wils went to the Pirs' home to obtain the car and the ownership papers. Wils stated that he waited for Vivian to leave, then removed a lock that he had installed himself in order to enter the house. He remained in the kitchen waiting for Vivian to return. Wils admits that he made himself a sandwich because he hadn't eaten in days and was starving.

After 45 minutes, Vivian returned and discovered Wils in the kitchen eating. She told him to get out before she called the police. Wils asked Vivian for the car again. Here, the testimony of Vivian and Wils differs -- Vivian stated that Wils began to approach her threateningly, whereupon Vivian grabbed a broom to protect herself. Wils then punched her in the shoulder, grabbed her purse, rummaged through it, and ran away.

Wils stated that after he asked for the car, Vivian grabbed a broom and threatened to hit him with it, whereupon he pushed her shoulder and took her purse, rummaging through it looking for the ownership papers. Not finding the papers in question, Wils took credit cards, a silver mirror and a cellular phone instead.

Wils pawned the mirror and the phone, then went to New York and ran up approximately $4000 in credit card debt on the Pirs' card because "that was what the Triumph was worth."

Wils was arrested on July 31st. He was convicted of burglary and robbery in Columbia Superior Court. The only jury instructions given concerned the elements of burglary, robbery and larceny.

As discussed further below, Wils has three meritorious claims of error on appeal: that the trial court (1) refused to instruct the jury on a bona fide belief in a claim or right to another personal property relating to burglary; (2) refused to instruct the jury on a bona fide belief in a claim or right to another's personal property relating to robbery; and (3) failed to instruct the jury sua sponte on trespass as a lesser included offense of burglary.

Argument

I. By failing to instruct the jury that a bona fide belief on the part of the taker of personal property in his right or claim to the property negates the intent to steal, the trial court erroneously instructed the jury on the crime of burglary.

It is well settled that a bona fide belief, even though mistakenly held, that one has a right to property negates larcenous intent. See Cutler, Alvarado. Wils has made it clear that he believed he was entitled to the car in payment for the work he had done for the Pirs. Whether or not he actually had such an arrangement is irrelevant, as is the fact that Vivian disputes Wils' account of the promise of the car. The important issue is that Wils had a bona fide belief that the car was owed to him, which he did.

Burglary comprised the entering of a dwelling without consent with the intent to commit larceny. Section 459 of Columbia Penal Code.

Crucial to the crime of burglary is the intent to commit larceny. A belief that the property taken belongs to the taker, or that he has a right or claim to it, is sufficient to preclude larcenous intent. See Cutler. Wils did not intend to rob Vivian when he went to her house, only to recover what he believed was owed to him: the car. The taking of property is not larceny in the absence of an intent to steal, according to the Cutler court.

The People, however, will argue that Wils waited until Arno was away on a business trip, broke into the Pirs' home and waited for Vivian alone. Furthermore, he helped himself to their food, without consent, while he was waiting. Even worse, the People will contend, when Vivian told him to get out of the house, Wils grabbed her purse and ended up taking credit cards and other items to which he had no arguable right or claim. The prosecution will argue that, like the defendant in Alvarado, Wils conducted a "general ransacking," indiscriminately taking items never specifically related to a right or claim.

However, this case is more like Cutler than Alvarado. In Alvarado, it is unclear that the defendant ever intended to retrieve the property she believed was hers, as opposed to merely taking items for the purpose of economic gain. In this case, Wils went to the Pirs' house with the express purpose of getting the car and the title. Believing, as Arno had told him, that the papers he wanted were in Vivian's purse, he grabbed her purse and rummaged through it.

His sole purpose when he grabbed her purse was to retrieve the papers he believed belonged to him. If, as in Alvarado, Wils truly wanted to simply take items for the purpose of economic gain, he could have easily ransacked the house instead of waiting 45 minutes in the kitchen for Vivian to return.

In Cutler, the defendant, believing he was owed money, took the [sic] Anderson's wallet when the opportunity presented itself while the two were struggling. Cutler did not intend to rob Anderson when he went to his house, only to recover money owed to him. The Cutler court found that an honest belief that he was entitled to the money was a defense, and that approval of the prosecutor's argument that no such defense exists was erroneous. The appeals court reversed the trial court's decision, and concluded that the trial court's approval of the prosecutor's argument removed completely from the consideration of the jury a material issue raised by substantial evidence, and resulted in a miscarriage of justice.

Wils' case is much like that of Cutler. He rummaged through the purse looking for ownership papers, and only when he and Vivian began to struggle did he take the other items and run away. His intent upon entering the house was to retrieve the car he honestly believed belonged to him. He may have changed his mind later in the heat of the moment, but the fact remains that he entered with the intent to retrieve his items only.

A key element of burglary is entering a dwelling with the intent to commit larceny. By refusing to give the jury instruction that a bona fide belief on the part of the taker of personal property in his right or claim to the property negates the intent to steal, the trial court did not allow the jury to consider a natural issue raised by substantial evidence -- that Wils believed he owned the car and entered only to retrieve his car.

Accordingly, the district court caused a miscarriage of justice pursuant to Article IV, Section 13 of the Columbia Constitution that requires reversal.

II.   <u>By failing to instruct the jury that a bona fide belief on the part of the taker of personal property in his right or claim to the property taken negates the intent to steal, the trial court erroneously instructed the jury on the element of intent in the crime of robbery</u>.

According to Section 211 of the Columbia Penal Code, robbery is the larcenous taking of the personal property of another, from his person or immediate presence, and without his consent, accomplished by means of force or fear.

Like burglary, robbery requires the requisite intent to steal. See Cutler. An essential element of robbery, stated the Cutler court, is the larcenous intent that accompanies the taking.

As explained under Section I above, substantial evidence was provided at trial that Wils did not have the requisite intent -- that he grabbed Vivian's purse (the act that would constitute robbery) with the sole intent of retrieving the ownership papers he believed belonged to him. Again, as stated previously regarding burglary, it is well settled that a bona fide belief that one has a right or claim to the property negates the larcenous intent required for robbery.

The People will argue that Wils ended up taking credit cards and other items to which he had no ownership interest. However, Wils stated that he took those items only because he was unable to locate the papers he wanted, and also that he only charged $4000 on the credit cards, or what he believed the car to be worth, and thus what was owed to him.

There is a stronger argument that Wils did not have the requisite larcenous intent when he entered the Pirs' house than there is in conjunction with the taking of the credit cards and other items. However, using Cutler, there is still sufficient support for an argument that the jury should have been instructed on a bona fide belief in a claim or right to another's personal property relating to robbery. Substantial evidence was given at the trial court such that if the jury should have been allowed to consider the issue of lack of intent to steal.

Accordingly, the district court caused a miscarriage of justice pursuant to Article IV, Section 13 of the Columbia Constitution that requires reversal.

III. By failing to include trespass as a lesser included defense of burglary, the trial court erroneously failed to instruct the jury sua sponte regarding trespass.

A trial court must instruct the jury sua sponte on a lesser included offense only if there is substantial evidence that, if accepted, would absolve the defendant from guilt of the greater offense but not the lesser. There must be substantial evidence showing the absence of the element distinguishing the greater from the lesser. According to Alvarado, evidence is substantial only if capable of inspiring belief on the part of the jury.

According to Section 602 of the Penal Code, every person who, without consent, enters any house, apartment, or other building is guilty of trespass. The crucial element distinguishing trespass from burglary is the intent to commit larceny within at the time of entering.

As discussed in Section I above, there was substantial evidence (capable of inspiring belief on the part of the jury) that Wils did not have the requisite intent for the crime of burglary.

The appeals court in Alvarado refused to reverse the judgment based on defendant's contention that the trial court failed to instruct the jury sua sponte on trespass as a lesser included offense of burglary. Wils' case, however, is distinguishable from Alvarado. In Alvarado the court did not find substantial evidence of lack of intent, whereas in Wils' case there is such substantial evidence.

Furthermore, the Alvarado court, citing People v. Watson, stated that a court may only come to the opinion that there has been a miscarriage of justice if it is reasonably probable that a result more favorable to the complaining party would have been reached in the absence of error.

Given the substantial evidence presented regarding Wils' belief that he was owed the car, there is a strong argument that Wils would have been found guilty of trespass instead of burglary had the court instructed the jury on the lesser included offense of trespass.

Therefore, the appeals court should find that the district court caused a miscarriage of justice pursuant to Article IV, Section 13 of the Columbia Constitution that requires reversal.

California
Bar
Examination

Performance Test A
INSTRUCTIONS AND FILE

ESTATE OF KEEFE

File

TABLE OF CONTENTS

<u>Estate of Keefe</u>

<u>INSTRUCTIONS</u>

1. You will have three hours to complete this session of the examination. This performance test is designed to evaluate your ability to handle a select number of legal authorities in the context of a factual problem involving a client.

2. The problem is set in the fictional State of Columbia, one of the United States.

3. You will have two sets of materials with which to work, a **File** and a **Library**. The **File** contains factual materials about your case. The first document is a memorandum containing the instructions for the tasks you are to complete.

4. The **Library** contains the legal authorities needed to complete the tasks. The case reports may be real, modified, or written solely for the purpose of this examination. If the cases appear familiar to you, do not assume that they are precisely the same as you have read before. Read them thoroughly, as if all were new to you. You should assume that cases were decided in the jurisdictions and on the dates shown. In citing cases from the **Library**, you may use abbreviations and omit page citations.

5. Your response must be written in the answer book provided. In answering this performance test, you should concentrate on the materials provided, but you should also bring to bear on the problem your general knowledge of the law. What you have learned in law school and elsewhere provides the general background for analyzing the problem; the **File** and **Library** provide the specific materials with which you must work.

6. Although there are no restrictions on how you apportion your time, you should probably allocate at least 90 minutes to organizing and writing.

7. This performance test will be graded on your responsiveness to instructions and on the content, thoroughness, and organization of your response.

McIntyre, Yost and Amrein, LLP

MEMORANDUM

TO: Applicant
FROM: Gretchen Pronko
DATE: February 26, 2002

Our client, Mason Finch, is the former caretaker of decedent, Sandra Keefe, who promised to leave him a life estate in certain real and personal property in exchange for Mr. Finch's agreement to care for her. We recently filed a complaint on behalf of Mr. Finch, asserting a simple cause of action against the administrator of Ms. Keefe's estate for specific performance of an oral contract. Defendant has filed a motion for summary judgment.

The file contains a number of documents and some relevant cases you will need to review in order to perform the following tasks:

A.   Draft declarations for all witnesses whose testimony will be useful in establishing that there are disputed issues of fact and in supporting our arguments. Don't take time to write out headings or other boilerplate language. Our client, the witnesses interviewed by our investigator, and the friend contacted by our client (see Mr. Finch's letter on this subject in the file) have all agreed to sign declarations if you think their testimony will help.

B. Draft only sections III and IV of a Memorandum of Points and Authorities in Opposition to Motion for Summary Judgment.

In performing this assignment, please comply with the Internal Memorandum regarding Oppositions to Motions for Summary Judgment.

McIntyre, Yost and Amrein, LLP
INTERNAL MEMORANDUM

TO: Associates
FROM: Myron Taylor
RE: Oppositions to Motions for Summary Judgment

DECLARATIONS

All facts asserted in opposition to motions for summary judgment must be supported by admissible evidence established in declarations or by judicial notice.

Declarations must:

- Be limited to facts relevant to the motion for summary judgment.

- Include only admissible evidence that the declarant could testify to if called as a witness.

- Be concise and direct statements of facts; a declaration should not be a summary of everything the declarant knows.

- Be drafted before the memorandum of points and authorities; then, the statements of undisputed and disputed facts and argument can cite to the declarations by paragraph number, and need not repeat all of the facts.

MEMORANDUM OF POINTS AND AUTHORITIES

The Memorandum of Points and Authorities in Opposition to Motion for Summary Judgment consists of five different sections, as follows:

Section I. Introduction: This consists of a concise one-paragraph summary of the nature of the underlying case, the basis for the summary judgment motion, and the basis for the opposition.

Section II. Response to Moving Party's Statement of Undisputed Facts: This is in two-column format. In the first column we restate the alleged Undisputed Facts. In the second column, we respond with "Agree" or "Disagree," indicating whether we agree or disagree that the fact alleged to be undisputed is in fact undisputed.

Section III. Responsive Party's Statement of Disputed Facts: This is a two-column section identical in format to the Moving Party's Statement of Undisputed Facts (Section II of their Memorandum). In the first column, we state those facts we believe are disputed. The second column lists citations to evidence that establish these facts.

Section IV. Response to Moving Party's Arguments: In this section, we draft arguments that respond point by point to the arguments made in the moving party's Memorandum of Points and Authorities in Support of Motion for Summary Judgment. In support of our arguments, we cite to our Disputed Facts by the number assigned in Section III, and to relevant cases to support our legal assertions. We also make any additional arguments that support the position that there are triable issues of fact or that there are legal issues precluding entry of judgment as a matter of law.

Section V. Conclusion: This is a brief statement asking the court to find in our favor.

Paul Price
HIMMLER & MATZEN
1 West Union Plaza, 15th Floor
Garden City, Columbia 00987
(555) 267–0001

Attorneys for Defendant

SUPERIOR COURT OF THE STATE OF COLUMBIA

IN AND FOR THE COUNTY OF CHESTER

In re ESTATE OF SANDRA KEEFE, Deceased.	Case No. 171757
_____/	**MEMORANDUM OF POINTS AND AUTHORITIES IN SUPPORT OF MOTION FOR SUMMARY JUDGMENT**
MASON FINCH,	
Plaintiff,	
vs.	
GRANT KEEFE, as Administrator of the Estate of Sandra Keefe,	
Defendant.	
_____/	

I. INTRODUCTION

This is an action for specific performance of an oral contract to make a will. Plaintiff, Mason Finch, claims that the decedent, Sandra Keefe, promised to leave him a life estate in certain real and personal property as consideration for his agreement to provide care for her. Defendant, Grant Keefe, seeks summary judgment on three grounds: the undisputed facts establish that there was no oral contract between plaintiff and decedent; this claim is barred by the statute of frauds; and, this claim is barred by the applicable statute of limitations.

II. DEFENDANT'S STATEMENT OF UNDISPUTED FACTS

Statement	Citation to Evidence
1. Defendant is the administrator of decedent's estate.	Declaration of Grant Keefe, ¶ 1
2. Defendant is decedent's nephew.	Declaration of Grant Keefe, ¶ 2
3. Defendant reviewed decedent's papers, documents, and personal effects, and found no writing signed by decedent promising interests in her estate to plaintiff.	Declaration of Grant Keefe, ¶ 3
4. Defendant spent significant time with decedent in the months before she died.	Declaration of Grant Keefe, ¶ 4
5. Defendant had many conversations with decedent in which she discussed defendant and plaintiff and Megan Finch.	Declaration of Grant Keefe, ¶ 5
6. Decedent indicated that she felt she had more than provided compensation to plaintiff for the services he provided.	Declaration of Grant Keefe, ¶ 6
7. Decedent indicated that she would not leave a will, as she knew and desired that defendant would inherit everything if she died intestate.	Declaration of Grant Keefe, ¶ 7
8. Decedent died on August 26, 1999.	Declaration of Grant Keefe, ¶ 8
9. This action was filed on January 11, 2002.	Request for Judicial Notice of Complaint

III. ARGUMENT

145

A.   Plaintiff's Claim Based on an Oral Contract to Make a Will Must Fail Because There is No Evidence to Establish the Existence of an Oral Contract.

The undisputed facts in this case show that there was no oral contract to make a will. Defendant was decedent's nephew. [Defendant's Undisputed Fact (hereafter DU Fact) 2.] Toward the end of decedent's life, defendant spent substantial amounts of time with her. [DU Fact 4.] Defendant had many conversations with decedent in which she discussed defendant and plaintiff and Megan Finch. [DU Fact 5.] Decedent indicated that she felt she had more than provided compensation to plaintiff for the services he provided. [DU Fact 6.] She further indicated that she would not leave a will, as she knew and desired that defendant would inherit everything if she died intestate. [DU Fact 7.]

These undisputed facts establish that decedent never promised to make a will with provisions in favor of plaintiff. Thus, no contract, oral or written, existed.

B.   Even if an Oral Contract Exists, It Cannot be Enforced Because It Is Not in Writing.

Defendant was named administrator of decedent's estate. [DU Fact 1.] In this capacity, he examined decedent's records, papers, and personal effects. [DU Fact 3.] He did not discover any will or any other writing signed by decedent indicating any promises made to plaintiff. [DU Fact 3.]

Columbia Probate Code §150 provides as follows:

A contract to make a will . . . can be established only by one of the following:

(a) Provisions of a will stating material provisions of the contract.
(b) An express reference in a will to a contract and extrinsic evidence proving the terms of the contract.
(c) A writing signed by the decedent evidencing the contract.

1   Probate Code §150 is clear in requiring a writing to establish the existence of a

2   contract to make a will. (*Riganti v. McElhinney* (Colum. Ct. App. 1967).) Because the

3   undisputed facts in this case establish that the provisions of Probate Code section 150

4   have not been met, this action is barred.

5

     C.   This Action Is Barred by the Statute of Limitations Because It Was Filed More
6   Than Two Years After Decedent's Death.

7

8   Columbia Code of Civil Procedure section 597 provides that actions to enforce the

9   terms of an oral contract must be brought within two years. An action to enforce a

10   contract to make a will arises upon the death of the promisor. (*Kennedy v. Bank of*

11   *Columbia* (Colum. Ct. App. 1965).) Decedent died on August 26, 1999. [DU Fact 8.]

12   This action was filed on January 11, 2002. [DU Fact 9.] Thus, plaintiff's action is

13   untimely and therefore barred.

14

15   IV. CONCLUSION

16   The law and undisputed facts in this case establish that plaintiff's action must fail.

17   Defendant respectfully requests that summary judgment in his favor be entered.

18

19   Dated: February 21, 2002   Respectfully submitted,

20   HIMMLER & MATZEN

21

                                           By_____
22   PAUL PRICE

23

                                           Attorneys for Defendant
24

25

26

27

28   147

Paul Price
HIMMLER & MATZEN
1 West Union Plaza, 15th Floor
Garden City, Columbia 00987
(555) 267–0001

Attorneys for Defendant

1

2

3

4

5

6

7

8

SUPERIOR COURT OF THE STATE OF COLUMBIA

IN AND FOR THE COUNTY OF CHESTER

9

10

11 In re ESTATE OF SANDRA KEEFE, Deceased.

12 _____/

Case No. 171757

DECLARATION OF GRANT KEEFE IN SUPPORT OF MOTION FOR SUMMARY JUDGMENT

13 MASON FINCH,

14   Plaintiff,

15 vs.

16 GRANT KEEFE, as Administrator of the Estate of Sandra Keefe,

17

18   Defendant.

19 _____/

20   I, Grant Keefe, declare as follows:

21   1. I am the defendant in this action, and I am the administrator of decedent

22 Sandra Keefe's estate.

23   2. I am also the nephew of decedent Sandra Keefe.

24   3. In my capacity as administrator, I reviewed my aunt's papers, documents and

25 personal effects, and found no writing signed by my aunt promising any interest in her

26 estate to plaintiff.

27

28

1   4. I spent on average two hours, three times per week with my aunt in each of the

2 six months before she died.

3   5. During the last six months of her life, I had many conversations with my aunt in

4 which she discussed Mason Finch, Megan Finch, and me.

5   6. In a number of these conversations, my aunt indicated that, while she

6 appreciated what Mr. Finch had done for her, she also felt she had more than provided

7 compensation to Mason Finch for the services he provided.

8   7. My aunt stated on several occasions that she would not leave a will, as she

9 knew that I would inherit everything if she died without a will. She made it clear to me

10 that this was her wish.

11   8. Sandra Keefe died on August 26, 1999.

12   I declare under penalty of perjury under the laws of the State of Columbia that the

13 foregoing is true and correct, and that this declaration was executed on February 16,

14 2002 in Garden City, Columbia.

15

16   _____

17   Grant Keefe

18

19

20

21

22

23

24

25

26

27

28

TRANSCRIPT OF INTERVIEW WITH MASON FINCH BY ATTORNEY GRETCHEN PRONKO

Ms. Pronko (Q): The tape recorder is on now. As I said, this will give us an accurate record of what you say for use later on.

Mr. Finch (A): That's fine with me.

Q: Good. First, let me tell you what I know about your case. An elderly woman whom you befriended some time ago promised to leave you certain property in her will, but she died without making a will.

A: Yeah, that's pretty much it in a nutshell, but of course there are lots of details □

Q: Why don't you begin with a little background information about yourself?

A: Okay. I'm 38 years old. I'm a single dad raising a daughter on my own. Her name's Megan and she's 16 years old. I've been an MFCC — a Marriage, Family and Children's Counselor — for about 12 years now. I got my Master's Degree in 1988, and opened my own practice in 1990. I've lived in Columbia for the last 16 years. Let's see, what else would you like to know?

Q: Why don't you tell me how you first met — what is the elderly woman's name?

A: Actually, there were two of them, sisters, Sandra and Mabel Keefe. I had just gotten my MFCC license and was looking for office space, so this was about 12 years ago. Sandra and Mabel owned a commercial building here in Columbia with six office spaces in it. I couldn't afford the rent they were asking, so I asked if they'd be willing to work out an exchange of some sort. They were very nice. We agreed I would manage the office building for them in exchange for a 50% discount in rent. I think what really clinched the deal was their meeting Megan. She was 4 years old at the time, and quite a charmer. Neither Sandra nor Mabel had children, and they absolutely fell in love with Megan. They invited us over for dinner, and after that, we became quite close. We reciprocated with dinners, and eventually took weekend trips together. Actually, they were quite adventurous, and we did lots of hiking and traveling together to quaint towns and sites throughout the country.

Q: How was their health?

A: About four years after we met, Mabel had a stroke. It was a pretty bad one. She was in the hospital for about six weeks. She moved to a rehabilitation facility for another six weeks. After that, Mabel was able to return home, but her mobility was very limited. She could get around with a walker, but really couldn't be left alone for long periods of time. It was difficult for Sandra to provide the level of care Mabel needed, so she approached me with an idea. Sandra was still well enough to do grocery shopping, and light housekeeping, and to provide care to Mabel in the mornings and on weekends. She asked if I would be willing to cut back my counseling practice to the mornings only. This way, I could provide care for Mabel in the afternoons. Sandra also asked me if I'd be willing to fix dinner for Mabel and Sandra in the evenings. In exchange, Sandra said that Megan and I could move in and live with them in a small in-law unit attached to their house. It was a converted garage. We'd be able to live there rent-free. Sandra also said I could use the office space rent-free. By this time in our friendship, this was a "no-brainer" decision for me. I had to do it.

Q: They must have felt very close to you to ask this of you.

A: It really was like having a wonderful second family, you know? They really felt like relatives to me, so, like I said, I had to do it.

Q: Well, you've described at least two different agreements, one involving the office rent, and a subsequent one involving taking care of Mabel. Do you have a sense of the respective market values of each of the arrangements?

A: Well, somewhat. The full rent for the office I leased was $500 per month, so half was $250. I would say that I spent an average of one-and-a-half hours per week on management tasks, such as taking calls about vacant offices, showing prospective tenants around, collecting rents, arranging for repairs, both routine and emergency, overseeing maintenance. I also know that similar positions charge a percentage of the gross rents, like five percent per month. So, either way, my management duties were worth about $250 per month. At first, I was charging $40 per hour for counseling, but I soon raised it, as my clientele built up, to $85 per hour. I'm telling you this so you may have an idea of what I feel my time was worth at the time.

Then, in terms of the second arrangement, I have no idea what my services were worth, but I was losing money, even with the free rent at both places. I'd estimate that I was losing about $1000 per month in income because of the reduction in work hours.

Q: How was your financial situation?

A: It was tough financially. I was just starting out. I had been living on student loans, and graduated with about $30,000 in loans to pay back. The first year I only made $12,000, so having a 50% reduction in rent really helped out. Four years later, though, my situation had changed pretty dramatically. I had a full-time practice, and was actually turning clients away.

Q: Were there any other consequences to your finances or otherwise as a result of the agreement?

A: Yeah, there were. First off, I spent a fair amount of time during the first four years building up my reputation in the community. I made lots of presentations, attended professional luncheons, seminars, and conferences, and actually started being asked to make presentations myself. That tailed off pretty much down to zero once I started caring for Mabel. I simply didn't have time anymore. It's hard to measure the effects of that sort of thing, but I'd have to say that my reputation has sort of plateaued now, instead of heading upward steadily like it was before. Oh yeah, I had also been thinking about getting my Ph.D. The local university offers a night program. I had to put that on hold indefinitely.

Q: How long did this arrangement continue?

A: Well, unfortunately, after about a year, Mabel passed away. Of course I helped Sandra as much as I could, but she was pretty devastated, as you can imagine. Just after the estate got settled, Sandra's health took a real turn for the worse — I think that Mabel's death took a lot out of her. She never really regained her spunk afterwards. Anyway, I ended up providing the same type of care for Sandra that I did for Mabel, only it was harder because I had to do it all myself. I had to cut down my practice some more, only working three mornings a week, about 33% of full time.

Q: Were you able to return to a full-time practice after Mabel died?

A: No, I had just started taking more clients when Sandra's health went downhill quite quickly.

Q: Did your care for Sandra differ from your care for Mabel?

A: Sandra's wasn't nearly as intensive, but because I had to do it myself I had to spend quite a bit of time doing errands like shopping, cleaning, and taking her to the doctors. Megan and I actually moved into the main house so I could be more available.

Q: It sounds like it must have been incredibly demanding.

A: Well, yes and no. I wouldn't have traded it for the world in a lot of ways. Mabel and Sandra lived life to its fullest, so if even a little of that rubbed off on me, I'm grateful.

Q: How long did you care for Sandra?

A: Five years. She was pretty lucid the entire time, except at the very end. She died the way she wanted to — at home.

Q: You mentioned that Sandra made some promises to you?

A: Yes, Sandra was extremely grateful. She realized all of the sacrifices I was making — not that I minded, you know. Anyway, she said she wouldn't forget me. Having inherited her sister's estate, Sandra now owned a 100% interest in the office building and residence. She said that she would meet with her lawyer and set it up so I would be able to live in the residence for the rest of my life and also get the income from the office building during my lifetime. In addition, Sandra made a series of cash contributions of $10,000 for each of five years to Megan's college fund.

Q: So Sandra gave you $50,000?

A: Yes.

Q: And she died without making the will she promised, right?

A: Yes, that's why I'm here. I actually thought things were going to work out fine. It turns out that Mabel and Sandra had a nephew they'd never even mentioned. Grant, the nephew, suddenly appeared about six months before Sandra died. He was named administrator of the estate because Sandra died without a will. I had a conversation with Grant soon after Sandra's death. I told Grant about the promises Sandra had made to me. Grant was noncommittal, but made no move to evict Megan and me from the house. As for the office building, Grant took over management of the building, but continued to charge me no rent. The income from the office building would have been nice, but I didn't really need it, and I thought Sandra and Mabel were very generous as it was. About two months ago, a real estate broker came by saying that Grant was going to sell the house, and I also got a 30-day notice terminating my use of the office. I called you right away.

Q: Did Grant Keefe say or do anything that led you to believe that he would honor the agreement?

A: No. Like I said, he was noncommittal, and I didn't push him. Maybe I should have. He said that his aunt had never mentioned anything about such promises. I think I just assumed that Grant was like his aunt, and that he would honor her promises. He's now taking the position that there were no such promises.

Q: When did Sandra die?

A: About two-and-a-half years ago. I thought that time might be a problem. That's why I was in such a hurry to find an attorney.

Q: Well, hopefully we'll be able to help you. What would you like the outcome of this situation to be?

A: To be honest, I'd like to get Grant to make good on the promises of his aunt.

Q: Let me ask you this. Was anything ever put into writing?

A: No, not that I ever saw.

Q: Were there any witnesses to any of these conversations you had with Sandra?

A: Well, there is Mildred Fowler. She helped with housekeeping for years. I'm sure Sandra talked to her. Oh, there was also Tori Phillips. She was a home-healthcare worker who helped out for about the last six months.

Q: Well, this gives me a good start. I will probably have my investigator talk to Ms. Fowler and Ms. Phillips, if that's all right with you.

A: That's fine. Anything that'll help.

Q: Mr. Finch, you'll probably have to sign a complaint, so you should hear from me by the end of the week, okay?

A: That's fine. Thank you very much.

TRANSCRIPT OF INTERVIEW WITH MILDRED FOWLER BY INVESTIGATOR CHARL MALONE

Ms. Malone (Q): Thank you for agreeing to talk to me, Ms. Fowler.

Ms. Fowler (A): Sure.

Q: I've asked your permission to tape-record this conversation, and you said that it would be okay, right?

A: Yes, that's right.

Q: My name is Charl Malone, and, as you know, I work for attorney Gretchen Pronko, who is representing Mason Finch in his dispute with Grant Keefe. I'm here to ask you questions about Sandra and Mabel Keefe. How long did you know them?

A: I first met them when I came to work for them about 20 years ago. They hired me to clean their house once a week.

Q: How well would you say you got to know them?

A: I'd say we got to know each other pretty well. They were around most of the time, so we'd chat about what was going on in our lives. They always asked about my family. They were both very sweet.

Q: That's certainly the impression one gets from Mason Finch. Speaking of Mason, what can you tell me about his relationship with the Keefes?

A: Mr. Finch rented an office space from Sandra and Mabel. They mentioned that he was managing the office building for them. They always spoke very highly of him. Then Megan and Mason moved in with Sandra and Mabel after Mabel's stroke, you know. Mason came home from work just as I was leaving, usually around lunchtime. Sandra told me that he took care of Mabel in the afternoons and fixed dinner in the evenings.

Q: Then Mason continued caring for Sandra after Mabel's death, right?

A: That's right. Over time he began to provide more and more care for her. At the end she was quite dependent on him to do just about everything.

Q: Did Sandra ever talk to you about whether she was paying him for the care?

A: Well, I didn't want to pry. She did mention quite frequently that she didn't know what she would have done without Mason. She also mentioned that she would help Megan with her college expenses and that she would make sure that she left Mason in good financial shape.

Q: Do you have any idea what she meant by leaving him in good financial shape?

A: She mentioned that she would be making a will so that Mason could use the house during his lifetime. I know that. Beyond that, I really don't know.

Q: Did she say this on more than one occasion?

A: Oh yes, definitely. I just can't say how many times for certain.

Q: Do you recall when she first mentioned it?

A: The first time must have been soon after Mabel died. She took it really hard. She was feeling quite lonely and depressed, I think. She'd never admit it, but she missed Mabel terribly. She was so grateful when Mason and Megan stayed on to help her out. I'm sure it was during this time that she decided she'd take care of Mason to show him how much it meant to her.

Q: This would have been in what year?

A: Well, Mabel died in 1995, so it was within six months or so of then.

Q: Do you have any recollection of other occasions when she mentioned taking care of Mason and Megan?

A: Sorry, I really don't, but it was a number of occasions over the next number of years, I'm sure.

Q: Did Sandra mention anything about the office building?

A: No.

Q: Well, thank you so much, Ms. Fowler. This has been very helpful. Here's my card. If you think of anything else, please get in touch with me, okay?

A: Yes, I certainly will.

TRANSCRIPT OF INTERVIEW WITH TORI PHILLIPS BY INVESTIGATOR CHARL MALONE

Ms. Malone (Q):   Ms. Phillips, my name is Charl Malone.   I've asked your permission to tape-record this conversation, and you indicated that this would be okay with you, right?

Ms. Phillips (A): Yes, that's fine.

Q: You probably know that I work for Attorney Gretchen Pronko, who has been retained by Mason Finch to represent him in an action against the estate of Sandra Keefe?

A: Yes, I understand.

Q: Please tell me about how you came to know Sandra Keefe.

A: I was hired by Grant Keefe to provide home healthcare for his aunt, Sandra Keefe.

Q: When were you hired?

A: I worked for about six months — until two weeks before she died, so I guess that would mean I was hired in early 1999.

Q: How many hours per week did you provide care?

A: I came in Monday through Friday, from 8:00 a.m. until 1:00 p.m., so that was 25 hours a week.

Q: How much were you paid and who paid you?

A: I was paid $27 per hour, and I was paid by my agency. Mr. Keefe hired me through my agency.

Q: What duties did you perform for Ms. Keefe?

A: She was confined to her bed. I had to assist her in getting her meals, administering medication, making sure that she changed positions in bed, emptying her catheter bag and changing bedding and clothing as necessary. I also provided companionship to her — someone to see to her needs, talk to her, cheer her up, that kind of thing.

Q: Could you describe Ms. Keefe's physical and mental state during this period?

A: Physically, she was pretty weak and, as I said, bedridden. Mentally, though, she was quite sharp, I would say.

Q: Did she ever talk to you about Megan and Mason Finch?

A: Oh, yes, she was quite fond of them. She was very glad that things had worked out for all of them.

Q: What do you mean by "things had worked out"?

A: She felt that Mason and Megan had provided her with companionship and care over the years, and that she had reciprocated by allowing them to live with her. She also mentioned that Mason had gotten some sort of deal with his office space. Oh yeah, I almost forgot. She also said that she had given Megan a pretty sizable sum of money for her college expenses.

Q: Did Ms. Keefe ever mention anything about making a will or making specific provisions in a will?

A: No, in fact she said she didn't really need one because she wanted her nephew to get everything. Since he was her only heir, he would get everything whether she had a will or not.

Q: Did she ever mention anything about allowing Mason and Megan to continue living in the house after her death?

A: No, she didn't.

Q: Did she ever say anything about letting Mason get income from the office building after she died?

A: No.

Q: You just mentioned her nephew, Grant Keefe. Was he around at all?

A: Yes, he came to visit Ms. Keefe pretty frequently, I'd say at least twice a week.

Q: Can you describe the interactions between Ms. Keefe and her nephew?

A: They obviously felt very warmly toward each other. I never heard her laugh as much as when he was in the room with her.

Q: Can you compare these interactions to those between Mr. Finch and Ms. Keefe?

A: To be honest, I didn't see that much of Mr. Finch. He came home at around 1:00 p.m., just when I was getting off.

Q: Did you see any interactions between Mr. Finch and Grant Keefe?

A: No, I can't say I did. As far as I know, Mr. Keefe only came when I was there. I don't think he visited when Mr. Finch was around.

February 23, 2002

Dear Ms. Pronko:

As we discussed, I contacted a close friend of mine named Ralph Sanchez. My career would have been closely parallel to his if I hadn't taken time off to care for Mabel and Sandra Keefe. He's also an MFCC, and we did both our undergraduate and masters degrees together, with very comparable academic records. Ralph is very willing to sign a declaration if it will help.

Here's a summary of his earnings compared to mine over the last 12 years:

	My net earnings (including rent savings)	Ralph's Earnings
1990	$15,000	$12,000
1991	$20,000	$20,000
1992	$30,000	$30,000
1993	$48,000	$48,000
1994	$33,000 (Mabel has stroke at mid-year)	$24,000 (Ralph in Ph.D. program)
1995	$45,000 (Mabel dies mid-year)	$24,000 (Ralph in Ph.D. program)
1996	$33,000 (begin caring for Sandra)	$65,000
1997	$31,000	$67,500
1998	$31,000	$71,000
1999	$35,000 (Sandra dies mid-year)	$72,500
2000	$45,000	$75,000
2001	$50,000	$78,000

I hope this helps. Remember, I would have entered the Ph.D. program the same year as Ralph and could have had similar earnings to his. By the way, I looked into whether I could enter the University of Columbia's Ph.D. program this coming year, and learned that the costs of doing so would be prohibitive at this point. In 1994 they would have waived tuition and even paid me a stipend. That program is no longer available.

Thanks,

Mason Finch

TUESDAY AFTERNOON
FEBRUARY 26, 2002

California
Bar
Examination

Performance Test A

LIBRARY

ESTATE OF KEEFE

LIBRARY

TABLE OF CONTENTS

RIGANTI v. McELHINNEY
Court of Appeal of Columbia (1967)

This is an action for quasi-specific performance of an oral contract between plaintiffs and one James R. Trissel, now deceased, wherein plaintiffs agreed to look after Trissel's improved real property, collect the rents, and account to him for same, and to care for Trissel so long as he lived, and show respect and obedience toward him as children toward a father. For this service, attention, and care, Trissel agreed plaintiffs should have free rent of the living quarters on his property that they then occupied, and that on his death he would leave them a part of his property by his will. Although plaintiffs carried out their part of the agreement, decedent failed to provide for them in his will.

The court rendered judgment in favor of plaintiffs. Defendant, Muriel McElhinney, niece of Trissel and the residuary devisee and legatee under the will, has appealed.

The judgment decrees, *inter alia*, that plaintiffs have quasi-specific performance of an oral agreement with Trissel; that plaintiffs are the sole and only beneficial and equitable owners of the improved real property here in question; that defendant has no right, title, interest, or estate whatsoever in and to said real property or the rents, issues, and profits therefrom, and that she and her heirs, representatives, transferees, or assigns, and each of them, is permanently restrained and enjoined from claiming or asserting any right, title, interest, claim, or estate whatsoever in, to, or over said real property.

Defendant pled the statute of frauds as embodied in Probate Code section 150 and the statute of limitations. But even though the agreement is oral, sufficient facts may be shown to take the case out of the statute of frauds.

Where a contract is within the statute of frauds, as it is here, the mere rendition of services is not usually such a part performance of a verbal agreement as will relieve the contract from the operation of the statute. If the services are of such a peculiar character, however, that it is impossible to estimate their value by any pecuniary standard, and it is evident that the parties did not intend to measure them by any such standard, and if the plaintiff, after the performance of the services, could not be restored to the situation in which he was before the rendition of the services, it is such a part performance of the verbal agreement as will remove the contract from the rule. Equity, where other objections are not present, will decree specific performance. But in such cases the reason for the interposition of equity is quite obvious. The plaintiff has rendered services of extraordinary and exceptional character, such service as in contemplation of the parties was not to be compensated for in money, and as in contemplation of law, cannot be compensated for in money; therefore, by no action at law could a plaintiff be restored to his original position. It would be in the nature of a fraud upon him to deny him any relief, and, the law failing by reason of its universality, equity, to promote justice, makes good its imperfections.

Applying these principles to the facts as found by the trial court, we conclude the judgment must be affirmed.

Plaintiffs had been living in Trissel's downstairs duplex at 623 South Catalina Avenue for a little more than five years when the oral agreement here in question was entered into. They had ample time and opportunity to get well acquainted and had apparently developed confidence and respect for each other. Trissel was without immediate family except for a son with whom his relations were not friendly and with whom he seldom communicated. His health was not good and he faced surgery. He was then 62 years of age. In these circumstances Trissel no doubt felt alone in the world and in need of "a family" who would take an interest in him and look after his needs and welfare, and treat him like a father. It seems that over the next two years plaintiffs gave Trissel the care and attention he needed and wanted and served him as though they were members of his family. He recognized this by referring to plaintiffs as "his kids" and stating to a friend that they were closer to him than the members of his own family had ever been. These services and this type of devotion for the rest of Trissel's life were of such a peculiar character that it was impossible to estimate their value by any pecuniary standard. Furthermore, it is evident that the parties did not intend to measure the value of these services by any such standard, for if they had so intended they could have fixed a fee therefor just as they had agreed that free rent would compensate for plaintiffs' taking care of Trissel's rental units and the collection of the rentals.

Having special skills as a mechanic and in certain trades of the building industry, Wade Riganti could have improved his station in life by leaving Trissel's living accommodations and "walking away" from his and his wife's obligations under their agreement with Trissel. But they did not do that. They honored their commitment with Trissel. As a result, plaintiffs, after the performance of their services, could not be restored to the situation in which they were before the rendition of the services. The failure therefore of Trissel to leave his will as agreed works a fraud upon plaintiffs and serves to remove the oral agreement from the statute of frauds. Equity then steps in, as it did in this case, and decrees what we call "quasi-specific" performance to avoid the perpetration of a fraud upon plaintiffs and unjust enrichment of defendant. Of course, equitable relief should not be granted where it would work a gross injustice upon innocent third parties. No such problem is presented in the case at bench, for the trial court drew the conclusion, *inter alia*, that plaintiffs were entitled to quasi-specific performance "to avoid . . . unjust enrichment of defendant."

There is no merit in defendant's suggestion that plaintiffs failed to show that the consideration rendered by them was adequate. It sufficiently appears that there was adequate consideration for the contract, for the extent of the consideration is to be measured by the breadth of the undertaking rather than by the eventuality. Plaintiffs might have had to serve and nurse Trissel for many years. Each party to the agreement knowingly stood to lose or gain by that contingency.

We can also dispose of the statute of limitations argument. An action for quasi-specific performance accrues on the death of the person who breached the agreement. Where quasi-specific performance by declaration of a constructive trust on real property is sought on the basis of an oral agreement pursuant to which that property was to have been left by will, a four-year period applies rather than the two-year period of limitation generally applicable to contracts not in writing.

The judgment is affirmed.

KENNEDY v. BANK OF COLUMBIA
Court of Appeal of Columbia (1965)

This appeal originated in an action brought by plaintiff against the Bank of Columbia National Trust & Savings Association, as executor of the will of Thomas J. McDermott, deceased (hereinafter referred to as executor). The complaint contained a single cause of action for quasi-specific performance of an alleged oral contract between plaintiff and decedent, by which decedent agreed to devise and bequeath his property to plaintiff by his will as compensation for personal services rendered and to impose a constructive trust upon the property. Executor filed a motion for summary judgment. The motion was granted, and judgment was entered.

The allegations of the complaint upon which plaintiff's case must stand or fall are these: On or about May 1, 1941, decedent offered to employ plaintiff in his home as a domestic servant and as an assistant in his retail gasoline station business, and orally promised that, if she would perform services for him and his family and would remain at Bakersfield and assist him in building up his business, he would execute an irrevocable will leaving her his entire estate; prior to May 1, 1941, plaintiff was a healthy woman and used her time to care for her own household and to earn money working at various tasks; plaintiff accepted decedent's offer of employment and worked for him substantially all of the time from May 1, 1941 until about June 15, 1953, at which time decedent orally informed her that he was retiring from business and he would no longer need her services, but that a will theretofore made by him in her favor would remain irrevocable.

Further, plaintiff alleged that, in order to fulfill her portion of said oral agreement between the parties, she gave up most of her own social life, opportunities to move to other cities with her husband, and opportunities to work for other persons so as to assist her husband in accumulating savings and property of their own. In general, plaintiff alleged, in reliance upon the oral agreement of decedent to leave all of his property to her by will upon his death, she put aside most of her personal pleasures, comforts, and affairs, and forsook many of her friends while she was performing services as housekeeper and assistant to decedent in his business.

Plaintiff alleged that in doing all of these things she was acting in reliance upon the promise of decedent to make her beneficiary of his will, and upon his promise that he would not change said will. Had it not been for such oral promises plaintiff would not have performed said services without receiving compensation therefor, which plaintiff did not receive, and were it not for said promises plaintiff would not have altered her way of life in the manner in which she did.

Plaintiff further alleged that the nature of her services and contributions was such that compensation therefor may not be measured, nor would compensation for services rendered be fair and reasonable under the circumstances; nor was it the intent of the parties that compensation be measured except by the total value of decedent's estate. Plaintiff alleged that she has no adequate or speedy remedy at law.

Executor filed a motion for summary judgment on the ground that the alleged contract is oral and unenforceable under our statute of frauds, section 150 of the Probate Code. The principal concern on this appeal is whether plaintiff has alleged evidence sufficient to demonstrate that triable issues of fact exist in this action.

In order to enforce an oral contract to bequeath or devise property in equity by quasi-specific performance, it must be shown that the contract is definite and certain, the consideration adequate, the contract is founded on good morals and not against public policy, the character of the services is such that a money payment would not furnish adequate compensation to the plaintiff, there is such a change in the plaintiff's condition and relations in reliance on the contract that a refusal to complete the contract would be a fraud upon him, and the remedy asked for is not harsh, oppressive, or unjust to innocent third parties.

The doctrine of estoppel, which lifts an agreement to make a will out of the operation of the statute of frauds, is based on either of two grounds. It has been applied where an unconscionable injury would result from denying enforcement after one party has been induced to make a detrimental change of position in reliance upon the oral agreement. It has also been applied where unjust enrichment would result if the party who has received the benefits of the performance of the other were allowed to invoke the statute.

Courts have found a detrimental change of position where there is a family relationship or close friendship, and the decedent has turned to the plaintiff for care, solace, comfort, and companionship. Oftentimes, at the decedent's supplication, the plaintiff has moved from an established home, leaving an established position or business in his or her hometown or state, to make a residence in the home of the decedent far from friends and family, and devoting himself or herself with dedicated care to the needs of the decedent, sometimes until the death of the decedent. Where the services rendered by the plaintiff consisted in nursing and caring for a person enfeebled and suffering from a horrible disease, requiring constant and unceasing watchfulness, harrowing to the mind, destructive to the peace and comfort of the one performing the services, and possibly injurious to the health, it has been held that it is impossible to estimate their value by any pecuniary standard; and where it is evident that the decedent did not intend so to measure them, it is out of the power of any court, after the performance of such services, to restore the plaintiff to the situation in which he was before the contract was made or to compensate him therefor in damages.

Plaintiff in this case has not submitted evidence sufficient to create triable issues as to either ground. The best description of the nature of the services that plaintiff can make is that she acted as a domestic servant and as an assistant in the retail gasoline station business operated by decedent. The services of both a domestic servant and a gasoline station assistant may be adequately compensated for in money. Such services are neither peculiar, nor exceptional, nor unique. They are performed for wages by thousands of employees similarly situated. It is not alleged that plaintiff made her home with decedent; or that she occupied a close or continuing familial relationship with him; or that she attended to his personal needs; or that she nursed him through any illness; or that she did anything that was "harrowing to the mind" or "destructive to her peace and comfort" or "injurious to her health" for which money cannot compensate. The allegation in the complaint that the nature of the services was such that compensation therefor may not be measured is a mere conclusion.

The allegations of the declaration that plaintiff gave up her social life, opportunities to move to other cities and to work for other persons, opportunities to assist her husband in accumulating savings and property of their own, and that she put aside most of her personal pleasures and forsook many of her friends are not sufficient.

Nor does the declaration establish sufficient facts to show that decedent or anyone else will be unjustly enriched if the purported oral contract is not enforced. There are no allegations that services rendered to decedent, either in his household as a domestic servant or in his service station business, substantially contributed to the value of the business or to the assets that comprise the estate. No unjust enrichment results, or may be implied, from mere allegations that plaintiff performed services of an impersonal nature for decedent.

We conclude that there are no triable issues of fact as to the inapplicability of the statute of frauds. The grant of the motion for summary judgment is affirmed.

HORSTMANN v. SHELDON
Court of Appeal of Columbia (1962)

Plaintiff, Ella Horstmann, brought this action to establish a trust in real and personal property held in the estate of her deceased mother, Bertha Horstmann. The complaint alleged that "on numerous occasions during the approximately 20 years before decedent's death, decedent urged plaintiff to reside with decedent and care for decedent; that decedent offered if plaintiff would so reside with and care for decedent and not undertake to obtain regular gainful employment outside the home of decedent, decedent would provide a home for plaintiff during the lifetime of decedent and would by a will leave the home of decedent, including the real property upon which it was situated and the furniture and furnishings therein, to plaintiff." The complaint further alleged that "plaintiff accepted each of decedent's offers and proposals and did all things required to be done in compliance therewith; that in connection therewith plaintiff refrained from undertaking any general employment outside the home and resided with decedent and cared for her and for her property for many years up to the time of the death of decedent; that during all of the aforesaid period of time decedent reiterated the aforesaid promises on numerous occasions." Plaintiff further alleged that she received no compensation for her services, and that decedent breached the alleged agreement by her will naming her brother-in-law, defendant George Sheldon, sole devisee and legatee of decedent's entire estate and the executor of her will.

The answer denied the existence of the contract and affirmatively asserted that plaintiff had been entirely supported by decedent during her lifetime.

At trial, plaintiff testified consistent with her complaint. In addition, several witnesses testified to extensive personal services rendered by plaintiff to decedent, including nursing and personal care, cooking, housework, serving meals, gardening, cutting wood, house repairs, and a multitude of other duties and responsibilities relating to the premises where the parties lived.

The trial court found the existence of the contract as alleged by plaintiff, and that plaintiff had fully performed her part of the bargain but that decedent had not performed her part of the agreement. The judgment imposed a trust upon the home property for the lifetime of plaintiff and also allowed her the life use of certain personal property.

The chief contention of defendant on appeal is that the evidence is insufficient to support the judgment. The record, however, is replete with evidence to support the making of the agreement between plaintiff and decedent and the full performance of the contract by plaintiff. Under long established rules it is not for this court to review the evidence and determine its weight and sufficiency. Where, as here, there is substantial evidence in the record to support the judgment, it will not be disturbed on appeal in the absence of some error requiring reversal on other grounds.

Defendant also urged that plaintiff filed no claim against decedent's estate and therefore the complaint does not state a cause of action. There is no merit in this contention, however. Plaintiff's suit here is not one for the recovery of damages for breach of contract, nor in quantum meruit for the value of her services. Plaintiff's suit is in equity for the purpose of enforcing her contract by having defendant declared trustee of the described property for plaintiff's benefit. She seeks no relief at law but only in equity, and under such a pleading no claim against the estate of the decedent need be filed.

Another question presented by this appeal is whether our statute of frauds, Probate Code section 150, bars the enforcement of plaintiff's contract. We conclude that it does not.

The doctrine of estoppel to assert the statute of frauds has been consistently applied by the courts of this state to prevent fraud that would result from refusal to enforce oral contracts in certain circumstances. Such fraud may contribute to the unconscionable injury that would result from denying enforcement of the contract after one party has been induced by the other seriously to change his position in reliance on the contract, or in the unjust enrichment that would result if a party who has received the benefits of the other's performance were allowed to rely upon the statute.

At the time of trial, plaintiff was 63 years of age. The understanding or agreement between plaintiff and decedent commenced about 1926, and from that date to the date of decedent's death plaintiff had been engaged in the performance of her part of the bargain. As the trial court found, many of the years of her youth and all of the years of her maturity were spent in the care and maintenance of decedent. The agreement was breached at a time when plaintiff was approaching the later years of her life. It can hardly be said that to permit this would not result in unconscionable injury to plaintiff. Having made this finding, we need not address the second prong.

If plaintiff is not permitted to pursue her remedy in a court of equity, she would be relegated to an action at law for damages for the breach of her contract, or left to pursue her quasi-contractual remedy for the value of services rendered. Neither is adequate for the breach of a contract to leave property by will in exchange for services of a peculiar nature involving the assumption or continuation of a close family relationship.

The judgment is affirmed.

ANSWER 1 TO PERFORMANCE TEST A

DECLARATIONS

Declaration of Mason Finch

I, Mason Finch, declare as follows:

1.   I am the Plaintiff in this action.

2.   I am a Marriage, Family and Children's Counselor and received my Master's Degree in 1988. I have been in practice for 12 years.

3.   I met Sandra and Mabel Keefe about 12 years ago 1990 through an agreement by which I managed an office building they owned for a 50% discount in rent so I could open my own practice. The rent before my half off was $500. I provided about an hour and half a week of my time for management duties and saved $250 in rent. At the time I was charging $40 and later $85 an hour. Therefore by the end my time was actually worth more than I was being compensated for with the rental agreement. (6 hours a month time $85=$440).

4.   My daughter Megan Finch and Sandra and Mabel Keefe and I developed a close friendship that included dinners and weekend trips together. I eventually considered them to be a wonderful second family.

5.   After Mabel Keefe suffered a stroke in 1994 I was approached by Sandra Keefe and asked to cut back my counseling practice to mornings only to care for Mabel in the afternoons and fix dinner for them both in the evenings. In exchange Sandra allowed my daughter and I to live with them in their converted garage

rent free and use the office space rent free.

6.   The reduction in hours resulted in a loss of about $1000 a month and I was in a tough situation financially. I had to turn clients away even before I reduced my hours. Also it resulted in a plateau in my reputation. I was not able to pursue speaking engagements as I had done before.

7.   I also was not able to pursue a PhD program which at the time would have paid for my tuition and provided me a stipend in a night program. This opportunity is no longer available to me at this time. I would have likely seen substantial increase in my salary comparable to the increase Ralph Sanchez saw after completing the PhD program I planned to take also.

8.   After Mabel passed away, I provided much needed emotional support to Sandra. After settling Mabel's estate, Sandra's health took a turn for the worse so I stayed on providing the same type of care I had for Mable, but now without anyone's help. I had to cut down my practice to only three hours a week and provided constant care for Mabel outside of the care her nurse gave her in the mornings.

9.   The type of care for Sandra included running errands, shopping, cleaning, taking her to the doctors.

10.   Megan and I moved into the main house to be more available.

11.   I cared for Sandra for five years this way. She was lucid until the very end, but required much physical care.

12.   Because of the care I provided for her, Sandra was extremely grateful and said she would not forget the way I cared for her and her sister. She owned 100% of the house and building after her sister's death and told me I could have the house to live in for the rest of my life and to get the income from the building

during my lifetime. She also made a series of cash contributions of $10,000 for each of five years to Megan's College Fund.

13.   Her nephew Grant Keefe who showed up about six months before she died was noncommital when I told him of her promises, but he made no move to evict me from the house so I assumed he would honor his aunt's promises. I received a 30- day notice two months ago from a real estate broker after staying in the house for two years as they were going to sell the house and to get out of the office.

Declaration of Mildred Fowler

1.   I, Mildred Fowler, declare as follows:

2.   I worked as a housekeeper for the Keefe sisters for 20 years. I cleaned their house once a week.

3.   I chatted often with them about what was happening in our lives.

4.   They told me they rented an office space to Mr. Finch and that he was managing the building for them.

5.   They always spoke very highly of Mr. Finch.

6.   Mr. Finch and Megan moved in with them after Mabel's stroke and took care of Mabel in the afternoons and fixed dinners in the evenings.

7.   He continued to take care of Sandra after Mabel's death and she grew

quite dependent on him to do just about everything.

8.   Sandra mentioned frequently that she did not know what she would have done without Mr. Finch. She was very grateful that Mr. Finch stayed on to help her after Mabel died as she was lonely and depressed. She said she would help Megan with her college expenses and make sure Mason was left in good financial shape.

9.   She specifically stated that she would make a will so Mason could use the house during his lifetime. She said this on many occasions, including soon after Mable died. And she said she wanted to take care of Mr. Finch to show him how much it meant to her that he took care of her.

Declaration of Ralph Sanchez

1.   I, Ralph Sanchez, declare the following:

2.   I did my undergraduate and masters degrees with Mr. Finch and we had similar academic records.

3.   We had similar earnings until Mr. Finch left his full time practice to care for the Keefe sisters.

4.   I received my PhD in 1995 and saw substantial increases in my salary.

III.   RESPONSIVE PARTY'S STATEMENT OF DISPUTED FACTS

Statement	Citation to Evidence
1. That an oral promise was made to Mr. Finch that he would receive the house for his lifetime.	Declaration of Mason Finch ¶ 12 Declaration of Mildred Flower ¶ 9
2. That an oral promise was made to Mr. Finch that he would receive the income from the office building for his lifetime.	Declaration of Mason Finch ¶ 12
3. Defendant [did] not spend significant amounts of time with decedent before her death. Rather he spent roughly 6 hours a week with her.	Declaration of Grant Keefe ¶ 4
4. Decedent did not feel that the compensation Mr. Finch had received was adequate. She was very grateful for his care and wanted to make sure he was left in good financial shape after her death.	Declaration of Mildred Flower ¶ 8
5. Decedent promised to leave a will leaving the house and office building to defendant.	Declaration of Mason Finch ¶ 12 Declaration of Mildred Flower ¶ 9

IV.   RESPONSE TO MOVING PARTY'S ARGUMENTS

A   Plaintiff's Claim Based on an Oral Contract to Make a Will is Sufficient as there is Evidence from the Declarations of the Oral Agreement.

Defendant asserts that the non-existence of a writing proves that decedent never promised to make a will with provisions in favor of plaintiff and therefore no oral or written contract ever existed. Although plaintiff cannot attest to the existence of a written provision, Mr. Finch has repeatedly and consistently maintained that he received oral promises from decedent for a life estate in the house and office building. [Finch DU Fact 12.] Ms. Fowler is able to support Mr. Finch's assertions of an oral promise as to the life estate in the house. [Flower DU Fact 9.]

Further the extensive nature of the services rendered, the lack of monetary compensation besides free rent for such services and the detrimental reliance by Mr. Finch that is the loss in revenue, clients, reputation, and opportunity to obtain a PhD, creates the reasonable assumption that an alternative means of compensation was intended. [Finch DU Fact 5-9, 12.]

Therefore there are triable issues of fact as to whether any such oral promises were made and the motion for summary judgment should be denied.

B.   The Oral Contract Does Not Fail for Lack of a Writing Because of the exceptions to the Statute of Frauds of Part Performance/Estoppel and Unjust Enrichment Which Apply.

Although the Statute of Frauds does apply to such an oral contract there are two defenses available. First is the doctrine of estoppel and second unjust enrichment.

Doctrine of Estoppel

Where a contract is within the statute of frauds as it is here, the mere rendition of services is not usually adequate part performance of a verbal agreement as to relieve the contract from the operation of the statute. However, if the services are of such a peculiar character, that it is:

(1)   impossible to estimate their value by any pecuniary standard, and

(2)   it is evident that the parties did not intend to measure them by any such standard, and

(3)   if the plaintiff after performance of the services could not be restored to the situation in which he was before the rendition of the services, it is such a part performance of the verbal agreement as will remove the contract from the rule of law. Riganti (Ct Appeal Col. 1967)

The policy behind this is equity as the plaintiff has rendered services of extraordinary and exceptional character, services as in contemplation of the parties was not to be compensated for in money and as in contemplation of law, cannot be compensated for in money. Id. Therefore, by no action of law could a plaintiff be restored to his original position. Id. It would be the nature of a fraud upon him to deny him relief and so equity in order to promote justice makes good the law's imperfections. Id. It would be inequitable to not enforce a contract after one party has been induced by the other to seriously change his position in reliance on the contract. Horstmann (Ct Appeal Col. 1962).

In addition to the above requirements the contract must be definite and certain, the   consideration adequate, the contract founded on good morals and not against public policy and the remedy is not harsh, oppressive or unjust to innocent third persons. <u>Kennedy</u> (Ct Appeal Col. 1965).

As to the requirement for definite and certain terms, Mr. Finch's oral agreement with Ms. Keefe was definite and certain. He was to have use of the house and income from the building for life. [Finch DU Fact 12.]

The requisite consideration for an agreement is found in measuring the breadth of the undertaking rather than the eventuality as the plaintiff may have had to serve and nurse the decedent for many years. <u>Id</u>. Here, Finch gave up over five years to care for Sandra alone and would have continued to perform such services as long as needed to his own professional and financial detriment therefore adequate consideration would be found. [Finch DU Fact 10.]

The contract was founded on good morals and not against public policy as it was a way to allow Ms. Keefe to provide for Mr. Finch in return for all the care he had provided her.

Finally, it would arguably not be harsh or unjust to a third person, here Mr. Keefe. This is arguable as he is a legal heir and appears to have had a relationship with Ms. Keefe. This is an issue to be further addressed and argued in court and requires the summary judgment motion to be denied.

We now turn to the first three requirements regarding service and pecuniary payments.

Exceptional Service - Impossible to Measure Value

The court in <u>Riganti</u> in finding performance of such services of extraordinary and exceptional character, looked to facts such as ample time to get acquainted and develop confidence and respect for each other. The court has also looked to such things as family relationship or close friendship that the decedent turned to for care, solace, comfort and companionship that is outside the normal realm of domestic or nursing services. Id. Further, relocating, devoting care until death such that the services rendered by the plaintiff consisted of nursing and caring for a person enfeebled and suffering from a horrible disease, requiring constant and unceasing watchfulness, harrowing to the mind, destructive to the peace and comfort of the one performing services, and possibly injurious to health, such services are impossible to have an estimated value by any pecuniary standard, especially where decedent did not intend to so measure them. Kennedy. Providing extensive personal services as the plaintiff did in Horstmann for her mother was also sufficient performance of exceptional and extraordinary character. Horstmann. [Note: Where the services provided by the plaintiff were purely as a domestic servant or a business assistant which could be adequately compensated for in money, services being neither exceptional or peculiar nor unique, quasi-specific performance is not available. Kennedy.]

Similarly here, such services of an extraordinary and exceptional character were performed by Mr. Finch. Mr. Finch reduced his office hours and took a substantial loss financially and professionally to spend all but three mornings a week caring for Ms. Keefe. He took care of all her shopping needs, cooked her meals in the evenings and provided her with her only company in the afternoons and evenings. Although she had a nurse, the nurse left by 1:00 [p.m.] and Mr. Finch took care of all her needs for the remainder and majority of the day. They had a close and personal relationship and she relied on him not only physically but for emotional support as well. Clearly, Mr. Finch provided much more than a domestic servant would and his services would be of an exceptional and extraordinary character, destructive to his peace and comfort to watch his dear friend deteriorate as he provided her main and substantial care. This was extraordinary care and service. [Finch DU Fact 5-12.]

Not Intend to Measure by Pecuniary Standard

The lack of a fixed fee for personal services where the parties entered an agreement for free rent as compensation for taking care of rental units and the collection of rentals was evidence the parties had not placed a monetary value on the personal services. Riganti. The courts look not only at a lack of an agreement to pay monetarily but also the inability to place a monetary standard on the services rendered.

Here, the Mr. Finch (sic) agreed to take care of Sandra for the majority of his time and with no monetary compensation. Mr. Finch was provided with free rent, but this was out of a necessity to be available to Sandra and care for her better. There was no benefit at any time monetarily to Mr. Finch; rather he suffered substantial monetary loss. Their agreement as to the management of the office building and the determination of his services and the reduction in rent evidenced Sandra's ability to enter contractual agreements for his services as a manager. The lack of such an agreement when we turn to his services caring for her shows they did not intend to place a pecuniary standard on his services. Further, the type services he provided her would not be conducive to placing a monetary standard on them. Therefore they were not intended and it would be impossible now to place a monetary value on his services.

Not be Restored

The court has also placed emphasis on the plaintiff's special skills, such as in Riganti where plaintiff was a mechanic and his choice to honor the commitment of taking care of the decedent and thereby denying himself the opportunity to improve his station in life. <u>Id.</u> This resulted in the plaintiffs' inability to be restored to the position they were in before rendition of the services. Id.

Could not restore him for his services and the loss he had in the reputation and PhD program. He forewent many opportunities and this could not be adequately compensated for in monetary standard.

Unjust Enrichment

An alternate basis is to limit unjust enrichment where a party would receive the benefits of the performance of the other if allowed to invoke the statute. <u>Kennedy.</u>

Unclear of unjust enrichment here as Mr. Grant entered late in the picture and did not care for her, only visited irregularly. This would be a triable issue for the court.

Therefore there are triable issues of fact as to whether the parties intended to place a monetary value on Mr. Finch's services, if this is possible and the amount of loss he suffered in his business and the loss of a PhD. Also legal issues as to whether Mr. Keefe would be unjustly enriched. Therefore the motion for summary judgment should be denied.

C. This Action is Not Barred by the Statute of Limitations Because It was Filed Within the Four Year Requirement Given to Requests for Quasi-Specific Performance by Declaration of a Constructive Trust on Real Property on the Basis of an Oral Agreement.

An action for quasi-specific performance accrues on the death of the person who breached the agreement. <u>Riganti</u>. Where quasi-specific performance by declaration of a constructive trust on real property is sought on the basis of an oral agreement pursuant to which that property was to have been left by will, a four-year period applies rather than the two-year period of limitation generally applicable to contracts not in writing. <u>Id</u>.

Here, the action is for quasi-specific performance by declaration of a constructive trust and therefore the relevant statute of limitations should be four years and not the two years claimed by defendant. [Moving Party's Motion for Summary Judgment.]

Here the breaching party was Ms. Sandra Keefe as she never created a written will and she died on August 26, 1999. [Moving Party's Motion for Summary Judgment.] Therefore the action started to accrue in August of 1999 and the statute of limitations will not toll until August 26, 2003. Plaintiff instituted his action on January 11, 2002, roughly two and a half years after decedent's death and well within the four year statue of limitations.

Further, Mr. Finch relied on Mr. Keefe not kicking him out of the house for two years, waiting until after the statute of limitations was up to kick him out. Even if the two year statute of limitation applies and Mr. Finch should have been alert as to his remedies, out of equity the court should not allow Mr. Keefe to use the statute of limitations as a way to cajole Mr. Finch into believing he would honor his aunt's promises until the statue of limitations expired. This is not the purpose of the statute of limitation provisions.

Therefore there are legal issues precluding entry of judgment as a matter of law as the statute of limitations has not tolled or alternately a trial issue of law/fact as to the proper form of relief and the applicable statue of limitations period and Mr. Keefe's bad faith in waiting till the statue of limitations tolled to try to evict Mr. Finch.

ANSWER 2 TO PERFORMANCE TEST A

A.   Draft declarations for all witnesses whose testimony will be useful in establishing that there are disputed issues of act and in supporting our arguments.

DECLARATION OF MASON FINCH

I, Mason Finch, declare as follows:

1.   I am the plaintiff in this action.

2.   I am the former caretaker of decedent Sandra Keefe, and decedent Mable Keefe (her sister).

3.   I've been a Marriage, Family and Children's Counsel for about 12 years.

4.   I got my Master's degree in 1988 and opened my own practice in 1990.

5.   It was also in 1990 that I met the decedent, Sandra Keefe.

6.   Sandra (and Mabel) owned a commercial building and asked that I manage the building for them in exchange for a 50% discount in rent.

7.   The full rent for my office was $500, so half was $250.

8.   During this period I spent about 1½ hours per week on management tasks (taking calls, showing units, collecting rents, repairs, etc).

9.   Similar positions at other commercial buildings charge a percentage of gross rents -- about 5% per month.

10.   At the same time I was earning between $45 - $85 dollars per hour ($85 towards 1994) for services in my MFCC business.

11.   In about 1994, Mabel had a stroke.

12.   Sandra asked me to cut back my counseling practice to mornings only so that I could provide care for Mable in the afternoon, and fix dinner for Sandra and Mabel,

13.   Sandra asked Megan (my daughter) and I to move into their in-law unit attached to their house (rent-free).

14.   Sandra also said I could use the office rent-free.

15.   Sandra, Megan and I were like a family so I agreed.

16.   This arrangement, albeit with rent-free living and rent-free office, cost me about $1000 per month in lost income because of the reduction in office MFCC work hours.

17.   This arrangement caused me to forgo a fair amount of reputation building and networking time in my professional community. Prior to the arrangement I had

attended and been asked to make professional presentations to the community. That ceased.

18.   The arrangement also prevented me from entering a PhD program at the local university.

19.   That university, Columbia, is now cost prohibitive for me to enter. Had I gone in 1994, I would have received a tuition waiver and a graduate stipend. This program is no longer available.

20.   After Mabel died, Sandra had us move into the main house to care for her.

21.   I cared for Sandra entirely by myself for the most part – doing shopping, cleaning and intervening with the doctors.

21b.   This care of Sandra, which I lovingly undertook, lasted about 5 years until her death.

22.   Sandra constantly thanked me for all the sacrifices I made, and told me that she would instruct her lawyer to give me a life estate in the residence for what I'd done.

23.   She said she would also instruct the lawyer to give me the income from the office building during my lifetime for what I'd done.

24.   Because Sandra loved Megan, almost as the daughter she never had, she also provided a cash gift for Megan's college fund of 50K.

25.   Upon Sandra's death, Megan and I continued to live in the house as agreed to with Sandra for 2½ years.

26. I informed Grant Keefe of Sandra's oral contract with me.

27. Last month I got an eviction notice from the house and the office.

28. Mildred Fowler witnessed several conversations in which Sandra promised me the house and the office life estates.

29. Toni Phillips witnessed the good work and peculiar services I rendered for Sandra.

30. My earnings from the MFCC profession began around 15K in my first year, and built steadily towards 48K, the year Sandra first asked me to reduce my work in half at the MFCC.

31. During the time I cared for Mildred and Sandra, my income dropped dramatically to 33K and below.

32. After Sandra died, my income increased slightly to pre-Mabel/Sandra days, but has not increased as appropriate to a professional with my years in the business.

33. At 2001, my income remained at 50K.

34. I am the sole support of my daughter, Megan, who relies on me to provide her the necessities of life.

DECLARATION OF MILDRED FOWLER

I, Mildred Fowler, declare as follows:

1)   I have been cleaning the Keefe house for Sandra and Mabel for 20 years.

2)   I clean regularly once a week.

3)   In my capacity as housekeeper I came to know Sandra as a friend.

4)   I knew her quite well by the time of her death.

5)   Mason and Megan moved in with Sandra and Mabel at Sandra's request to care for Mabel after her stroke.

6)   I witnessed Mason coming home right around lunch every time I was there.

7)   Sandra told me that Mason cared for her and Mabel, and she didn't know what she'd do without him.

8)   I personally came to see that Sandra had become quite dependent on Mason and relied upon him to do most everything.

9)   Sandra said she'd help Megan with college.

10)   Sandra said she'd make sure Mason was in good financial shape by making a will so that Mason could use the house during his lifetime to compensate him.

11)   She told me about her intent to make this provision on many occasions starting in 1995 and repeating it many times after that.

DECLARATION OF TORI PHILLIPS

I, Tori Phillips, declare as follows:

1.   I am a home healthcare worker.

2.   I was hired by Grant Keefe in early 1999 to provide care for Sandra.

3   I worked about 6 months until her death.

4.   I came Monday through Friday 8:00 a.m. to 1:00 p.m. and was paid $27 per hour.

5.   I assisted her with meals, medications, certain personal hygiene issues, and provided companionship.

6.   Sandra told me Megan and Mason were ones she was quite fond of.

7.   Sandra told me that she wanted Mason and Megan to live with her.

8.   I personally witnessed Grant Keefe coming to visit about twice a week during my duty shift.

9.   To my knowledge, that was the only time Grant Keefe visited.

10.   Mason Finch came every day at 1:00 p.m. to care for Sandra.

DECLARATION OF RALPH SANCHEZ

I, Ralph Sanchez, declare as follows:

1.   I am a colleague of Mason Finch.

2.   Mason and I did our undergrad and masters work together, with very comparable academic records.

3.   I entered the PhD program the same year as Mason should have, but didn't in order to care for Ms. Keefe.

4.   My net earnings paralleled Mason's during the first four years of our professional career – starting at about 12K – and rising to 48K.

5.   During the two years I attended the PhD program my earnings dropped to 24K.

6.   Immediately upon graduation my earnings skyrocketed to 65K and have steadily increased each year.

7.   They are now 78K.

B.   Draft Section III and IV of a Memorandum of Points and Authorities in Opposition to a Motion for Summary Judgement.

III.   RESPONSIVE PARTY'S STATEMENT OF DISPUTED FACTS:

Facts that are Disputed	The Citation to Evidence
1. Defendant did not spend significant time with the decedent in the months before she died.	Declaration of Tori Phillips at ¶ 8-9.
2. Decedent did not indicate she she had more than provided compensation to plaintiff for the services he provided.	Declarations of Mason Finch at ¶ 22, 23 Mildred Fowler at ¶10.
3. Decedent promised plaintiff she'd leave him a life estate in her house in her will.	Declarations of Mason Finch at ¶22 and Mildred Fowler at ¶10 and 11.
4. Decedent promised plaintiff she'd leave him a life estate in the rental income from the office building in her will.	Declaration of Mason Finch at ¶23.
5. Plaintiff rendered extraordinary and exceptional services to the decedent.	Declaration of Mason Finch at ¶12 and 21
6 Plaintiff's devotion to the decedent were (sic) of such a character as it was impossible to estimate by any primary standard.	Declaration of Mason Finch at ¶12 and 21.

7.	Plaintiff put aside his primary MFCC career in order to care for decedent.	Declarations of Mason Finch at ¶12.
8.	Plaintiff's MFCC career will not recover from the time he spent not tending to it.	Declaration of Mason Finch at ¶30 - 33 and Ralph Sanchez at ¶4 - 7.
9.	Plaintiff passed by other opportunities, such as a tuition free PhD to take care of decedent.	Declaration of Mason Finch at ¶18 and 19 and Ralph Sanchez at ¶3.
10.	Plaintiff's expected MFCC earnings are irreversibly hurt for life.	Declaration of Mason Finch at ¶17 and 30 - 33.
11.	Plaintiff and Decedent have enjoyed a long, familia – like relationship in which Plaintiff has gone the extra mile for Decedent in every way, albeit to his personal and professional detriment.	Declaration of Mason Finch at ¶24, 28, 16, 17.
12.	Decedent did not indicate she would not leave a will. In fact, she told Plaintiff she would instruct her attorney to draft one.	Declaration of Mason Finch at ¶22 and 23.

Section IV of the Memorandum of Points and Authorities in Opposition to Motion for Summary Judgement.

IV   <u>Argument</u>

A. Defendant's claim that there is no Oral Contact to Make a Will fails because there is substantial evidence to establish the existence of the Oral Contract.

The disputed facts in this case show that there was an oral contract to make a will. [Disputed Fact, hereafter DF, at ¶3 and 4.]
Toward the end of Decedent's life, Defendant did not spend substantial amounts of time with decedent [DF at 1]. Rather, plaintiff spent most of the time with decedent. [DF at 6.]

During this time, decedent mentioned to Plaintiff her intention to leave him a life estate in the house and in the income from the office building [DF at 3 and 4]. Decedent also indicated to housekeeper that same intention [DF at 3].

These disputed facts establish that decedent intended that her attorney make the will with provisions in favor of the plaintiff.

B. The Oral Contract cannot be defeated because it isn't in writing – rather it is removed from the Statute of Frauds.

The doctrine of estoppel, which lifts an agreement to make a will out of the question of the statute of frauds, is satisfied if one of two grounds are met [<u>Kennedy v. Bank of Columbia</u>.] or if the result would be unconscionable, [<u>Horstsmann</u>].

1) it has been applied where an unconscionable injury would result from denying enforcement after one party has been induced to make a detrimental change in position in reliance upon the oral agreement.

Here, in reliance on the promise, the plaintiff gave up advancing his profitable MFCC business [DF at 7] and put aside his goals of professional academic advancement [DF at 9]. As a result, plaintiff's career and long-term earning potential are irrevocably harmed. [DF at 8 and 10.] Failure to enforce the contract would be unconscionable.

2) It has also been applied where unjust enrichment would result if the party who has received the help would be allowed to invoke the Statute of Frauds.

Here, the decedent's estate (Grant O'Keefe) would be unjustly enriched. Grant didn't spend time with his aunt until she was on her deathbed – and even then only minimal [DF at 1]. To allow him to recover would be unjust. Even if this is not held unjust, the plaintiff meets the first prong of the test solidly.

Therefore, the oral contract can not be barred because of the statute of frauds.

C. This action is not barred by the statute of limitations because a four-year period applies rather than a two-year period [is] generally applicable.

Where quasi-spec. performance by declaration of a constructive trust on real property is sought on the basis of an oral agreement pursuant to which that property was to have been left by will, a four-year period applies rather than the 2-year statute of limitations (<u>Riganti v. McElhinney</u>).

Here, since Plaintiff is seeking a constructive trust on real property, the four-year statute has been abided by. Sandra died on August 26, 1999 and the action was filed January 11, 2002, well under four years after the death of Sandra.

Hence, the plaintiff's action is timely and not barred.

D. Moreover, even if the court finds that the 2-year statute applies (and it doesn't) the defendant is barred from asserting it because of the doctrine of laches.

The defendant was aware of Plaintiff's assertion that Sandra left the life estate in the house to Plaintiff [DF at 2]. He left Mason in possession of the house for the next 2½ years before evicting him. Hence, under the doctrine of laches, the action to assert the statute of frauds is barred.

THURSDAY AFTERNOON
AUGUST 1, 2002

California
Bar
Examination

Performance Test B
INSTRUCTIONS AND FILE

U.S. v. ALEJANDRO CRUZ

U.S. v. ALEJANDRO CRUZ

INSTRUCTIONS

1. You will have three hours to complete this session of the examination. This performance test is designed to evaluate your ability to handle a select number of legal authorities in the context of a factual problem involving a client.

2. The problem is set in the fictional State of Columbia, one of the United States.

3. You will have two sets of materials with which to work, a **File** and a **Library**. The **File** contains factual materials about your case. The first document is a memorandum containing the instructions for the tasks you are to complete.

4. The **Library** contains the legal authorities needed to complete the tasks. The case reports may be real, modified, or written solely for the purpose of this examination. If the cases appear familiar to you, do not assume that they are precisely the same as you have read before. Read them thoroughly, as if all were new to you. You should assume that cases were decided in the jurisdictions and on the dates shown. In citing cases from the **Library**, you may use abbreviations and omit page citations.

5. Your response must be written in the answer book provided. In answering this performance test, you should concentrate on the materials provided, but you should also bring to bear on the problem your general knowledge of the law. What you have learned in law school and elsewhere provides the general

background for analyzing the problem; the **File** and **Library** provide the specific materials with which you must work.

6. Although there are no restrictions on how you apportion your time, you should probably allocate at least 90 minutes to organizing and writing.

7. This performance test will be graded on your responsiveness to instructions and on the content, thoroughness, and organization of your response. Grading of the two tasks will be weighted as follows:

Task 1 — 70%

Task 2 — 30%

Law Offices of
Miles, Read and Paulete
605 Crawford Street
Carpenter, Columbia

MEMORANDUM

To: Applicant

From: Matt Mato

Re: U.S. v. Alejandro Cruz

Date: August 1, 2002

Our client, Alejandro Cruz, is threatened with criminal prosecution by the United States Department of the Treasury's Office of Foreign Assets Control (OFAC) following a trip to Cuba. OFAC has sent Mr. Cruz a letter requesting information concerning a possible criminal violation of Section 515.201 of the Trading With the Enemy Act.

> 1. Prepare a memorandum for me that (a) identifies the elements of a criminal violation of Section 515.201 of the Trading With the Enemy Act, (b) indicates the evidence the government now possesses to establish each element, and (c) determines whether the government may constitutionally use the presumption contained in the Trading With the Enemy Act at any ensuing criminal trial.

> 2. Prepare a memorandum for me on the ethical considerations that I must take into account as I undertake to draft a letter on Mr. Cruz's behalf in response to OFAC's request for information. As you will see, the request inquires into such matters as travel-related transactions, licenses, and fully-hosted travel. As you will also see, Mr. Cruz has provided us with much information relating to such matters, and has provided it quite candidly. Please tell me what I am ethically required or allowed to say, or not to say, in response to the request, and give me your reasons.

TRANSCRIPT OF
ALEJANDRO CRUZ INTERVIEW

Matt Mato: OK, Alejandro, it was good to catch up on what you've been doing since we were in the Peace Corps in Nepal.

Alejandro Cruz: Indeed it was, Matt.

MATO: Well, let's get to work. We've covered the basics, costs, retainer, and information that you and I will need to keep in touch. So, as I told you, I've turned on the tape recorder to get the full story. Do you have any questions before we start?

CRUZ: I don't think so. This whole thing is overwhelming. I don't feel that I'm on familiar or solid ground. I went on a tropical vacation and now I'm facing fines of six figures and even prison.

MATO: I'm sure it is a shock. Thanks for the documents you've brought. We'll go over them in a minute. Let's go back to what's happened and start at the beginning.

CRUZ: Certainly. About a year ago, I began looking at a trip to Cuba. I was reading a lot of news stories about Cuba. There was the Pope's visit in 1998, the 40th anniversary of Castro's revolution the next year, and then all the news coverage on the little boy, Elían González, who was the center of the controversy involving Cuban-Americans in Miami. For a couple of years, it's seemed as though there was a news story every week about Cuba. I was curious about Cuba, and frankly I wanted to learn for myself what was left of communism in the 21st century. I'm not of Cuban extraction myself, but I was interested.

MATO: Would it be fair to say that as a result of the news coverage you were aware of the U.S. embargo?

CRUZ: Yes. For example, in 2000 there were many stories about the possibility of the U.S. easing the embargo against the sale of food and medicine to Cuba, even though it didn't actually succeed. I definitely recall reading those with interest. Running my own business, I couldn't believe that the United States Congress would prohibit U.S. farmers from selling their agricultural commodities to Cubans.

MATO: So you knew about the legal problems of going to Cuba before you went?

CRUZ: Let me think about that. There was extensive coverage on doing business with Cuba, for example, comparing the conflicting U.S. policies toward China and Vietnam and toward Cuba, but I can't recall ever reading about the travel restrictions. I don't think that many people in America realize that a trip to Cuba could land them in federal prison for 10 years.

MATO: So you knew about the trade embargo, but perhaps not about the travel restrictions?

CRUZ: I think that I discovered those only after I decided to go, and began doing research on traveling there.

MATO: What did you do?

CRUZ: I went to a bookstore and checked out the Internet. All the major guidebook publishers have guides to Cuba. I scanned many of them, and finally chose the Freedom one, probably because I've liked using their guides on trips to Latin America.

MATO: That's the guidebook you've shown me?

CRUZ: Yes.

MATO: So, before going, how would you describe your understanding of the legality of traveling to Cuba?

CRUZ: That it was illegal, but that the travel restrictions were a relic of the long dead and buried Cold War, that thousands of Americans were going, and there was no punishment, not even a slap on the wrist. Everyone seemed to be going. I had received announcements of organized tours from my university alumni association.

MATO: Did you keep any of them?

CRUZ: I don't think so. No, I didn't. I preferred to go on my own, traveling independently rather than on a packaged tour. Perhaps that was a mistake. Are the tours legal?

MATO: I really don't know. So would it be fair to say that you understood that without some kind of permission, a license I think it says, it was illegal to go?

CRUZ: Yes.

MATO: You knew the rules, you just did not think that there would be any consequences?

CRUZ: Yes, and, I guess, that it was so commonplace, that I would not be caught.

MATO: So how did you go?

CRUZ: I followed the guide's instructions. I booked flights to Montego Bay and then to Havana. It's very easy to do on the Internet, except that you can't pay for the flight to Havana with a U.S. credit card. Only cash is accepted, but it's easy. It's the same in Cuba. You cannot use your American credit card, but the dollar is the common currency. There's no need to change any money for Cuban pesos.

MATO: How long were you there?

CRUZ: Two weeks.

MATO: Any idea what you spent?

CRUZ: Less than $2,000, including airfare.

MATO: What was that for?

CRUZ: Hotel rooms, meals, and transportation basically.

MATO: Again, is it fair to say that those were the kinds of expenditures that you believed were prohibited?

CRUZ: Pretty much. I just did not think it mattered to anyone.

MATO: Any records of your expenditures?

CRUZ: I can't recall any that I retained.

MATO: So, when you came back to the U.S., what happened?

CRUZ: I was not even thinking that there would be a problem. I took a few precautions, and then forgot about it until I was suddenly searched and given the "third degree" by Customs.

MATO: What precautions?

CRUZ: I stashed the Cuban cigars and rum I'd bought. And I removed the baggage tags from the flights to and from Havana.

MATO: But they found the cigars and rum?

CRUZ: Just bad luck to be the one they picked out to search. As I said, I was not prepared for it. I tried to think of an explanation, but I did not do it very well. The Customs guy could tell I wasn't being straight.

MATO: That comes through in his report.

CRUZ: I felt that he could see right through me. I finally decided to tell him the truth: I had been to Cuba. And then not say anything else. At least I had the presence of mind to remember that from the guidebook.

MATO: I don't know how this is going to turn out, Alejandro, but I think that you made the right decisions on both counts. Is the inspector's report accurate?

CRUZ: It embarrasses me to say that it is. He probably could have put in some more shuddering and stammering while I tried to think of something to say. I don't think that I raised my voice as he claims, but I did go through a phase of being angered that I was caught, because I recalled reading of Little Leaguers being able to get away with going to Cuba. I guess I thought of myself as an experienced world traveler, and I felt very foolish.

MATO: Then what?

CRUZ: I thought that giving up 70 or 80 dollars worth of cigars and rum at the airport was the end of it. That's ironic: I bought them on the black market, so the money did not go to the Cuban government, but to some Cuban undercutting the government stores.

MATO: Then what? You received the letter from OFAC?

CRUZ: Yes, the "Request to Furnish Information" from a "Sanctions Coordinator." That is when I decided that this was getting out of control and called you.

MATO: This is obvious, but I assume that you don't have one of the licenses mentioned in the OFAC request?

CRUZ: No. I do not know who gets them or how. Although I guess the tour companies have that figured out.

MATO: Probably. I notice that OFAC has to ask if you have a license. But I guess that's what they're stuck with. They can't send the FBI to Cuba to prove that you committed a crime. Are these then the only documents you have?

CRUZ: Yes. It's my entire Cuba file, guidebook and all.

MATO: I'll look them over. As I said, the Trading With the Enemy Act is not something I'm familiar with, so I'll probably ask one of our associates to look into it. We will probably want to respond in some way to the request, since criminal sanctions are being threatened. We'll draft something and be in touch.

CRUZ: Thank you.

FREEDOM'S CARIBBEAN: THE CHOICE FOR AMERICANS

* * * * * *

CHAPTER 4

The Choice For Americans: Licensed or Unlicensed Travel

Travel to Cuba itself is not difficult, but it is very difficult to understand or reconcile the technicalities and the realities of travel to Cuba. For those not interested in tackling the details of the grotesquely named Trading With the Enemy Act or licenses to qualify for legal travel to Cuba, these key facts may be sufficient:

- Thousands of Americans, perhaps 200,000, are illegally traveling to Cuba annually through Canada, Mexico, and the Caribbean.

- Many other Americans are going legally on tours for apparent educational, religious, and cultural purposes.

- Despite the flow of travelers, prosecution by U.S. authorities for violating the travel ban is rare.

Although there is a travel ban, it is flouted with impunity by thousands, and unevenly and inconsistently applied by the United States.

To begin with, what is legal or permitted involves TWO governments: the U.S. and Cuba. So, when one asks, "What is allowed?" The answer may be, "According to whom, the U.S. or Cuba?"

On the Cuban side, the situation is much clearer. Cuba welcomes tourists, including those from the United States. (An exception is returning Cuban-Americans whose right to return is tightly regulated.) The Cuban government wants tourists to come and spend money. Cuban airport immigration officials facilitate U.S. tourism and usually will not stamp American passports. In general, travel to and within Cuba is not restricted, although there are many harsh, incomprehensible restrictions on the Cubans with whom tourists may travel, stay, and eat.

FREEDOM'S CARIBBEAN: THE CHOICE FOR AMERICANS

In terms of U.S. law, travel to Cuba is either (1) legal, more accurately "licensed," or (2) illegal, that is, "unlicensed." From this point on, the rules get complicated and arbitrary, and even simple rules are inconsistently and sometimes inexplicably applied.

Contrary to popular belief, U.S. law does not technically prohibit U.S. citizens from visiting Cuba. However, tourism is effectively banned by the U.S. embargo, which prohibits U.S. citizens or residents from spending any money there to rent a room, buy a meal, or use transportation, or buying anything from or selling anything to Cuba, and threatens those who do so with 10 years imprisonment and fines of $100,000 for individuals and $1,000,000 for businesses. The law does not allow minimal travel-related transactions or minor purchases. Any amount is unlawful. Do not try to tell Customs that you stayed in a cheap hotel or bought only one box of cigars. You will only be getting yourself into more trouble.

The trade embargo and travel restrictions are rooted in the Trading With the Enemy Act, which, in effect, puts Cuba in the category of Iraq, Libya, and North Korea. It authorizes the President to prohibit or regulate trade with hostile countries **in time of war**. According to a 1998 Pentagon report, Cuba poses no national security threat, and its military capabilities are only defensive. The State Department says that Cuba no longer actively supports armed struggle in Latin America or elsewhere. Nevertheless, U.S. Presidents, both Democrats and Republicans, annually sign declarations putting Cuba in the official and legal category of an enemy. There was a brief opening of travel to Cuba in the 1970s, but ever since President Reagan reimposed the prohibition on travel-related transactions in Cuba, it has been practically illegal to travel to Cuba.

The legal prohibition is about controlling dollars; thus, enforcement and applications for licenses to travel to Cuba are handled by the U.S. Treasury Department, not the State Department. Specifically, it is the Office of Foreign Assets Control (OFAC), U.S. Department of the Treasury, Washington, D.C., telephone (202) 622-2520.

The U.S. sanctions for unlicensed travel to Cuba **are not limited** to U.S. citizens. Any person subject to U.S. jurisdiction who engages in any travel-related transaction in Cuba violates the law. Thus, foreign nationals who are U.S. residents should also not risk a Cuban entry stamp in their foreign passports.

FREEDOM'S CARIBBEAN: THE CHOICE FOR AMERICANS

Although it is possible to travel to Cuba through a third country, such as Canada or Mexico, the circuitous route is not legal. However, if a traveler can prove that she or he did not spend any money in Cuba, then travel there may be legal. One of the categories of legal travel has been "fully-hosted travel"; that is, trips where the Cuban government or some non-U.S. organization picks up all travel expenses in Cuba. "Venceremos Brigades" used to go (and perhaps still do) to help the Revolution cut sugar cane. The Cuban government continues to operate fully-hosted trips, which reportedly are long on indoctrination and short on food and amenities. The U.S. government will not just take your word that you were "fully-hosted." You will be asked to provide a day-to-day explanation of who paid for your meals, lodging, transportation, and even gratuities.

Other than a "fully-hosted" visit, U.S. law permits only a few categories of "licensed" travel, such as to gather news or attend professional conferences and athletic competitions. "General" licenses are available to diplomats, full-time journalists, and full-time academic researchers. Everyone else must apply for and obtain a "specific license." These include religious organizations, human rights groups, and projects to directly benefit the Cuban people.

The largest category of licensed travel comprises Cubans in the U.S. who are permitted, once a year, to visit close relatives in "humanitarian need." One of the ironies of the Elían González saga is that if Congress had succeeded in making Elían a U.S. citizen or resident, he could have visited his own father only once a year and only if there was a humanitarian need.

The U.S. travel restrictions state repeatedly that all tourism or recreational travel is prohibited. However, in fact and in law, it is not so. A fully-hosted trip can be totally recreational; a Cuban who legally visits family in Cuba is free to engage in recreation.

Furthermore, in the last few years, there has been a steady flow of celebrities, tour groups, and just plain tourists going to Cuba. For example, newspapers and the Web have reported that visitors to Cuba have included:

- 60 Baltimore Little Leaguers;
- Basketball coach Bobby Knight, to fly fish and conduct basketball clinics;

- Delegations from the U.S. Chamber of Commerce (even though U.S. businesses cannot do business there).

U.S. travel companies advertise apparently legal trips for cigar aficionados, photo enthusiasts, and music and dance fanatics. The National Geographic Society and many cultural, alumni, senior, and even veteran's groups run cultural trips to Cuba; yet U.S. law does not include an exception for cultural travel. One U.S. company advertises trips to Cuba's nightlife and beaches. These licensed trips would seem to be recreational.

In total, somewhere between 160,000 to 300,000 U.S. citizens visit Cuba annually; only about 100,000 do so legally, while the rest slip in through third countries. Going through Canada, Mexico, or the Bahamas is not legal, of course, but thousands of Americans do it annually.

Prosecutions are rare, although they do occur. If you are caught, do not lie, but do not admit that you bought anything in Cuba or that you spent any money in Cuba.

DEPARTMENT OF THE TREASURY
Office of Foreign Assets Control
WASHINGTON, D.C.

OFAC No. 02-53-0798

July 26, 2002

Alejandro Cruz
463 Cespedes
San Cabo, Columbia 60001

Request to Furnish Information Regarding Possible
Criminal Violation of Section 515.201 of Trading With the Enemy Act

Dear Mr. Cruz:

This is in reference to your entry into the United States on July 2, 2002 at San Cabo International Airport, State of Columbia. At that time, you acknowledged to a Customs Service Inspector that you had been to Cuba. The Customs Report is enclosed.

Section 515.201 of the Trading With the Enemy Act, administered by the Office of Foreign Assets Control (OFAC) of the United States Department of the Treasury, prohibits all persons subject to the jurisdiction of the United States from travel-related transactions in Cuba, unless authorized under a license.

The Trading With the Enemy Act provides that, unless otherwise authorized, any person subject to the jurisdiction of the United States who has traveled to Cuba shall be presumed to have engaged in prohibited travel-related transactions. This presumption may be rebutted by a statement signed by the traveler providing specific supporting documentation showing that (1) no transactions were engaged in by the traveler or on the traveler's behalf by other persons subject to the jurisdiction of the United States, or (2) the traveler was fully-hosted by a third party not subject to the jurisdiction of the United States, and payments made on the traveler's behalf were not in exchange for services provided to Cuba or any national thereof.

Accordingly, would you provide to this Office a signed statement under oath explaining whether you engaged in travel-related transactions in Cuba pursuant to a license? If you claim to have traveled pursuant to a license, provide documentation of the purpose and activities of your travel to Cuba; provide the number, date, and name of the bearer of the license; and, if still in your possession, provide a copy of the license itself.

If you claim not to have engaged in travel-related transactions in Cuba, provide a statement under oath describing the circumstances of the travel and explain how it was possible for you to avoid entering into travel-related transactions such as payments for meals, lodging, transportation, bunkering of vessels, visas, entry or exit fees, and gratuities.

If you claim to have been a fully-hosted traveler to Cuba, provide a statement under oath describing the circumstances of the travel and explain how it was possible for you to avoid entering into travel-related transactions such as payments for meals, lodging, transportation, bunkering of vessels, visas, entry or exit fees, and gratuities. The statement should also state what party hosted the travel and why. The statement must provide a day-to-day account of financial transactions waived or entered into on behalf of the traveler by the host, including but not limited to visa fees, room and board, local or international transportation costs, and Cuban airport departure taxes. It must be accompanied by an original signed statement from the host, confirming that the travel was fully-hosted and the reasons for the travel.

Since there is no question that you traveled to Cuba, the failure to establish that your travel was pursuant to a license, or that there were no travel-related transactions in Cuba, or that you were a fully-hosted traveler, could result in a criminal prosecution for violation of the Trading With the Enemy Act.

Your response should be mailed within 10 days to: Sanctions Coordinator, OFAC, U.S. Department of the Treasury, Washington, D.C.

OFFICE OF FOREIGN ASSETS CONTROL

Clara Charles
Washington Sanctions Coordinator

DEPARTMENT OF THE TREASURY
UNITED STATES CUSTOMS SERVICE

Report (Customs Form 110 A)

Case No.   CS: 02-53-0798

Report Type: Seizure/Forfeiture of Cuban-origin commodities

Officer's Name Badge: Customs Inspector Paul Nardella, #26262

Office/Location: San Cabo International Airport, State of Columbia

Report Date/Time: July 2, 2002, 3 p.m.

Suspect/Victim/Reporting Party: Alejandro Cruz, U.S. Passport #0534123132.

Address: 463 Cespedes, San Cabo, Columbia 60001 Telephone: (301) 703-6034

DOB: 3/30/66, Falls Church, Columbia. M. Cauc, 5-9, 160, Brn eyes

Seized or Forfeited Property: 2 boxes, 25 cigars each of Cohiba Esplendidos. 1 box, 25 cigars of Cohiba Habanos. Total 75 cigars. 2 bottles Havana Club Anejo Reserva Rum. 5 "Che" key chains. One Cuban 3-peso coin.

Action Taken: Forfeiture of Cuban-origin commodities and referral to OFAC, Washington Office.

Narrative: On date of report, Customs Inspector (CI) Nardella was assigned to an Inspector's secondary examination station, San Cabo Customs. Alejandro Cruz was selected for a random inspection by a roving inspector and referred to CI's inspection station. Passport in order. Entry and exit stamps from Jamaica, Montego Bay, in accord with Customs Declaration (Form 6059B), listing arrival on Air Jamaica # 666. No entry or exit stamps indicating travel to Cuba. Passport not retained. No commodities declared. CI asked Cruz if he had anything to declare. Cruz responded no. "No tobacco or alcohol products?" CI asked. Cruz again responded no.   CI performed hand search of luggage. Discovered Cuban-origin commodities listed above wrapped in dirty clothing and stuffed inside an empty camera bag. CI asked Cruz why he had not listed the commodities on Customs Declaration. Cruz said that he estimated that they were within $400 duty-free exemption and it was not necessary to write in. CI responded that that is correct if items are orally declared. Cruz responded, "That's been done now, right?" CI responded that was correct but these are Cuban-origin commodities. Cruz volunteered that he had bought the Cuban-origin commodities in Jamaica, so he did not believe that they "were a problem with the Cuba embargo." CI responded, "So you did not buy these commodities in Cuba?" Cruz said, "No. I bought them in the duty-free store leaving Montego Bay, Jamaica." (This Customs Officer has observed the same items carried by passengers coming from Montego Bay.) CI informed Cruz that it did not matter where he bought them, as U.S. law does not permit the importation of Cuban-origin commodities even if purchased in another country. CI informed Cruz that Cuban-origin commodities would have to be seized and that unless he was licensed to import or transport Cuban-origin commodities, he would be required to forfeit the Cuban-origin commodities. CI informed Cruz that he would have to wait while CI filled out a Seizure Report identifying the Cuban-origin commodities. Cruz was observed to be agitated and nervous. Cruz volunteered that he "misspoke." He had not bought the items. They were gifts. He said several times, "I did not pay for them." Cruz said he had read that the U.S. embargo of Cuba was "over." CI asked Cruz where he'd read that, and Cruz said, "Right here," waving a copy of the Freedom's Caribbean he was carrying. Cruz said that he read that no one had ever been prosecuted for violating the embargo. "Why did you single me out?" Cruz said in a raised voice. CI responded by asking Cruz to calm down. CI said that he thought that Cruz said he had not been to Cuba. Cruz responded, "I did not spend any U.S. dollars" on the Cuban-origin commodities. CI responded OK, that he would put on the seizure form that the commodities had not been purchased in Cuba and that Cruz had not been in Cuba. Cruz responded the CI had "misunderstood me. I was in Cuba. I received the cigars as gifts in Cuba." CI inquired what Cruz was doing in Cuba. Cruz responded that he thought he "better not say anything else." Thereafter Cruz refused to respond and repeated that he "better not say anything else." CI explained to Cruz that not all travel to Cuba was prohibited, that if he was in a category that qualified for a general license he could travel there and bring into the U.S. up to $100 worth of Cuban-origin commodities. CI explained that if he had family members in Cuba or was a journalist or a professor working in Cuba he could bring in the Cuban-origin commodities. CI asked Cruz whether he had traveled to Cuba as part of a specific license held in the name of another, such as an educational or professional tour. Cruz's response to each of these suggestions was that he "better not say anything else." CI offered Cruz the opportunity to talk to a Custom Service supervisor-on-duty if he wanted to explain his presence in Cuba. Cruz declined. CI explained process to reclaim property or accept forfeiture. Cruz said, "Keep it. You and your buddies can enjoy the cigars." CI informed Cruz that the contraband would be smoked — in the Customs Service incinerators.

Page____2____of____2

California

Bar

Examination

Performance Test B

LIBRARY

U.S. v. ALEJANDRO CRUZ

LIBRARY

SELECTED PROVISIONS OF THE TRADING WITH THE ENEMY ACT

*   *   *

Section 515.201. Transactions involving designated foreign countries or their nationals.

(a) All of the following transactions are prohibited, except as authorized by the Secretary of the Treasury by means of licenses, if such transactions involve money or property in which any foreign country designated under this section, or any national thereof, has any interest of any nature whatsoever, direct or indirect:

    (1) All dealings in, including, without limitation, transfers, withdrawals, or exportations of, any money, property, or evidences of indebtedness or evidences of ownership of property by any person subject to the jurisdiction of the United States; and

    (2) All transfers outside the United States with regard to any money, property, or property interest subject to the jurisdiction of the United States.

(b) For the purposes of this section, and subject to the President's declaration, the term "foreign country designated under this section" includes . . . Cuba . . . .

(c) Any person subject to the jurisdiction of the United States who engages in any of the foregoing transactions is in violation of this section and is subject to civil action and remedies and, if such person engages in any such transaction willfully, to criminal prosecution and sanction.

*   *   *

Section 515.420. Fully-hosted travel to Cuba.

A person subject to the jurisdiction of the United States who is not authorized to engage in travel-related transactions in which Cuba has an interest will not be considered to violate the prohibitions of Section 515.201 when a person not subject to the jurisdiction of the United States covers the cost of all transactions related to the travel of the person subject to the jurisdiction of the United States.

Section 515.421. Presumption of travel-related transactions.

Unless otherwise authorized, any person subject to the jurisdiction of the United States who has traveled to Cuba shall be presumed to have engaged in travel-related transactions prohibited by Section 515.201. This presumption may be rebutted by a statement signed by the traveler providing specific supporting documentation showing that no transactions were engaged in by the traveler or on the traveler's behalf by other persons subject to the jurisdiction of the United States or showing that the traveler was fully-hosted by a third party not subject to the jurisdiction of the United States and that payments made on the traveler's behalf were not in exchange for services provided to Cuba or any national thereof. The statement should address the circumstances of the travel and explain how it was possible for the traveler to avoid entering into travel-related transactions such as payments for meals, lodging, transportation, bunkering of vessels, visas, entry or exit fees, and gratuities. If applicable, the statement should state what party hosted the travel and why. The statement must provide a day-to-day account of financial transactions waived or entered into on behalf of the traveler by the host, including but not limited to visa fees, room and board, local or international transportation costs, and Cuban airport departure taxes. Travelers fully-hosted by a person or persons not subject to the jurisdiction of the United States must also provide an original signed statement from their sponsor or host, specific to that traveler, confirming that the travel was fully-hosted and the reasons for the travel.

* * *

SELECTED COLUMBIA RULES OF PROFESSIONAL CONDUCT

* * *

Rule 3.21. Meritorious claims and contentions

A lawyer shall not bring or defend a proceeding, or assert or controvert an issue therein, unless there is a basis for doing so that is not frivolous. A lawyer for the defendant in a criminal proceeding may nevertheless so defend the proceeding as to require that every element of the case be established. A lawyer for a person who may become subject to a criminal proceeding may decline to aid in the investigation of the case.

* * *

Rule 4.1. Truthfulness in statements to others

In the course of representing a client a lawyer shall not knowingly:

(a) make a false statement of material fact to a third person; or

(b) fail to disclose a material fact to a third person when disclosure is necessary to avoid assisting a contemporaneous or future criminal act by a client, unless disclosure would reveal confidential information obtained from the client and the criminal act in question is not likely to result in imminent death or substantial bodily harm.

COMMENT

Misrepresentation. A lawyer is required to be truthful when dealing with others on a client's behalf, but generally has no affirmative duty to inform an opposing party of relevant facts. A misrepresentation can occur if the lawyer incorporates or affirms a statement of another person that the lawyer knows is false.

Confidential Information. A lawyer is generally under a duty to preserve client confidences. A lawyer is also generally required to be truthful to others. Rule 4.1(b) effects an accommodation between the general requirement of truthfulness to others and the general duty to preserve client confidences.

*　　*　　*

SANDSTROM v. MONTANA
Supreme Court of the United States, 1979

Defendant had confessed to the slaying of Annie Jessen. In a Montana state court prosecution for deliberate homicide, defendant's attorney informed the jury that, although defendant client admitted killing Jessen, he did not do so "purposely or knowingly," and was therefore not guilty of "deliberate homicide" but of a lesser crime. Defendant presented no evidence. At the prosecution's request, the trial court instructed the jury that "the law presumes that a person intends the ordinary consequences of his voluntary acts." The jury found defendant guilty of deliberate homicide. Defendant, who was 18 at the time, was sentenced to 100 years in prison. The Montana Supreme Court affirmed, and certiorari was granted.

The question presented is whether, in a case in which intent is an element of the crime charged, the jury instruction, "the law presumes that a person intends the ordinary consequences of his voluntary acts," violates the requirement of the Fifth and Fourteenth Amendments' due process clauses that the prosecution prove every element of a criminal offense beyond a reasonable doubt. We hold that it does and reverse.

The threshold inquiry in ascertaining the constitutional analysis applicable to this kind of jury instruction is to determine the nature of the presumption it describes. Defendant's jurors were told that "the law presumes that a person intends the ordinary consequences of his voluntary acts." They were not told that they had a choice, or that they might infer that conclusion; they were told only that the law presumed it. It is clear that a reasonable juror could easily have viewed such an instruction as mandatory, as "conclusive," that is, not technically as a presumption at all, but rather as an irrebuttable direction by the court to find intent once convinced of the facts triggering the presumption. Alternatively, the jury may have interpreted the instruction as a direction to find intent upon proof of defendant's voluntary actions (and their "ordinary" consequences), unless defendant proved the contrary by some quantum of proof which may well have been considerably greater than "some" evidence — thus effectively shifting the burden of persuasion on the element of intent. Numerous federal and state courts have warned that instructions of the type given here can be interpreted in just these ways. Although the Montana Supreme Court held to the contrary in this case, Montana's own Rules of Evidence expressly state that the presumption at issue here may be overcome only "by a preponderance of evidence contrary to the presumption." Such a requirement shifts the ultimate burden of persuasion on the issue of intent.

In In re Winship (U.S. Supreme Ct. 1979), we stated:

> Lest there remain any doubt about the constitutional stature of the reasonable-doubt standard, we explicitly hold that the Due Process Clauses of the Fifth and Fourteenth Amendments protect the accused against conviction except upon proof beyond a reasonable doubt of every fact necessary to constitute the crime with which he is charged.

We do not reject the possibility that some jurors may have interpreted the challenged instruction as permissive, or, if mandatory, as requiring only that defendant come forward with "some" evidence in rebuttal. However, the fact that a reasonable juror could have given the presumption conclusive or persuasion-shifting effect means that we cannot discount the possibility that defendant's jurors actually did proceed upon one or the other of these latter interpretations.

Thus, the question is whether the challenged instruction had the effect of relieving the prosecution of the burden of proof enunciated in Winship on the critical question of defendant's state of mind.

We conclude that under either of the two possible interpretations of the instruction set out above, precisely that effect would result, and that the instruction therefore represents constitutional error, which on the facts presented must be deemed prejudicial.

Reversed.

BUSTOS v. IMMIGRATION AND NATURALIZATION SERVICE
United States Court of Appeals, Fifth Circuit, 1990

Pedro Bustos appeals from the Board of Immigration Appeals' final order of deportation. Because the immigration judge did not err in admitting an Immigration and Naturalization Service (INS) Form I-213, Record of Deportable Alien, and because Bustos did not refute any of the statements in the form which were sufficient for a prima facie showing of deportability, we affirm.

At the deportation hearing, Bustos identified himself, but refused to plead to the order to show cause and refused to answer the immigration judge's questions. The INS submitted a Form I-213 Record of Deportable Alien relating to a Pedro Bustos, which stated that he is a native and citizen of Mexico who had been in the United States since 1981. Attached to the form is an attestation by the INS's trial attorney that it is authentic and a true and correct copy of the original document taken from the INS's files. No further evidence was presented, and the judge found Bustos deportable.

We must decide whether the information in Form I-213 is by itself sufficient to make a prima facie showing of deportability, requiring the alien to produce evidence of legal presence in this country.

First, it is well established that a deportation hearing is a purely civil proceeding and that the alien is not entitled to all the constitutional safeguards of a criminal defendant.

Nonetheless, due process standards of fundamental fairness extend to the conduct of deportation proceedings. The test for admissibility of evidence in a deportation proceeding is whether the evidence is probative and whether its use is fundamentally fair. The affidavit of the examining officer shows that the information in the Form I-213 is based upon statements of Bustos, and Bustos does not contest their validity.

Although the government has the ultimate burden of proving deportability by clear and convincing evidence, in a deportation case charging deportability of an alien who entered the country without inspection, the government need only show alienage.

8 U.S.C. §1361 provides in pertinent part:
   In any deportation proceeding, the burden of proof shall
   be upon such person to show the time, place, and

manner of his entry into the United States . . . . If such
burden of proof is not sustained, such person shall be
presumed to be in the United States in violation of law.

Thus, 8 U.S.C. §1361 imposes a statutory presumption that the alien is in the country illegally, and that the burden shifts to the alien to prove that he is here legally.

Once the form was properly admitted, the INS's prima facie case of deportability was made. The burden of proof then shifted to Bustos. No abridgement of his constitutional rights was involved in imposing that burden on him.

Affirmed.

UNITED STATES v. FRADE
United States Court of Appeals, Eleventh Circuit, 1985

Father Joe Morris Doss, Rector of Grace Episcopal Church in New Orleans, and Father Leopold Frade, Curate of Grace Episcopal Church and Chairman of the National Commission for Hispanic Ministry, appeal their convictions for criminal violation of Section 515.415 of the Trading With the Enemy Act (TWEA). This provision makes unlawful any transaction "when in connection with the transportation of any Cuban national . . . unless otherwise licensed." The prohibited transactions included "transportation by vessel," the "provision of any services to Cuban nationals," and "any other transactions such as payment of port fees and charges in Cuba and payment for fuel, meals, lodging."

The events giving rise to the convictions are those of the now famous Mariel boatlift, or freedom flotilla, of spring 1980, by which some 114,000 Cuban refugees, in nearly 1,800 boats, crossed the 90 miles of ocean and great political divide between Cuba and the United States. In early April 1980, some 10,800 Cuban citizens claiming status as political refugees sought sanctuary in the Peruvian Embassy in Havana. On April 14, 1980, President Carter declared that up to 3,500 of these refugees would be admitted into the United States. An airlift was started, but within three days Castro stopped the flights, announcing that anyone who wanted to leave could do so through the harbor of Mariel. Almost immediately, small boats, funded by the members of the Cuban-American community, began leaving Key West.

Cuban-American parishioners of Grace Church implored Fathers Frade and Doss to help in arranging for a boat to bring their relatives from Cuba. A meeting held by the priests at Grace Church on May 3 to organize the rescue mission was attended by 650 people and met with immediate overwhelming response. Within forty-eight hours, $215,000 was raised.

Fathers Frade and Doss commenced negotiations with the Interest Section of the Cuban Government in Washington to obtain the release of family members and political prisoners. They obtained assurances that they would not be forced to bring back criminals, the mentally ill, or other undesirables that the Cuban government was then forcing into the Mariel boatlift. The Cuban Interest Section insisted that Fathers Frade and Doss turn over the list of the people they proposed to pick up. The priests submitted a list of 366 names which were immediately telexed to Havana. Although Fathers Frade and Doss understood that, in the week following their meeting at the Cuban Interest Section, the Administration's attitude towards the boatlift had changed, they realized that, once the names had been telexed, they had passed the point of no return. Father Frade had been told by a Cuban official that a "national purge was taking place," those applying for permission to leave Cuba were losing jobs, houses, and ration cards, and sometimes being attacked, beaten and killed. As the district judge observed at sentencing, "Once the list of names had been given over to the Cuban officials . . . it would have been very difficult, a very difficult decision of conscience to stop at that time."

On May 26, 1980, the God's Mercy, a large, safe vessel, equipped with $10,000 in added safety equipment, and manned by an experienced crew, including a doctor and a nurse, set sail for Mariel. After two weeks of intense negotiation, Fathers Frade and Doss succeeded in obtaining commitments to release the persons on their lists. On June 12, 1980, the God's Mercy arrived in Key West, with the priests and 402 refugees including 288 persons from the lists.

The God's Mercy was escorted into Key West by two Coast Guard cutters. Fathers Frade and Doss were arrested immediately, and the indictment under the TWEA was brought. After trial, Fathers Frade and Doss received $431,000 in fines and the God's Mercy was forfeited to the government.

Fathers Frade and Doss contend that the trial court erred in denying their motion for judgment of acquittal on the ground that there was no evidence to establish the requisite mental state for a criminal violation of Section 515.415 of the TWEA.

To be criminal, violation of the TWEA must be "willful." "Willfulness" is expressly required in some provisions of the act, such as Section 515.201, and impliedly required in the rest, including Section 515.415, with which we are concerned here. When used in a criminal statute, the word "willfully" generally connotes a voluntary breach of a known legal duty. Section 515.415, under which the priests were convicted, was enacted into its operative form unexpectedly and with little publicity on May 15, 1980 — after the list of names had been tendered to Cuba. It criminalized behavior (travel to, from, and within Cuba), which previously had been expressly authorized and which, in fact, remained lawful for a time, except when done in connection with the transportation of Cuban nationals, an activity which also is not generally criminal. It penalized the paying of port fees in a foreign harbor and duly incurred hotel, motel and restaurant bills if done to assist the transportation of Cubans to the United States. These are activities which laymen do not consider wrong nor lawyers classify as malum in se.The government argues that the evidence demonstrated the necessary mental state for a criminal violation of Section 515.415 of the TWEA. The government relies principally on the testimony of government officials who stated that they had warned the priests that the venture might be against the law. The government also relies on the priests' knowledge that they might be liable for repeat trips or boat safety violations; that they might be subject to forfeiture of their vessel under civil statutes; and that the government generally disapproved of the boatlift as dangerous and inadvisable.

However, the finding that a defendant is aware of matters such as those stated above is insufficient to sustain a finding of guilt under a statute requiring a voluntary breach of a known legal duty.

The government also argues that the priests' own behavior, including their fears and expressed concerns, indicated a voluntary breach of a known legal duty. The government relies on the priests' decision to captain the God's Mercy on the return voyage so that any possible onus might fall personally on them, and their own trial testimony that they would have gone ahead with the mission regardless of the law because of their moral commitment to those whose names were on the list submitted to the Cuban government. Their fears and expressed concerns, however, were understandable as normal caution and worry for the welfare of all concerned. They were simply insufficient to sustain a finding of a voluntary breach of a known legal duty. The judgment of the district court must be reversed.

UNITED STATES v. MACKO

United States Court of Appeals, Eleventh Circuit, 1999

Defendant Ralph Macko was accused of selling cigarette-packaging machinery and supplies to Cuba in violation of Section 515.201 of the Trading With the Enemy Act (TWEA). After a jury found Macko guilty, the district court held that the evidence was insufficient to support the guilty verdict. The United States appealed.

The evidence presented during the government's case-in-chief shows that the sales were through freight forwarders in Panama. The invoices did not disclose that Cuba was the ultimate destination. Macko visited Cuba by going through third countries.

In its order explaining the judgment of acquittal, the district court described the government's evidence as "primarily a paper case, made up of letters, faxes, shipping invoices, and other documents." This "paper trail," the court stated, "has too many twists and turns and dead ends to establish more than a tenuous inference that Macko acted with the requisite mental state for a criminal violation of Section 515.201 of the TWEA." The district court observed that the circumstantial evidence against Macko "is susceptible of more than one interpretation." The jury could reasonably infer that Macko knew that his conduct was generally unlawful, the court says, but such a general awareness of illegality is not sufficient to establish guilt here. Only by "mere speculation" could a jury conclude that Macko acted with the mental state required.

According to the government, the evidence against Macko, though circumstantial, established that he was aware of the prohibitions of the Cuban trade embargo and that he acted with the intent to avoid them to his profit.

In Section 515.201, the TWEA prohibits the sale of merchandise to Cuba or Cuban nationals without a license from the Office of Foreign Assets Control. Though a child of the Cold War that ended seven years ago with the Soviet Union's extinction, the Cuban embargo remains very much alive. The TWEA limits transactions with Cuba for many purposes, including both trade and travel, although subject to many exceptions. Its primary purpose is to stop the flow of hard currency from the United States to Cuba.

In United States v. Frade (11th Cir. 1985), we held that "willfulness" under the TWEA entails a voluntary breach of a known legal duty.

To establish that Macko voluntarily breached a known legal duty, the government had to prove that he knew of the prohibition against dealings with Cuba and nevertheless violated it.

In United States v. Frade, the defendants were two Episcopal priests who arranged for a ship to bring 402 Cuban refugees to the United States in 1980 during what became known as the Mariel boatlift. While the priests were laying their plans, President Carter's administration attempted to gain some control over the sudden mass immigration by amending the TWEA to generally criminalize travel to or from Cuba in connection with the transportation of Cuban nationals. We held that the evidence did not establish that the priests voluntarily breached a known legal duty, principally because the government failed to establish that the priests had knowledge of any such duty.

The case against Macko is more convincing than the case against the priests in Frade. Indeed, Frade recites considerable evidence that the priests did not know about the provision of the TWEA at issue there. That provision barred conduct that until then had been expressly authorized by a different provision. Although U.S. officials warned the priests that their boatlift might be illegal, that is all that they did, and that was insufficient. Furthermore, the priests did not attempt to hide their travel to and from Cuba.

In this case, on the other hand, the trade ban in Section 515.201 of the TWEA was promulgated neither quietly nor unexpectedly. It was in effect long before Macko involved himself in the Cuban cigarette plan, and it was widely publicized. The provision does not apply only to certain goods or activities but states a broad prohibition against transactions with Cuba or Cuban nationals. We also find it telling that Macko actively concealed his travel to Cuba as well as the final destination of the cigarette machinery and supplies. He did not attempt to shield his contacts with Panama or Panamanians, nor did he hide the fact that he was acquiring cigarette-packaging machinery and supplies. The one aspect of the operation that he kept secret was the Cuban connection. Macko traveled to Cuba through Panama in a manner that left no reference to Cuba on his passport. Macko initially lied to U.S. Customs agents about traveling and sending equipment to Cuba. Macko's correspondence about the project with other participants scrupulously avoided mentioning Cuba by name. Macko had experience in exporting machinery from the United States and was involved in international sales of various goods.

The inference that Macko acted as though it was illegal to deal directly with Cuba would seem to satisfy the element of voluntary breach of a known legal duty. A jury could reasonably conclude that Macko's secrecy about this single fact resulted from his knowledge of the Cuban embargo. Consequently, the district court erred in granting Macko's motion for a judgment of acquittal on the charge of criminal violation of Section 515.201 of the TWEA.

Reversed.

1) PT-B *(Essay)*

1. Prepare for me a memorandum that (a) identifies the elements of a criminal violation of Section 515.201 of the Trading with the Enemy Act, (b) indicates the evidence the government now possesses to establish each element, and (c) determines whether the government constitutionally may use the presumption contained in the Trading With the Enemy Act at any ensuring criminal trial.

2. Prepare a memorandum for me on the ethical considerations that I must take into account as I undertake to draft a letter on Mr. Cruz's behalf in response to OFAC's request for information. As you will see, the request inquires into such matters as travel-related transactions, licenses, and fully-hosted travel. As you will see, Mr. Cruz has provided us with much information relating to such matters, and has provided it quite candidly. Please tell what I am ethically required or allowed to say, or not to say, in response to the request, and give me your reasons.

MEMORANDUM

TO: Matt Mato

FROM: Applicant

RE: U.S. v. Alejandro Cruz

DATE: August 1, 2002

_____

You have asked that I prepare a memorandum that (a) identifies the elements of a criminal violation of Section 515.201 of the Trading with the Enemy Act, (b) indicates the evidence the government now possesses to establish each element, and (c) determines whether the government constitutionally may use the presumption contained in the Trading With the Enemy Act at any ensuing criminal trial.

A. The elements of a criminal violation of Section 515.201 of the Trading with the Enemy Act (TWEA) are as follows:

(1) any person
(2) subject to the jurisdiction of the United States
(3) willfully
(4) engages in a transaction

(5) involving money or property in which Cuba or any national thereof has any interest of any nature whatsoever, direct or indirect,

(6) including (A) transfers, withdrawals, or exportations of any money, property, or evidences of indebtedness of evidences of ownerships of property by any person subject to the jurisdiction of the United States, and (B) transfers outside the United States with regard to any money, property, or property interest subject to the jurisdiction of the United States.

Three exceptions exist:

(I) transactions pursuant to license,

(II) "fully-hosted travel," that is, where a person not subject to the jurisdiction of the United States covers the cost of all transactions related to the travel of the person subject to the jurisdiction of the United States,

(III) "no transactions travel," that is, where a person travels to Cuba and no transactions were engaged in by the traveler or on the traveler's behalf by other persons subject to the jurisdiction of the United States.

In some sense exceptions II and III are not really exceptions; when their terms are true, it means that no prohibited transactions occurred so that element 6 was not met.

B. Evidence the government now possesses to establish each element

"ANY PERSON"

This is not defined in the statute or materials in the file, but it is safe to assume that "any person" includes an individual human being and the government surely can prove Cruz is an individual, through his presence. That is, the fact finder will be able to observe that Mr. Cruz is an individual.

"SUBJECT TO THE JURISDICTION OF THE UNITED STATES"

This important operative phrase similarly is not defined. However, it is safe to assume that it includes a U.S. citizen. I assume that Mr. Cruz is a United States citizen. Although I cannot find a statement to that effect in the file, the Customs Service Report notes that Cruz has a U.S. Passport (#0534123132). The Customs Report says that Cruz's passport was returned to Cruz, but the government could obtain it from him by a subpoena. The 5th Amendment right against testimonial self-incrimination, which applies to the federal government, which would be the prosecuting government here, does not extend to non-testimonial things like passports. Thus, the government can acquire the passport by subpoena and use it to prove Cruz is a U.S. citizen and subject to the jurisdiction of the United States.

"WILLFULLY"

This is doubtless the most important element in our case. Macko and Frade cases interpreted the meaning of willfully in this context. Technically Frade, a 1985 case, interpreted "willfully" as used in Section 515.415 of the TWEA. However, Macko, a 1999 case, interpreted willfully as used in Section 515.201 and cited Macko. Hence it appears that willfully has the same meaning in both sections so that both cases are relevant in construing willfully as used in 515.201. Note as well that Macko and Frade are 11th Circuit cases, which is understandable as Florida is located in the 11th Circuit and many of these cases would be expected to arise there. I do not know what circuit in which Columbia is located. The US Constitution requires that a federal criminal trial be brought in the district in which the crime allegedly occurred. The crime/alleged crime here occurred in Cuba, and I do not know how the venue would work for that; probably venue would lie in the district in which the defendant resides. Cruz resides in Columbia, so he would be tried in federal district court in the relevant district of the Columbia Federal District Court. Such court would be bound by the decisions of its circuit and not necessarily bound by the decisions of the 11th Circuit (assuming of course that Columbia is not in the 11th Circuit). Nonetheless the Macko and Frade cases are persuasive, if not binding, authority.

Macko, citing Frade, defines willfully as used in Section 515.201 as "the voluntary breach of a known legal duty." To prove that Macko voluntarily breached a known legal duty, the government had to prove that he "knew of the prohibition against Cuba and nevertheless violated it."

Macko is a very problematic case for Cruz. It permitted an inference that the defendant knew of the prohibition against Cuba and nevertheless violated it under facts remarkably similar to ours.

Presently the government has the following evidence to prove that Cruz "knew of the prohibition against Cuba and nevertheless violated it."

First I note that, from the interview, Cruz has said that the customs report is embarrassingly accurate.

One, Cruz actively concealed his travel in two regards: Cruz traveled to Cuba in a manner that left no reference to Cuba in his passport and Cruz did not attempt to hide his dealings with the third country, Jamaica, through which Cruz cleansed his travel. Macko did the exact same two things (his third country was Panama) and the court found this evidence of active concealment, that is, a scheme to make it appear that travel had been only to the third country. The government can prove these two elements from the customs report and Cruz's passport. According to the Customs Report, Cruz virtually admitted to traveling to Cuba [see discussion below] and Cruz's passport did not bear any indicia of having visited Cuba.

233

[Note that your question to me does not specifically whether [sic] the government's evidence would be admissible in a criminal trial, but I'll briefly address. Although the Customs Report is hearsay, many exceptions exist. In fact, the entire report probably will be admissible under the "business records" exception since the customs service regularly makes such reports, and the reports are made by customs service employees with personal knowledge of the events, and the practice is to accurately record the events. The business records exception has an exception for reports prepared in anticipation of litigation, but it is not clear that customs reports are in anticipation of litigation. Even if they are, the government could call CI Nardella and she [sic] could testify about what Cruz said. Such statements would not be hearsay, as they would be statements of a party.]

Two, Cruz initially lied to US Customs Agents about his transactions involving Cuban items. Macko identified that as relevant evidence as to willfulness. The Customs Report shows that Cruz initially said in answer to the question "So you did not buy these commodities in Cuba?" "No, I bought them in the duty-free store leaving Montego Bay, Jamaica." Later, Cruz said that he had not bought the items, that they were gifts. Still later, "CI said that he thought that Cruz had said he had not been to Cuba." Cruz did not answer that remark except to say that "I did not spend any U.S. dollars." The parsing of this language is intricate. From it, Cruz did not say, "I never have been to Cuba." However, Cruz did not affirmatively deny CI's statement, "I thought that you said you had not been to Cuba." Because Cruz did not deny it, it could be regarded as an admission that Cruz had been to Cuba. However, that affirmation by silence cannot be made if the affirmative statement would be incriminating as it would have been here. Nonetheless, the statements in the Customs Report would be strong circumstantial evidence to allow a fact finder to conclude that Cruz had been to Cuba. Indeed, the government has so concluded. Its letter states, "You admitted going to Cuba; tell us how you did not violate the TWEA." Thus, while we could intricately parse the conversations between CI and Cruz and argue that Cruz never admitted going to Cuba, a fact finder could infer that he had been there. However, the fact finder could find otherwise.

Three, Cruz otherwise lied to and was deceitful with Customs. Cruz specifically denied that he had tobacco or alcohol products, but he had them. As well, Cruz's statement that he thought they were within a $400 allowance is negated by the secretive nature in which he packed them – wrapped in dirty laundry, stuffed inside an empty camera bag. The lying and secretive nature are deadly evidence as they show knowledge of the prohibition and strongly indicate Cruz's willful violation.

Fourth, Cruz is a well-versed traveler. Macko indicated that this was relevant to a conclusion that the defendant knew of the prohibition. As well, in the report Cruz is heard to say that he thought the US embargo of Cuba was over. That was not true, and even as the statement stands, it suggests that Cruz was aware of the embargo. In addition, Cruz waved the Freedom's Caribbean book and if put into evidence it would show that it informed Cruz that what he was doing was illegal and it also gave the roadmap for deceit that Cruz followed.

ENGAGES IN A TRANSACTION

The government has the following evidence, cigars and rum and a Cuban 3-peso coin. It also has the above evidence tending to prove that Cruz traveled to Cuba. The coin is the most damaging. It gives a strong inference that Cruz engaged in a transaction with a Cuban national.

INVOLVING MONEY OR PROPERTY IN WHICH CUBA OR ANY NATIONAL THEREOF HAS ANY INTEREST WHATSOEVER, DIRECT OR INDIRECT

The government has the cigars, rum and Cuban 3-peso coin. It also has the above evidence tending to prove that Cruz traveled to Cuba.

INCLUDING (A) TRANSFERS, WITHDRAWALS, OR EXPORTATIONS OF ANY MONEY, PROPERTY, OR EVIDENCES OF INDEBTEDNESS OR EVIDENCES OF OWNERSHIP OF PROPERTY BY ANY PERSON SUBJECT TO THE JURISDICTION OF THE UNITED STATES, AND (B) ALL TRANSFERS OUTSIDE THE UNITED STATES WITH REGARD TO ANY MONEY, PROPERTY OR PROPERTY INTEREST SUBJECT TO THE JURISDICTION OF THE UNITED STATES

The government has the cigars, rum and Cuban 3-peso coin. It also has the above evidence tending to prove that Cruz traveled to Cuba.

C. Determine whether the government constitutionally may use the presumption contained in the Trading With the Enemy Act at any ensuing criminal trial.

The government may not.

Section 515.421 provides that any person subject to the jurisdiction of the United States who has traveled to Cuba shall be presumed to have engaged in travel-related transactions prohibited by Section 515.201.

The due process clause of Fifth Amendment to the US Constitution requires that the prosecution prove each and every element of a criminal offense beyond a reasonable doubt. (US Sup Ct case of Sandstrom, which technically construed the 14th Amendment due process clause but indicated that for this purpose the clauses are the same, so did In re Winship).

The question of the permissible reach of presumptions in criminal cases is an intricate issue. Certainly a presumption cannot create an irrebuttable or conclusive presumption. That is, upon proof of the primary fact, travel to Cuba, the jury may not be told that it must conclude that the presumed fact, engaging in travel-related transactions, exists. However, the presumption under

515.421 permits the rebuttal of the presumption by evidence to the contrary. But this is still like the presumption in Sandstrom. In Sandstrom the presumption was not irrebuttable, the defendant was permitted to offer evidence against it, but there the presumption could be overcome only if the defendant showed "by a preponderance of evidence contrary to the presumption."

Thus the presumptions in Sandstrom and the TWEA are indistinguishable. Neither was an irrebuttable presumption, as each permitted a rebuttal, but each required the defendant to rebut it by evidence. Although the TWEA does not expressly state that the counter evidence must create a preponderance of the evidence, that can be fairly inferred from the text. Under Sandstrom, the government may not create a presumption in a criminal case in which an element of the offense is proven by a presumption capable of being overcome only if the defendant shows the contrary by a preponderance of the evidence. Such a requirement shifts the ultimate burden of persuasion, and the prosecution must prove each and every element of a criminal offense.

Note that such a presumption is proper in a civil case, even one in which a significant interest like deportation is at issue. Bustos. The TWEA has both civil and criminal sanctions. The presumption in Sec. 515.421 properly could be applied to the civil aspects of the TWEA.

MEMORANDUM

TO: Matt Mato

FROM: Applicant

RE: U.S. v. Alejandro Cruz

DATE: August 1, 2002

You have asked that I prepare a memorandum on the ethical considerations that I must take into account as I undertake to draft a letter on Mr. Cruz's behalf in response to OFAC's request for information. As you will see, the request inquires into such matters as travel-related transactions, licenses, and fully-hosted travel. As you will see, Mr. Cruz has provided us with much information relating to such matters, and has provided it quite candidly. Please tell me what I am ethically required or allowed to say, or not to say, in response to the request, and give me your reasons.

First, given our knowledge from the Cruz interview, we know that Cruz is guilty of violating the TWEA. Cruz "knew of the prohibition against Cuba and nevertheless violated it." Cruz, with knowledge of the prohibition, traveled to Cuba and engaged in prohibited transactions with Cuban nationals. Thus, if the government proceeds against Cruz civilly under the TWEA, we cannot defend because we would know that such a defense is frivolous. We would violate Rule 3.21.

However, under that same rule, "A lawyer for the defendant in a criminal proceeding may nevertheless so defend the proceeding as to require that every element of the case be established.

Is The OFAC Letter a Civil or Criminal Matter?

The letter threatens criminal prosecution. It says that since there is no question that Cruz traveled to Cuba, failure to document one of the three exceptions could result in a criminal prosecution for violating TWEA.

237

The most appropriate response is for Cruz to decline to answer on the grounds that an answer might incriminate him. The Fifth Amendment to the US Constitution provides that no person can be made to testify against himself. Ethically we can advise Cruz to take such a position, because under Rule 4.1, a lawyer has no affirmative duty to inform the opposing party, here the federal government, of relevant facts.

We cannot counsel Cruz to answer the letter in any way other than silence. The letter asks Cruz to establish one of the three exceptions to the TWEA travel rule. We know that none are met. Cruz did not have a license; his was not hosted travel; nor did he engage in no transactions (we know he spent about $2000). Thus, if Cruz were to answer and claim any of those exceptions we know that he would be lying and we cannot permit a client to lie. Thus, we have to tell him that he either takes the Fifth or he incriminates himself in a truthful answer. If he wanted to falsely reply, we would have to counsel him against that, and, if he insisted, we would have to withdraw.

In addition, we are in the delicate position of knowing that our client has committed a crime. We know that all the elements of the offense were met, and although the government may have some difficulty proving them, ethically we can require the government to establish every element of the case.

As well, we are not required to disclose the fact that Cruz has committed a crime. We learned that information through a confidential communication. Under Rule 4.1 we must not knowingly fail to disclose a material fact to a third person when disclosure is necessary to avoid assisting a contemporaneous or future criminal act by a client unless disclosure would reveal confidential information obtained from the client and the criminal act in question is not likely to result in imminent death or substantial bodily harm. That rule does not require us to disclose. First, Cruz's crime was in the past; it is not contemporaneous or future. Second, disclosure would reveal confidential information obtained from the client. Third, the crime did not involve death or substantial bodily harm.

CONCLUSION

"Please tell me what I am ethically required or allowed to say, or not to say, in response to the request, and give me your reasons."

Ethically you are required to say to Cruz that he should assert his Fifth Amendment right against self-incrimination and not answer the letter. If Cruz insists on writing a letter that is untruthful (and he might, as his conduct with the Customs Officer indicates that absolute truthfulness with government officials does not come naturally to him), you have to counsel him against making false statements, especially as any response has to be under oath and would subject Cruz to a perjury prosecution, and, if Cruz insists, you have to withdraw from the representation.

On this point, we will want to point out to Cruz that this matter is a big deal. He seems to think that this is a foot fault in tennis and that his claim of selective prosecution has some merit. No matter how many other persons subject to US jurisdiction may have gone to Cuba illegally, Little Leaguers from Baltimore or not, Cruz did violate the statute and do [sic] so knowingly. In fact he had quite good knowledge of the prohibition and went to some lengths to conceal his travel. If the facts come to light, he will be convicted as surely as Macko was convicted.

Other Ethical Issues

Your interview notes that you and Cruz agreed on costs and retainer. However, you will want to ensure that you have a signed retainer agreement. Some jurisdictions like California require signed agreements when fees are expected to exceed $1000 unless there is a prior professional or familial arrangement.

ANSWER 2 TO PERFORMANCE TEST – B

MEMO

To:	Matt Mato
From:	Applicant
Re:	U.S. v. Cruz – Elements of Criminal Violation of §515.201
Date:	August 1, 2002

Per your request, this memorandum identified the elements of a criminal violation of Section 515.201 of the Trading With the Enemy Act (TWEA), the facts that the government now possess[es] to establish element, and whether the government may constitutionally use the TWEA presumption at a criminal trial. The first two items are discussed under Section I of this memo. The constitutionality of the presumption is discussed under Section II of this memo.

I.   Elements and Evidence of Criminal Violation of Section 515.201

There are four elements to a criminal violation of 515.201:

(1) A person subject to the jurisdiction of the U.S., (2) engages in a prohibited transaction (3) with a designated foreign country, and (4) the person engages in the transaction willfully.

A.   Element I: Person Subject to the Jurisdiction of the U.S.

1.   Definition:

Although TWEA does not define this specifically, the general understanding from the cases on TWEA suggests that any person who is either a U.S. national or a U.S. resident is a person subject to the jurisdiction of the U.S. (Frade; Macko.)

Also, anyone trying to enter the U.S. may be subject to the jurisdiction of the U.S. (Frade: also "Freedom's Caribbean".)

2.   Evidence Gov't. Now Possesses

Cruz tried to enter the United States. Cruz had a United States passport, which shows that Cruz is a U.S. national. (Customs Report.) This is sufficient to establish this element.

B.   Element 2: Engaging in Prohibited Transaction

1.   Definition

A transaction is prohibited if it involves any exchange or expenditure of money that directly or indirectly interests a foreign country designated by TWEA (§515.201(a).)

Since both direct and indirect interests are implicated, this could include direct purchases or purchases from another locale.

2.   Evidence Gov't. Now Has

The government has the seized property of Cuban origin listed in the Customs Report, including cigars, rum, key chains, and a Cuban coin.

The government also has Cruz's statement, later contradicted, that he bought the items in Jamaica at a duty-free shop. Since TWEA covers both direct and indirect purchases or transactions, the government may use this statement to establish a prohibited transaction.

The government also has Cruz's subsequent statement that he got these items as gifts. If uncontroverted and believed, this could show that no prohibited transaction took place because no money exchanged hands.

Also, a transaction is NOT prohibited if Cruz has a license or was fully-hosted, or that his expenses were fully covered by someone not under U.S. jurisdiction. The government does not have any evidence that Cruz does not have a license, or that he was not fully-hosted, since Cruz had declined to answer those questions.

The government also does not have any statements from Cruz that be engaged in any prohibited transactions.

Section 515.421 allows for a presumption that prohibited transactions took place if Cruz traveled to Cuba. Whether the government can employ this presumption at trial will be discussed below. For now, the government has Cruz's statement that he was in Cuba.

C.   Element 3: Foreign Country Designated By TWEA

1.   Definition

Section 515.201(b) includes Cuba as a country so designated.

2.   Evidence Gov't. Now Has

The gov't. has Cruz's statement that he was in Cuba, as well as the item[s] seized that were of Cuban origin.

D.   Element 4: Willfulness

1.   Definition

The government must show that Cruz willfully engaged the [sic] aforementioned prohibited transactions.

The 11th Circuit Court has defined "willful," as used in Section 515.201, necessary for a criminal conviction, to mean a "voluntary breach of a known legal duty." (Frade, Macko.)

In order to convict, the government must show that Cruz knew of the prohibition beyond suspicion that the activities "might" be illegal, or that the government "generally disapproved" of them. Also, the court considers whether the activities are "malum in se," or whether laymen such as Cruz generally would know or consider to be illegal. (Frade)

The government, however, can establish the requisite knowledge through inference. (Macko.) A jury may reasonably infer willful conduct based on (1) whether the prohibition was widely publicized, (2) whether the defendant actively concealed travel to Cuba, including lying to Customs Agents, and (3) whether the defendant was experienced or involved in international transactions.

242

2.   Evidence the Gov't. Now Posses[es]

The government has Cruz's statement that he did not believe items purchased in Jamaica "were a problem with the Cuba embargo." This statement shows that Cruz did know of the embargo and its prohibitions. But the statement also show[s] that Cruz did not know that his action violated the law.

The government has the Freedom's Caribbean article, which Cruz referred to. The discussions in the article may show that Cruz knew that certain transactions may be illegal. Again, however, it may also show that Cruz did not know his specific actions were illegal, since the article discussed many exceptions, including that certain recreational trips and expenses may not be illegal.

The government also has Cruz's conflicting statements about where be obtained the Cuban items. Cruz fist stated that he bought them in Jamaica, then said he got them as gifts. These may be used to show that Cruz was lying to the Customs Agent and/or trying to actively conceal Cuban connections, which may support in inference that he knew what he was doing was wrong.

The government has Cruz's statement that there is [sic] nothing to declare before items were found. This may be inferred as a lie. But Cruz may have been correct in estimating them to be within the $400 exemption, and an oral declaration was given.

The government did not retain Cruz's passport, but the Customs Agent noted that there was no indication of traveling to Cuba. This may be the basis for an inference that Cruz was trying to cover up his Cuban connections. (Macko.) But, the inference was created in Macko because the defendant in the case traveled extensively and did not conceal his other journeys. Here, the government does not have any evidence of the extent of Cruz's travel plans and experience.

Overall, the government has evidence to suggest that Cruz knew generally of the embargo, but not evidence that he specifically knew that his particular actions were illegal and breaching a known legal duty.

II.   The Gov't. Use of the 515.421 Presumption

        A.   The Presumption

243

Under §515.421 of TWEA, Cruz is presumed to have engaged in travel-related transactions prohibited by Section 515.201 if he has traveled to Cuba. Since Cruz admitted to being in Cuba to the Customs Agent, 515.421 puts the burden on Cruz to rebut the presumption.

B.   Constitutionality of the Presumption

The government may <u>not</u> constitutionally use the presumption at any criminal trial against Cruz.

In <u>Sandstrom</u>, the U.S. Supreme Court held that the government may not use a presumption to shift the burden of proof onto a criminal defendant when the presumption involves an element of the crime charged. Such a presumption would shift the burden of persuasion onto the defendant regarding an element of crime, contrary to the constitution.

As the court pointed out in <u>In re Winship</u>, the due process clause of the 5th and 14th Amendment[s] requires the government prosecution to prove "beyond a reasonable doubt of every fact necessary to constitute the crime" charged.

Here, "prohibited transaction" is an element of a criminal violation of §515.201. The 515.421 presumption alleviates the government of proving such a transaction by presuming that Cruz engaged in them by virtue of his presence in Cuba. Since the transaction is an element of the crime charged, the government's use of the presumption would violate the constitution.

The government may argue that presumptions requiring defendant to carry the burden of proof was permitted by the 5th Circuit in <u>Bustos</u>. <u>Bustos</u> is not applicable here, however, because <u>Bustos</u> involved a deportation hearing, which the court characterized as a "purely civil proceeding." The <u>Bustos</u> court specifically pointed out that criminal defendants are entitled to more procedural safeguards.

Thus, although the government my employ the presumption against Cruz at a civil proceeding under §515.201, the government cannot use the presumption at any <u>criminal</u> trial against Cruz.

MEMO

Re: U.S. v. Cruz – Ethical Considerations

Per your request, below are discussions of the ethical considerations implicated as you draft a response letter on Cruz's behalf. I discussed the general ethical rules on disclosure first, then explain[ed] my reasoning as to why particular pieces of information requested by OFAC should or should not be disclosed.

I.   Your Duties

A.   To Mr. Cruz

First, the Columbia Rules of Professional Conduct requires you to preserve client confidences.

Here, the information Cruz gave you during the interview was all candidly shared in the course of your attorney-client relationship. Thus, you must preserve the confidentiality.

The only applicable exception is when disclosure is necessary to avoid assisting a contemporaneous or future criminal act that is likely to result in imminent death or substantial bodily harm.

Here, there is clearly no assistance of any crime, and certainly not any that is likely to result in imminent death or bodily harm. This is a routine government inquiry into Cruz's past travel activities. Thus, the exception to confidentiality does not apply, and Cruz's confidence must be strictly preserved.

B.   To OFAC

You also have a duty to be truthful when dealing with another party, such as OFAC, or Cruz's behalf.

You cannot make a false statement affirmatively to OFAC in your letter or other dealings with them. You do not, however, have the affirmative duty to inform them of any relevant facts. But you cannot incorporate or affirm any statements that Cruz has made that you know are false. (Rule 4.1, Comment.)

II. What You Can and Cannot Say

The OFAC letter requests three pieces of information: (1) whether Cruz had a license to travel to Cuba and information regarding any license, (2) how Cruz avoided engaging in travel-related expenses, and (3) details of expense if Cruz was a fully-hosted traveler.

A. Regarding the License

You are not required to, and should not, inform OFAC either [sic] Cruz does or does not have a license.

You are not required to do so because you do not have an affirmative duty to disclose this material fact. As mentioned above, there is no imminent death or harm at risk, so you are not required to disclose.

You should not disclose this information because you obtained it by way of representing Cruz, and you are under a duty to preserve its confidentiality.

Also, Cruz has not made any false statements in this regard that can be affirmed by your silence. He said nothing when asked about a license by the Customs Agent.

Lastly, you are not required to disclose this information, and not doing so would not constitute a frivolous controversy because, as a criminal defense representative, you may defend Cruz by requiring the government to prove the elements of its case.

Here, having a license takes any transaction out of the "prohibited" category. Thus, it is up to the government to prove that Cruz is _not_ licensed.

Travel-Related Expenses

You are not required and should not disclose what Cruz told you concerning his travel expenses.

Cruz has told you that he spent $2,000 on his trip to Cuba, and that he bought cigars and rum. As discussed above, you must preserve his confidentiality, because the exception does not apply here.

Cruz told the Customs Agent that he did not pay for the items. Although that was false, you are not required to disclose what you know, and cannot disclose and breach your duty of confidentiality.

You cannot, however, in any way affirm Cruz's false statement by referring to it or incorporating it into your letter, because you may be adopting his misrepresentation.

Thus, the best thing to do is to decline to answer. As noted above, you are within your professional obligations to require that the government prove this element of the crime.

C.   Regarding Fully-Hosted Travel

The considerations here are similar to those discussed under licenses.

If Cruz's travel is fully-hosted then transaction would not be "prohibited" as required by the element of the offense. Thus, you are not required to disclose your knowledge that Cruz's trip was in fact NOT fully-hosted, because you do not have a duty to affirmatively inform OFAC of this fact, and because you are permitted to require the government to meet its burden of proof.

You should not disclose what you know, that Cruz was not fully-hosted, because your duty to preserve his confidence is not excepted by any threat of death of harm.

In sum, you are ethically required to decline OFAC's request for information because you are obligated to preserve Cruz's confidence, and because you are allowed to require the government to meet its burden of proof, as long as you don't give false statements or affirm any that Cruz has made.

California
Bar
Examination

Performance Test B
INSTRUCTIONS AND FILE

MARRIAGE OF EIFFEL

MARRIAGE OF EIFFEL

INSTRUCTIONS

1. You will have three hours to complete this session of the examination. This performance test is designed to evaluate your ability to handle a select number of legal authorities in the context of a factual problem involving a client.

2. The problem is set in the fictional State of Columbia, one of the United States.

3. You will have two sets of materials with which to work: a **File** and a **Library**.

4. The **File** contains factual materials about your case. The first document is a memorandum containing the instructions for the tasks you are to complete.

5. The **Library** contains the legal authorities needed to complete the tasks. The case reports may be real, modified, or written solely for the purpose of this performance test. If the cases appear familiar to you, do not assume that they are precisely the same as you have read before. Read them thoroughly, as if all were new to you. You should assume that cases were decided in the jurisdictions and on the dates shown. In citing from the **Library** you may use abbreviations and omit page citations.

6. Your response must be written in the answer book provided. You should concentrate on the materials provided, but you should also bring to bear on the problem your general knowledge of the law. What you have learned in law school and elsewhere provides the general background for analyzing the problem; the **File** and **Library** provide the specific materials with which you must work.

7. Although there are no restrictions on how you apportion your time, you should probably allocate at least 90 minutes to reading and organizing before you begin writing your response.

8. Your response will be graded on its compliance to instructions and on its content, thoroughness, and organization. Grading of the two tasks will be weighted as follows:

Task A	----	30%
Task B	----	70%

i

LAW OFFICES OF
ALEJANDRO RUZ AND RENA TISHMAN
THE CANYONS, COLUMBIA

MEMORANDUM

To: Applicant

From: Rena Tishman

Re: **Marriage of Eiffel**

Date: February 24, 2005

I want you to help me prepare Appellant's Opening Brief for our client, Angela Eiffel, nee Killian. The appeal is from an order following a trial on the sole issue of the enforceability of the Marital Settlement Agreement ("MSA"). Her husband wrote an agreement they both agreed to and signed. Then they had the agreement formalized into a complete MSA, which they also signed. The lawyer who prepared the MSA for them had previously represented each of them in other, unrelated matters. The trial court, despite finding that both the wife and husband had knowingly and voluntarily entered into the MSA, invalidated the agreement on the ground that the attorney drafting it did not make an adequate conflict of interest disclosure.

I have attached the trial court decision and trial transcript. The complete record (including the petition for dissolution of marriage, response, complete MSA, and judgment) is not necessary for your task.

Please draft for my approval _only_ the following two sections of an Appellant's Opening Brief:

    A. A statement of facts.

    B. An argument demonstrating that the trial court erred.

For each section, please follow the guidelines set out in the Office Memorandum on the Drafting of Appellant's Opening Briefs. I shall draft the remaining sections of the brief.

LAW OFFICES OF
ALEJANDRO RUZ AND RENA TISHMAN
THE CANYONS, COLUMBIA

OFFICE MEMORANDUM

To: Associates

From: Rena Tishman

Re: **Drafting of Appellant's Opening Briefs**

All Appellant's Opening Briefs ("AOB") must conform to the following guidelines:

• All AOBs must include the following sections: a table of contents; a table of cases; a summary of argument; a statement of the jurisdictional basis of the appeal; a procedural history; a statement of facts; an argument comprising one or more claims of error; and a conclusion.

• The *statement of facts* must contain the facts that support our client's claims of error and must also take account of the facts that may be used to support the opposition. It must deal with all such facts in a persuasive manner, reasonably and fairly attempting to show the greater importance of the ones that weigh in our client's favor and the lesser importance of the ones that weigh in the opponent's favor. Above all, it must tell a compelling story in narrative form and not merely recapitulate each witness's testimony.

• The *argument* must analyze the applicable law and bring it to bear on the facts in each claim of error, urging that the law and facts support our client's position. It need not attempt to foreclose each and every response that the opponent may put forth in their brief, but it must anticipate their strongest attacks on our client's weakest points, both legal and factual. It must display a subject heading summarizing each claim of error and the outcome that it requires. The subject heading must express the application of the law to the facts, and not a statement of an abstract principle or a bare conclusion. For example, do *not* write: DEFENDANT HAD SUFFICIENT MINIMUM CONTACTS TO ESTABLISH PERSONAL JURISDICTION. *Do* write: A RADIO STATION LOCATED IN THE STATE OF FRANKLIN THAT BROADCASTS INTO THE STATE OF COLUMBIA, RECEIVES REVENUE FROM ADVERTISERS LOCATED IN THE STATE OF COLUMBIA, AND HOLDS ITS ANNUAL MEETING IN THE STATE OF COLUMBIA, HAS SUFFICIENT MINIMUM CONTACTS TO ALLOW COLUMBIA COURTS TO ASSERT PERSONAL JURISDICTION.

IN THE SUPERIOR COURT OF THE STATE OF COLUMBIA

COUNTY OF AVENTURA

4 In re the Marriage of Eiffel

5 ANGELA EIFFEL,

6   Petitioner

7   v.   Case No. 140733

8 PAUL ALEXANDRE EIFFEL,   **Memorandum of Decision**

9   Respondent

10 _____/

11   On July 13, 2002, petitioner Angela Eiffel (Wife) and respondent Paul Alexandre

12 Eiffel (Husband) filed a joint petition for summary dissolution of marriage. The matter

13 proceeded to trial in May, 2003.

14   This Memorandum of Decision shall constitute the Court's findings of fact and

15 conclusions of law:

16   1. Wife (now known as Angela Casey Killian) and Husband were married on

17 September 24, 1994. During the marriage Husband became unemployed, and Wife, who

18 was still working, put Husband through paralegal school.

19   2. In February 2001, Husband was arrested in Aventura County on a no-bail warrant

20 issued by San Joaquin County for Husband's failing to appear in a criminal paternity case.

21 Wife then sought the services of attorney Robert Gant to defend Husband. The very next

22 day, Wife was arrested in Aventura County on a no-bail warrant issued by San Joaquin

23 County for allegedly making criminal threats concerning the San Joaquin County District

24 Attorney handling Husband's case. Wife too was thereafter represented by Mr. Gant. The

25 criminal case against Husband was dismissed following a separate acknowledgement and

26 settlement of the paternity claim. Wife was acquitted in a trial on the criminal threats

27 charge.

28   3. In May and June 2002, Husband and Wife discussed their marital problems and

29 community debts, and Husband agreed to refinance and borrow money against real

30 property in his name in Texas to pay community debts and to fund the separation of the

1 parties. Whether the Texas property is characterized as community or separate property,
2 Husband agreed to donate the loan proceeds from refinancing to liquidate community
3 debts.

4   4. By July, 2002, Husband and Wife had agreed to separate. As part of the
5 separation they agreed on a division of property and payments of debts.

6   5. Husband and Wife contacted attorney Robert Gant about drafting a Marital
7 Settlement Agreement ("MSA") for them. Mr. Gant reluctantly agreed.

8   6. Husband and Wife each agreed to and signed an agreement on July 19, 2002.
9 The agreement is attached as Exhibit A. Husband drafted and freely executed the July 19,
10 2002 agreement. Husband faxed Exhibit A to Mr. Gant after it was signed by Husband and
11 Wife.

12   7. Based upon this fax and his conversations with Husband and Wife, Mr. Gant
13 prepared an eleven-page MSA. The majority of the MSA contained the standard provisions
14 of a marital settlement agreement, and these provisions are not in dispute.

15   8. The MSA contained the agreements set forth in Exhibit A, and an additional
16 provision that Husband would repay the entire loan on the Texas property. Husband
17 agreed with all of the provisions.

18   9. Prior to execution of the MSA, Mr. Gant had Husband and Wife execute a written
19 waiver of conflict. That written conflict waiver statement read:

20   "This will confirm that Angela Eiffel and Paul Alexandre Eiffel have been advised that
21   Robert Gant's mere typing of an agreement made between the parties may be a
22   potential conflict of interest, despite the fact that he was not in an advisory capacity,
23   nor involved in the negotiation of the agreement. Each party knowingly waives any
24   potential conflict of interest in the preparation of the parties' agreement. In addition,
25   each party has been advised to seek independent counsel and advice with respect
26   to this statement and the agreement."

27   10. Pursuant to the terms of the MSA, Wife assumed and paid a substantial amount
28 of community debt, including the attorney fees she owed to Mr. Gant. Husband made one
29 spousal support payment, but failed to make further payments. Wife then petitioned this
30 Court for enforcement of the Marital Settlement Agreement.

1   11. The Court finds the MSA was in fact the free and voluntary agreement of the

2   parties as of the date it was made, and specifically rejects the claim that Husband was

3   forced to consent to its terms as a result of fraud, duress, or undue influence.

4   12. The Court also concludes that Mr. Gant's testimony on the admonitions,

5   warnings, and conflicts disclosures he made to the parties was clear, credible and

6   convincing, and specifically concurs in Mr. Gant's observation that there was nothing to

7   suggest that the MSA was anything other than what the parties freely and genuinely

8   "wanted" and consented to at the time it was signed. The Court concludes that Mr. Gant

9   was not motivated to obtain payment of the attorney fees that were due him. He was not

10 trying to "protect himself" nor guilty of "overreaching," as Husband now contends.

11 13. Notwithstanding the above findings, the Court also finds that the MSA is subject

12 to attack and is not enforceable because the conflict disclosures made by Mr. Gant were

13 inadequate to permit his dual representation of the parties under the circumstances. Under

14 *Klemm v. Superior Court* (Columbia Court of Appeal, 1977), he could proceed with dual

15 representation only after making full disclosure of all facts and circumstances necessary

16 to enable both parties to make a fully informed decision regarding such representation.

17 The evidence in this case regarding disclosure was inadequate to meet this standard. As

18 a result, under the Court's equitable powers, the agreement is not enforceable.

19 14. The Court is persuaded that the weight of authority in Columbia is that a lawyer

20 may represent both parties only in exceptional circumstances. [*Marriage of Vandenburgh*

21 (Columbia Court of Appeal, 1993); *Klemm v. Superior Court*, supra.] Even when a party

22 waives separate representation, confusion can arise and the party may think that he or she

23 is getting legal representation. The theory that a lawyer can serve both parties and be a

24 mere "scrivener" does not absolve the lawyer should a dispute arise. At the very least such

25 agreements are subject to heightened scrutiny. (*Marriage of Vandenburgh*, supra.) As

26 experts on ethics and family law have concluded, "most lawyers *refuse* dual representation

27 in all cases. Despite the spouses' assurances they are in agreement on all issues, all

28 marital cases involve a potential conflict of interests." [*Klemm v. Superior Court*, supra,

29 quoting from Elrond and Elrond, "Common Ethical Problems In Family Law Practice," 82

30 *Col. State L. J.* (1975) (emphasis original).]

1   15. The Court emphasizes that the only issue before this Court is the enforceability

2 of the September, 2002, MSA.

3

4 Dated: July 21, 2003._____ *Kevin J. Burke*_____

5   Kevin J. Burke

6   Judge of the Superior Court

7

8

9

10

11

12

13

14

15

16

17

18

19

20

21

22

23

24

25

26

27

28

29

EXHIBIT A

Angela and I agree to the following terms:

1) Until a new lease is signed Angie will receive from me by the 3rd of each month $750.

2) After the new lease is signed Angie will receive 50% of the new lease income after the money for the loan is taken into account. This money will be paid directly by Northland Corporation to Angie.

3) Should the new lease account for less than $2,000 a month for Angie, I agree to make up the difference.

4) Angie will receive 50% of the yearly percentage income given by Northland for the lease.

5) This agreement will be in effect for a maximum of five years or until Angie has regained her feet to include a stable job.

6) Angie will be responsible for $15,000 in legal fees for her defense and I will be responsible for those fees remaining that were incurred in my paternity case.

7) Angie will receive a copy of the new lease after it is signed.

I hereby agree to the above: I hereby agree to the above:

_Angela Eiffel_____   _Paul Alexandre Eiffel_____
Angela Eiffel   Paul Alexandre Eiffel

July 19, 2002

Date

July 19, 2002

Date

BY THE COURT: Let's begin. First, let me review the state of the record. In the Marriage of Eiffel, the essential facts of the marriage, separation, and jurisdiction have been admitted. This trial is solely on the issue of the validity and enforceability of a Marital Settlement Agreement executed by the parties. Its authenticity is also admitted, and it is already in the record. You may proceed, Ms. Tishman. The witness, Mrs. Eiffel, has been sworn.

BY THE WITNESS: Excuse me, your honor, I don't use that name anymore. My name is Angela Casey Killian.

BY PETITIONER'S COUNSEL, RENA TISHMAN:

Q: Thank you for the correction, Ms. Killian. You are married to Paul Alexandre Eiffel?

A: Yes. We were married on September 24, 1994.

Q: Where do you live?

A: Here in The Aspens. At the Creek Side Apartments, number C 16.

Q: Ms. Killian, please look at the document that the clerk has marked as Exhibit A. Do you recognize the document?

A: Yes. It is the settlement agreement that Paul wrote. My husband, Paul Eiffel.

Q: Is that your signature on the document?

A: Yes, and that of Paul, too.

Q: I assume that you are familiar with his signature. Is that Paul Eiffel's signature under the statement "I hereby agree to the above?"

A: I saw him sign it. The signature is Paul's.

PETITIONER'S COUNSEL, MS. TISHMAN: Move to admit as Exhibit A.

THE COURT: Admitted as Petitioner's Exhibit A.

Q: Would you please describe the document?

A: It is the agreement Paul and I made when we split up. Each of us was to take care of our bills. Paul got to keep his property in Texas but I was to get at least $2000 a month for five years, but Paul only made the first payment, and he's still getting the profits.

1	**Q:**	To put this in context, Ms. Killian, this one-page agreement that you and Paul signed
2		is the one that then was used by the lawyer that represented you and Mr. Eiffel to
3		write the much longer marital settlement agreement, correct?
4		**BY RESPONDENT'S COUNSEL, RICHARD HENKE:** Objection. The question assumes
5		that the lawyer who drafted it was representing Mr. Eiffel.
6		**THE COURT:** I'll allow it. It's preliminary, and we know that whether and by whom Mr.
7		Eiffel was represented is the matter now at issue.
8	**A:**	Yes, it was the basis of the legal settlement agreement.
9	**Q:**	Let's look at each paragraph. Now, number 1 says "Until a new lease is signed
10		Angie will receive from me by the 3rd of each month $750." What is the lease?
11	**A:**	Before we got married, Paul inherited a dry cleaning business in Houston. When
12		we married, he moved here, and since then he's rented the space out, when he
13		could. Mostly it has been vacant, but a convenience store was going to rent it, and
14		that's why we put in that my share was 50%.
15	**Q:**	How much was the new rental income to be?
16	**A:**	They were negotiating the exact amount, but it was supposed to be between $4,000
17		or $5,000 a month, plus another payment at the end of the year, a percentage of the
18		profits on the sales. I was to get one-half, and that was to be at least $2,000 a
19		month and one-half of the annual profits.
20	**Q:**	Had both you and Paul been making the mortgage payments on the building?
21	**A:**	At first Paul did since it was in his name. But since Paul wasn't working most of the
22		time, I made the payments. For the last 8 years at least.
23	**Q:**	How much was the mortgage on the Texas building?
24	**A:**	It was $460.90 each month. When we agreed to separate and needed money to
25		pay off our bills, Paul refinanced, and so the monthly loan payment was more. I
26		never made those payments, since we were separated.
27	**Q:**	Before separation did you handle most of the money?
28	**A:**	Yes, although we each had our own checking accounts and credit cards. Paul's
29		account was used mostly for the Texas property, paying taxes and repairs, and
30		depositing rent checks, but as I said, since for many years there was no income, I

1		paid the mortgage from my account. I paid both credit cards also. Paul and I had
2		serious problems, but we did not fight about money.
3	**Q:**	Was the division at the time of your separation amicable?
4	**A:**	Well, we both saw divorce was coming, and spent time the last couple of months
5		together working out how we'd split things, and mainly get out of debt. We owed our
6		lawyer Mr. Gant $21,000. And together we owed over $20,000 on our credit cards.
7		So we decided that, since renting the Texas building looked very likely and the
8		mortgage was paid down, that Paul would refinance the mortgage and we'd try to
9		pull out about $50,000, so that each of us could start off fresh.
10	**Q:**	Is that roughly what you did?
11	**A:**	Yes. We paid off Mr. Gant and the credit cards. Paul got $5000 for first and last
12		months' rent on a new place and to buy some new furniture. And we split the stuff
13		we'd accumulated in 10 years.
14	**Q:**	You were able to agree on personal possessions as well?
15	**A:**	It wasn't that much. Each of us had our own car, Paul's was almost new. Our
16		furniture was old, and none of it expensive or valuable any more. Paul collected
17		avant garde art, and he insisted on keeping all of it, even the paintings that he
18		bought and had given me as gifts. I didn't like that, and objected at first, but in the
19		end all I wanted was to be free. I never liked them anyway. I took them down the
20		day Paul moved out, even before he picked them up.
21	**Q:**	The cars and art. How were they bought or paid for?
22	**A:**	With our -- my account. Since Paul wasn't working and the Texas building wasn't
23		rented, my salary was all our income. I guess we did sometimes argue whenever
24		Paul found a painting he just had to have.
25	**Q:**	So, everything in the agreement was done, except what Paul was to pay you?
26	**A:**	Exactly. I got $750 once. I know that the building is rented, but I haven't gotten any
27		of my share, or even seen the lease, as Paul promised. He's kept it all.
28	**Q:**	How did this typed agreement, Exhibit A, come about?
29	**A:**	In about May or June of last year, when we were splitting up, dividing the property
30		and all that, Paul said we needed a legal agreement. He had studied to be a

1		paralegal, but never really did it. We said we'd go see our lawyer Mr. Gant and
2		have it drawn up for us. So, we made an appointment. When he heard that we
3		were there to get divorced and for him to help us, he said no, actually he said, "No
4		way."
5	**Q:**	What was the reason?
6	**A:**	He said a lawyer couldn't represent both of us, that it would be a conflict, a conflict
7		of interests. In fact, he stated each of us had to get our own lawyer. Two new
8		lawyers, because Mr. Gant would not even help one of us. We hadn't counted on
9		hiring any more lawyers. Paul really argued with Mr. Gant. Telling him that we had
10		agreed on everything. That we had no disputes. That it was all done.
11	**Q:**	Did you agree, or say that to Mr. Gant?
12	**A:**	Yes. We had agreed on everything, and divided things up. Paul had rented a place,
13		and the bank in Texas was about to send us the money to pay everything off. Paul
14		finally persuaded Mr. Gant that he could write up our agreement and that Mr. Gant
15		was just to make it a legal agreement. We were doing the divorce ourselves and
16		Paul had already typed out the forms and filed them.
17	**Q:**	Mr. Gant did agree to draft the settlement agreement?
18	**A:**	Finally. But you could tell he did not want to. He insisted that we write out and sign
19		a document of all our agreements, and send him only that. No other
20		communications, he said. He said that he'd only be a draftsman for us. That was
21		the word he used.
22	**Q:**	Did you and Paul do as Mr. Gant said?
23	**A:**	Yes, we met at Paul's new place, and sat at his computer, and Paul typed out the
24		agreement, the one you call Exhibit A. He printed it. We each signed it, and faxed
25		it to Mr. Gant.
26	**Q:**	You agreed with and signed the agreement?
27	**A:**	Yes, although Mr. Gant called me a day or two later to ask about who was going to
28		pay off the mortgage. He said that it should be in there as well. Of course, I agreed
29		that it belonged there. A couple of weeks later his office called and said that we
30		should come in to sign the legal agreement. I guess they called Paul too, and we

1		met there to go over the legal documents. We signed them, and I thought that it
2		was done until Paul didn't pay.
3	**Q:**	Did you read the documents at Mr. Gant's office?
4	**A:**	Yes. He made us read every word, and explained it all. I realized that it was much
5		more complicated than I'd thought. I had had my doubts that we needed a legal
6		document, perhaps that Paul was just saying that because he liked playing lawyer,
7		but Mr. Gant had included provisions that belonged there.
8	**Q**	Did Mr. Gant actually say that for him to represent you both was a conflict of
9		interests?
10	**A:**	Yes, he was extremely clear about that, telling us again and again that he was not
11		advising us on how to divide our assets or how much support I should get. He even
12		had us read and sign another document saying that he had told us that and that it
13		was okay with us.
14	**Q:**	I was coming to that. Mr. Gant also had you sign a written waiver of conflict?
15	**A:**	We had to read that too. Read each paragraph. Mr. Gant would ask if we had
16		questions. And even though we didn't, he would explain what it meant.
17	**Q:**	Did Mr. Gant go through the same steps on the marital settlement agreement?
18	**A:**	Yes. It took a long time. Mr. Gant kept asking us if he had written down what we
19		had agreed to. Was it everything? Was there anything else we wanted in it?
20	**Q:**	When you signed the waiver and the marital settlement agreement did you believe
21		that you fully understood what you were doing?
22	**A:**	Yes. Although I thought I understood before, Mr. Gant then made sure.
23	**Q:**	In sum, Ms. Killian, did you think that the agreement was fair?
24	**A:**	Yes. It would have allowed each of us a fresh start. Paul had gotten training and
25		education, even though it was his choice not to take advantage of it. Now it was my
26		turn to improve my situation. Paul knew that it was fair.
27	**Q:**	You stated that you understood that Mr. Gant was not giving you legal advice, but
28		now you have a lawyer, and have been given legal advice about the agreement.
29		Do you believe that the agreement was fair?
30	**A:**	Yes I do.

1   **Q:**   No further questions.

2   **RESPONDENT'S COUNSEL, MR. HENKE:**

3   **Q:**   Ms. Killian, Mr. Gant was your lawyer? He had defended you in a serious criminal

4   case just last year?

5   **A:**   Yes, he did, and I was acquitted.

6   **Q:**   You were charged with threatening the life of a public official here in Columbia?

7   **PETITIONER'S COUNSEL, MS. TISHMAN:** That's irrelevant. Mr. Gant represented both

8   Mr. and Mrs. Eiffel regarding the disputes arising from Mr. Eiffel's adultery and his

9   paternity case. Both of these people were in debt because of his irresponsibility.

10 **THE COURT:** This is unnecessary. You have stipulated in chambers that Mr. Gant had

11   represented both parties. Mr. Eiffel first, when he was charged in a criminal

12   paternity case, and perhaps in an overly aggressive defense of her husband, Mrs.

13   Eiffel -- Ms. Killian -- was charged, tried and acquitted of threats against the District

14   Attorney of San Joaquin County.   Let's have nothing further on either of these

15   matters.

16 **Q:**   Thank you, Your Honor. Ms. Killian, as I understand your present situation, you still

17   work, that is, you have the same job as before, you aren't making payments on huge

18   credit card debt, and you aren't making mortgage payments. Your rent is the same.

19   Aren't you better off, financially, than you were before?

20 **A:**   I am supporting myself, as I was before, but I haven't been able to get more training

21   or education, as Paul did.

22

23   **TESTIMONY OF ROBERT GANT**

24

25 **PETITIONER'S COUNSEL, MS. TISHMAN:** Mr. Gant, you are here pursuant to a

26 subpoena, correct?

27 **A:**   Yes. I am not here voluntarily to testify for or against Angela or Paul. They are both

28   my clients.

29 **Q:**   Would it be fair to say that based on your past representation, you had a very good

30   understanding of their situation, their financial situation?

1	**A:**	Yes. At least up until their separation. I had to defend Paul in the paternity case,
2		and negotiate a settlement based on what he could afford. I represented Angela in
3		a several day trial, so I think I knew her pretty well too.
4	**Q:**	What was your reaction when they came to see you to draft a marital settlement
5		agreement?
6	**A:**	I refused to do it, and advised them in the strongest manner I could that they each
7		needed to have another lawyer. I tried my best to persuade them that property
8		divisions could be complicated, and that each of them should have a lawyer to
9		advise them on their rights. They were insistent, however.
10	**Q:**	Would you say that either one of them was more interested in having one lawyer,
11		or conversely was one more reluctant to follow your advice?
12	**A:**	No, not at all. They were both alternately arguing with me. One would say they
13		couldn't afford it. The other would say that both of them trusted me. Finally, Paul
14		said he'd write their agreement, and all they wanted was for me to add the so-called
15		"boilerplate" of a MSA, a marital settlement agreement.
16	**Q:**	Did that finally persuade you?
17	**A:**	I concluded that they had talked extensively, even negotiated, and had worked out
18		a settlement that each of them thought was fair and workable. These are two
19		intelligent people. Paul has completed a paralegal program. No one takes
20		advantage of him. Paul says it is because his heritage makes him wary. Angela is
21		a competent public administrator in the city planning office. The San Joaquin
22		County DA learned when he tried to browbeat her into turning against Paul that no
23		one walks over Angela. I was persuaded that they really understood that I was not
24		going to give them advice and would do no more than translate their agreements
25		into a marital settlement agreement. When I said that I would not help one of them
26		against the other, they got it. I have no doubt of that, and subsequent events
27		showed that they understood it.
28	**Q:**	How so?
29	**A:**	Well, after I told them that if they would write up and agree upon their complete
30		agreement, I'd have it typed into a MSA, Paul faxed the agreement over. When I

1		went to dictate the terms into a standard MSA form, I noted that they had put in
2		language about deducting the mortgage from the rent, but they hadn't said who
3		would pay the mortgage. I knew from talking to them that it was to be Paul, but
4		rather than adding it, I called each and asked whether they wanted it in the
5		agreement. Angela said yes. Paul did likewise, but then he asked me, "Is this
6		something I have to do?" I told him that I would not say, and if he had any question
7		about it, he must see a lawyer. He laughed and said that he knew I'd say that and
8		he was just testing me.
9	**Q:**	Angela and Paul thereafter returned to review and sign the agreement?
10	**A:**	In September, 2002, the MSA was done, and I called them to come in.
11	**Q:**	You also had prepared a waiver, a written statement that there was a waiver of any
12		potential conflict of interests?
13	**A:**	Yes, I dictated it myself. I didn't want legalese. Simple, direct, plain English. Then,
14		I had them read it. I read each of the two paragraphs aloud, and explained what
15		they meant, such as, my just being a drafter, and that I wasn't acting in an advisory
16		capacity, and that my only advice was to get another lawyer. I recall saying, if I
17		were in their shoes, I would not do it.
18	**Q:**	But they did?
19	**A:**	Yes, they both signed, and then we moved on to the MSA, and, once again, they
20		read each paragraph, and I'd explain what it meant. When I thought they
21		understood, we'd move on to the next provision. We were there for two hours.
22	**Q:**	At any time, in either of your meetings or conversations, did you think that either
23		Angela or Paul was under duress or pressure to go along with the agreement?
24	**A:**	Never. This agreement was voluntary, something each genuinely wanted.
25	**Q:**	At any time, did you think that either had been misled or tricked?
26	**A:**	No, never. They knew each other, knew what they were doing.
27	**Q:**	Thank you. Nothing further.

28 **RESPONDENT'S COUNSEL, MR. HENKE:**

29	**Q:**	Mr. Gant, you never gave Mr. Eiffel a written disclosure of each type of conflict that
30		could arise?

1	**A:**	Do you mean in addition to the one that both Paul and Angela signed?
2	**Q:**	Well, I'd say that document is a waiver of your conflict of interests, not a disclosure
3		of adverse consequences. For example, did you provide Mr. Eiffel a written
4		statement of each area of potential conflict involved in dividing all of their community
5		property and paying community obligations?
6	**A:**	No. That would be quite a job, and I can't imagine how you would do it without
7		seeming to be arguing against what they had agreed to.
8	**Q:**	Ethical obligations can be like that. Specifically did you provide a written statement
9		stating that an area of potential conflict was whether Ms. Killian was entitled to
10		spousal support, or for how long and in what amount?
11	**A:**	No.
12	**Q:**	For all she knew, she might have been entitled to more, without knowing it?
13	**A:**	Yes. With her own lawyer, as I urged, she could have found out.
14	**Q:**	Did you notify Mr. Eiffel, orally or in writing, that his separate property in Texas was
15		an area of potential conflict?
16	**A:**	No.
17	**Q:**	Thus, Mr. Eiffel agreed to put his separate property into the agreement without any
18		disclosure that he might have a right to retain the proceeds of this property?
19	**A:**	He knew that the property was in his name, and that I explicitly refused to give him
20		advice on it. I neither urged nor opposed any provision. I stayed completely away
21		from the pros and cons of their agreements.
22	**Q:**	Would you agree that telling either of them the pros and cons might have persuaded
23		one of them to withdraw?
24	**A:**	That is possible.
25	**Q:**	And you didn't want to talk either of them into withdrawing?
26	**A:**	That was not my job. The only thing I tried to talk them into was obtaining separate
27		independent advice. Then, they could decide for themselves.
28	**Q:**	If one of them withdrew, your fee of over $20,000 might not be paid, correct?

1 **A:** No, my payment was in no way dependent on the agreement. I had complete
2 confidence that both Angela and Paul were going to pay the amount due me for past
3 services.

4 **Q:** But, it is true that you were reluctant to undertake this dual representation, that you
5 conditioned your representation on their signing a document absolving you of
6 responsibility, that you devoted considerable time to the task, and I understand
7 charged neither party a fee. You did all this without any thought that it might be the
8 only way to collect the $20,000 that they owed you?

9 **A:** That's what I did.

10 **Q:** Let me ask another specific question. Did you disclose to either party that by
11 choosing to have one lawyer, they had given up the attorney-client privilege, and
12 in any future dispute, such as this one, nothing they said was privileged and
13 confidential?

14 **A:** No.

15 **Q:** Mr. Gant, it appears that the only disclosure you made was to protect yourself with
16 a waiver, with nothing to protect Mr. Eiffel or Ms. Killian.

17 **A:** I do not agree with that. I would not have helped them if I had not thought that
18 basically what they had agreed to was fair to each of them.

19 **Q:** Thank you, Mr. Gant. Will there be redirect or anything further, Ms. Tishman? No?
20 Then, Respondent calls Mr. Paul Alexandre Eiffel.

21

22 **TESTIMONY OF RESPONDENT PAUL ALEXANDRE EIFFEL**

23

24 **RESPONDENT'S COUNSEL, MR. HENKE:**

25 **Q:** Mr. Eiffel, before you and your wife drew up the one-page document identified as
26 Exhibit A had either of you consulted a lawyer other than Mr. Gant?

27 **A:** No, we did that strictly on our own.

28 **Q:** Before signing the MSA in Mr. Gant's office did you consult with any other lawyer?

29 **A:** Just Mr. Gant.

1	**Q:**	You had agreed with Ms. Killian to refinance, borrowing about another $50,000,
2		secured by the property in Texas, that the loan proceeds would be used to pay off
3		family debts, including the $15,000 she owed Mr. Gant for her own criminal defense,
4		and then that you alone would be responsible to pay back the entire loan. Is that
5		correct?
6	**A:**	Yes. When you put it that way, it sounds foolish, but that is what I did.
7	**Q:**	You further agreed that even though Ms. Killian was not going to help pay the
8		mortgage on the building, she would get one-half of the income and profits?
9	**A:**	Yes. That too.
10	**Q:**	Before making these agreements with respect to the loan proceeds, repayment or
11		income, did you obtain any advice from a lawyer?
12	**A:**	No, none.
13	**Q:**	What were you thinking?
14	**A:**	As I said, I thought that we had to do something. We owed Mr. Gant $21,000 and
15		another $20,000 on two credit cards. I thought that there was no other way. I was
16		under immense pressure to come up with a solution. I thought I had no choice. It
17		never occurred to me that the property might be just mine.
18	**Q:**	If someone had told you that you might have the right to retain the proceeds of the
19		Texas property, that is, the loan proceeds and income, would you have made the
20		same agreement?
21	**A:**	I doubt it. Certainly, I would first have wanted to know if that was correct before
22		making a legally binding agreement.
23	**Q:**	Did you try to get help from Mr. Gant on your rights with regard to the Texas
24		property?
25	**A:**	Yes. After that first time we saw him, he called to ask whether he should put into the
26		MSA that I was going to pay off the entire mortgage myself, and I asked him
27		whether I had to do it. He got upset, and told me there was a huge potential conflict
28		of interests and that he wanted to remain as neutral as possible.

1	**Q:**	So, knowing that you were unsure about whether you were obligated to share the
2		loan proceeds but be saddled with all the debt, Mr. Gant went ahead and wrote the
3		MSA to say exactly that?
4	**A:**	Yes. He went ahead and wrote it that way.
5	**Q:**	I think that should be enough. Nothing further.
6		**PETITIONER'S COUNSEL, MS. TISHMAN:**
7	**Q:**	Good afternoon, Mr. Eiffel. As I understand it, you refinanced the mortgage on the
8		Texas property through a bank in Texas, and thereby obtained cash?
9	**A:**	Yes, after fees, we received around $46,000.
10	**Q:**	What did you do with the money?
11	**A:**	I turned it over to Angela. She paid our bills.
12	**Q:**	So, you agreed that the money would be used to pay the family debts?
13	**A:**	Yes, and, well, the money couldn't go into my checking account because there was
14		a court order garnishing the funds in my account for child support arrears.
15	**Q:**	Hadn't you and Angela agreed many years ago that all family income would go into
16		Angela's bank account?
17	**A:**	Yes, we thought that would be the best way to manage our affairs.
18	**Q:**	You and Angela agreed that she would receive at least $2,000 a month for five
19		years once the building was leased?
20	**A:**	Yes, that is what the agreement said.
21	**Q:**	And she was to get that amount even if the 50% of the net on the lease did not add
22		up to $2,000, correct?
23	**A:**	Yes, that too was in the agreement.
24	**Q:**	The building is leased.
25	**A:**	Yes.
26	**Q:**	How much are you receiving a month from Northland?
27	**A:**	I don't receive direct payment. The rent goes to the Texas bank for the mortgage,
28		and the balance goes into an account I set up in Texas. My net has been $4,400
29		a month.
30	**Q:**	And you have paid none of that to Angela, right?

1   **A:**   No. I've been advised that those proceeds are my property.

2   **Q:**   Mr. Eiffel, when you wrote and signed the one-page agreement, Exhibit A, you

3   agreed with everything in it, correct?

4   **A:**   Yes, at that time.

5   **Q:**   And when you signed the MSA, you agreed with everything in it?

6   **A:**   Yes, as I said, based on what I knew, I went along with it.

7   **Q:**   No more questions.

8

9

10

11

12

13

14

15

16

17

18

19

20

21

22

23

24

25

26

THURSDAY AFTERNOON
FEBRUARY 24, 2005

California
Bar
Examination

Performance Test B
LIBRARY

MARRIAGE OF EIFFEL

LIBRARY

Rule 3-310. Avoiding the Representation of Adverse Interests

(A) For purposes of this rule:

(1) "Disclosure" means informing the client or former client of the relevant circumstances and of the actual and reasonably foreseeable adverse consequences to the client or former client;

(2) "Informed written consent" means the client's or former client's written agreement to the representation following written disclosure.

*　*　*　*　*

(C) A member shall not, without the informed written consent of each client:

(1) Accept representation of more than one client in a matter in which the interests of the clients potentially conflict; or

(2) Accept or continue representation of more than one client in a matter in which the interests of the clients actually conflict; or

(3) Represent a client in a matter and at the same time in a separate matter accept as a client a person or entity whose interest in the first matter is adverse to the client in the first matter.

*　*　*　*　*

Discussion:

Rule 3-310 is not intended to prohibit a member from representing parties having antagonistic positions on the same legal question that has arisen in different cases, unless representation of either client would be adversely affected.

Some tasks commonly performed by lawyers require no distinctly legal skill. Some courts in an earlier era determined that the lawyer was then a mere "scrivener" and that communications relating to such tasks were not privileged. The older decisions reflected a culture in which many clients were illiterate and lawyers were employed because they could read and write, rather than employed because of their legal skills or knowledge. (See *Blevin v. Mayfield*) [Columbia Court of Appeal, 1961], where the court upheld the deed an attorney had drafted, because "the agreement had already been reached between the two parties and therefore the only service performed [by the attorney] was that of a scrivener.")

However, in contemporary practice it will be unusual for a lawyer to prepare a document without communication with the client to determine, at a minimum, the client's objectives. Except in unusual circumstances clearly indicating otherwise, no distinction under this Section should be drawn between situations where the lawyer performs perfunctory services and those involving greater complexity or moment.

Subsection (C)(1) has its origins in the case law beginning with *Lessing v. Gibbons*, (Columbia Court of Appeal, 1935). That court held that it was proper for one lawyer to negotiate a contract for two parties, despite potential conflicts, since the parties retained one lawyer with the goal of working out a mutually satisfactory agreement. In *Lessing*, the court found that the attorney developed an attorney-client relationship with both parties. Since that time, many courts have upheld the principle of one lawyer representing multiple parties in transactional settings.

Subparagraphs (C)(1) and (C)(2) are intended to apply to all types of legal employment, including the concurrent representation of multiple parties in litigation or in a single transaction or in some other common enterprise or legal relationship. Examples of the latter include the formation of a partnership for several partners or a corporation for several shareholders, the preparation of an antenuptial agreement, or joint or reciprocal wills for a husband and wife, or the resolution of an "uncontested" marital dissolution. In such situations, for the sake of convenience or economy, the parties may well prefer to employ a single counsel, but a member must disclose the potential adverse aspects of such multiple representation and must obtain the informed written consent of the clients thereto pursuant to subparagraph (C)(1). Moreover, if the potential adversity should become actual, the member must obtain the further informed written consent of the clients pursuant to subparagraph (C)(2). Subparagraph (C)(3) is intended to apply to representations of clients in both litigation and transactional matters. There are some matters in which the conflicts are such that written consent may not suffice for nondisciplinary purposes. (See *Marriage of Vandenburgh*) [Columbia Court of Appeal, 1993.]

Klemm v. Superior Court

Columbia Court of Appeal (1977)

The ultimate issue herein is to what extent one attorney may represent both husband and wife in a noncontested dissolution proceeding where the written consent of each to such representation has been filed with the court.

Dale Klemm (hereinafter "husband") and Gail Klemm (hereinafter "wife") were married and are the parents of two minor children. They separated after six years of marriage, and the wife filed a petition for dissolution of the marriage *in propria persona*. There was no community property, and neither party owned any substantial separate property. Both parties waived spousal support. The husband was a carpenter with part-time employment.

At the dissolution hearing attorney Catherine Bailey appeared for the wife. Bailey is a friend of the husband and wife and because they could not afford an attorney she was acting without compensation. The attorney had consulted with both the husband and wife and had worked out an oral agreement whereby the custody of the minor children would be joint, that is, each would have the children for a period of two weeks out of each month, and the wife waived child support.

The trial judge granted an interlocutory decree and awarded joint custody in accord with the agreement. However, because the wife was receiving Aid for Families with Dependent Children (AFDC) payments from the county, he referred the matter of child support to the Family Support Division of the County District Attorney's office for investigation and report.

The subsequent report from the Family Support Division recommended that the husband be ordered to pay $25 per month per child (total $50) child support and that this amount be paid to the county as reimbursement for past and present AFDC payments made and being made to the wife. Attorney Bailey, on behalf of the wife, filed a written objection to the recommendation that the husband be required to pay child support.

At the hearing on the report and issue of child support on April 25, 1977, Bailey announced she was appearing on behalf of the husband. She said the parties were "in agreement on this matter, so there is in reality no conflict between them." No written consents to joint representation were filed. On questioning by the court the wife expressed uncertainty as to her position in the litigation. The wife said, "She (Bailey) asked me to come here just as a witness, so I don't feel like I'm taking any action against Dale." The judge pointed out that she (the wife) was still a party. When first asked if she wanted Bailey to continue as her attorney she answered "No." Later she said she would consent to Bailey's being relieved as her counsel. She then said she didn't believe she could act as her own attorney but that she consented to Bailey's representing the husband. After this confusing and conflicting testimony and a request for permission to talk to Bailey about it, the judge ordered, over Bailey's objection, that he would not permit Bailey to appear for either the husband or the wife because of a present conflict of interest and ordered the matter continued for one week.

At the continued hearing on May 2, 1977, Bailey appeared by counsel, who filed written consents to joint representation signed by the husband and wife and requested that Bailey be allowed to appear for the husband and wife (who were present in court). The consents, which were identical in form, stated:

> "I have been advised by my attorney that a potential conflict of interest exists by reason of her advising and representing my ex-spouse as well as myself. I feel this conflict is purely technical and I request Catherine Bailey to represent me."

The court denied the motion, stating,

> "Under our canons of ethics and rules of conduct it would be improper for Ms. Bailey to appear in this proceeding on behalf of the respondent where there is not in the court's opinion a theoretical conflict, but an actual conflict of interest. There is obviously a potential if not actual point in time when the petitioner may not be receiving public assistance, in which case whatever order, if any, is made to her benefit on account of child support in this proceeding would be the amount subject to modification that she would receive on account of child support at least for some

period of time."

The husband and wife have petitioned this court for a writ of mandate to direct the trial court to permit such representation.

Rule 3-310 of the Columbia Rules of Professional Conduct prohibits an attorney from representing conflicting interests, except with the written consent of all parties concerned. The Columbia cases are generally consistent with Rule 3-310 permitting dual representation where there is a full disclosure and informed consent by all the parties, at least insofar as a representation pertains to agreements and negotiations prior to a trial or hearing. For example, in *Lessing v. Gibbons* (Columbia Court of Appeal, 1935), the court approved an attorney acting for both a studio and an actress in concluding negotiations and drawing agreements. The court refers to the common practice of attorneys acting for both parties in drawing and dissolving partnership agreements, for grantors and grantees, sellers and buyers, lessors and lessees, and lenders and borrowers.

Where, however, a fully informed consent is not obtained, the duty of loyalty to different clients renders it impossible for an attorney, consistent with ethics and the fidelity owed to clients, to advise one client as to a disputed claim against the other.

Though an informed consent be obtained, no case we have been able to find sanctions dual representation of conflicting interests if that representation is in conjunction with a trial or hearing where there is an actual, present, existing conflict and the discharge of duty to one client conflicts with the duty to another. As a matter of law a purported consent to dual representation of litigants with adverse interests at a contested hearing would be neither intelligent nor informed. Such representation would be *per se* inconsistent with the adversary position of an attorney in litigation, and common sense dictates that it would be unthinkable to permit an attorney to assume a position at a trial or hearing where he could not advocate the interests of one client without adversely injuring those of the other.

However, if the conflict is merely potential, there being no existing dispute or contest between the parties represented as to any point in litigation, then with full disclosure to and informed consent of both clients there may be dual representation at a hearing or trial.

In our view, the case at bench clearly falls within the latter category. The conflict of interest was strictly potential and not present. The parties had settled their differences by agreement. There was no point of difference to be litigated. The position of each *inter se* was totally consistent throughout the proceedings. The wife did not want child support from the husband, and the husband did not want to pay support for the children. The actual conflict that existed on the issue of support was between the county on the one hand, which argued that support should be ordered, and the husband and wife on the other who consistently maintained the husband should not be ordered to pay support.

While on the face of the matter it may appear foolhardy for the wife to waive child support, other values could very well have been more important to her than such support, such as maintaining a good relationship between the husband and the children and between the husband and herself despite the marital problems thus avoiding the backbiting, acrimony, and ill will. Thus, it could well have been if the wife was forced to choose between AFDC payments to be reimbursed to the county by the husband and no AFDC payments she would have made the latter choice.

Of course, if the wife at some future date should change her mind and seek child support, and if the husband should desire to avoid the payment of such support, Bailey would be disqualified from representing either in a contested hearing on the issue. There would then exist an actual conflict between them, and an attorney's duty to maintain the confidence of each would preclude such representation.

We hold on the facts of this case, wherein the conflict was only potential, that if the written consents were knowing and informed and given after full disclosure by the attorney, the attorney can appear for both of the parties on issues concerning which they fully agree. It follows that if we were reviewing the order of the trial court after the first hearing held on April 25, 1977, the petition for mandate would have to be denied on the ground that no written consents to joint representation had been procured at that time. Moreover, as a result of the judge's questioning of the wife, he could have reasonably concluded that the wife's consent was not given after a full disclosure and was neither intelligent nor informed.

The order before us, however, is the order entered after the second hearing held on May 2, 1977, at which time the written consents of both the husband and wife, dated that date, were received by the judge without further inquiry of the clients or of the attorney. It could well have been that between April 25 and May 2 and before signing the written consents the parties became apprised of sufficient information to make the written consents intelligent and informed. The situation on May 2 was not necessarily the same as it was on April 25. The record of the May 2 hearing reflects no inquiry whatsoever as to whether the written consents were knowing, informed and given after full disclosure.

Thus it appears the trial judge failed to exercise his discretion in accordance with proper legal principles. Accordingly, the cause must be returned to the trial court to make the determination of whether the consents were knowing, informed, and given after a full disclosure.

Finally, as a caveat, we hasten to sound a note of warning. Attorneys who undertake to represent parties with divergent interests owe the highest duty to each to make a full disclosure of all facts and circumstances which are necessary to enable the parties to make a fully informed decision regarding the subject matter of the litigation, including the areas of potential conflict and the possibility and desirability of seeking independent legal advice. Failing such disclosure, the attorney is civilly liable to the client who suffers loss caused by lack of disclosure. In addition, the lawyer lays himself/herself open to charges, whether well founded or not, of unethical and unprofessional conduct. Moreover, the validity of any agreement negotiated without independent representation of each of the parties is vulnerable to easy attack as having been procured by misrepresentation, fraud, and overreaching. It thus behooves counsel to cogitate carefully and proceed cautiously before placing himself/herself in such a position. As some commentators have stated,

"For these reasons, it has been our observation that most lawyers *refuse* dual representation in all cases. Despite the spouses' assurances they are in agreement on all issues, all marital cases involve a potential conflict of interests. In our opinion, dual representation is ill-advised, even if arguably permissible under Rule 3-310." Elrond and Elrond, "Common Ethical Problems In Family Law Practice," 82 *Columbia State Law Journal*, 1150, 1163, (1975).

It is an attorney's duty to protect his client in every possible way, and it is a violation of that duty for him to assume a position adverse or antagonistic to his client without the latter's free and intelligent consent given after full knowledge of all the facts and circumstances. By virtue of this rule an attorney is precluded from assuming any relation which would prevent him from devoting his entire energies to his client's interests. Nor does it matter that the intention and motives of the attorney are honest. The rule is designed not only to prevent the dishonest practitioner from fraudulent conduct, but also to preclude the honest practitioner from putting himself in a position where he may be required to choose between conflicting duties, or be led to an attempt to reconcile conflicting interests, rather than to enforce to their full extent the rights of the interest which he should alone represent.

It is ordered that a peremptory writ of mandate issue directing the trial court to reconsider Bailey's motion to be allowed to represent both husband and wife, that the court determine if the consent given by each was knowing and informed after a full disclosure by the attorney, and to decide the motion in accordance with the principles set forth in this opinion.

Marriage of Vandenburgh

Columbia Court of Appeal (1993)

This is an appeal from a judgment granting the plaintiff-husband a divorce and, *inter alia,* setting aside the parties' separation agreement. The marriage of these parties was both short and stormy. After a bitter all-night quarrel extending through to the morning, wife demanded that husband leave the marital home. He refused to leave without a written separation agreement, in response to which wife contacted an attorney who agreed to meet with them at 8:00 A.M. that very morning. They reconciled that afternoon and returned to the attorney's office to delay any further action. A separation agreement had already been prepared which the parties executed together with several supporting documents to be utilized in the event their reconciliation failed. The agreement provided that wife could purchase husband's interest in the marital home for $2,500, but no mention of the parties' significant marital savings was made. Subsequently, another violent argument erupted resulting in husband's peaceful departure from the residence.

Husband and wife reaffirmed the separation agreement in writing, which included the statement that each agreed the attorney could represent them both in the preparation of the agreement. Husband received $2,500 in exchange for the previously executed deed. On the very next day, husband learned that wife had become a secretary to the attorney who prepared the separation agreement and immediately sought to rescind it and regain title to the marital home. Following a trial, the court set aside that portion of the separation agreement with respect to the marital residence and directed that the property be sold and the net proceeds divided equally between the parties. On this appeal wife challenges that part of the judgment which modified the separation agreement.

The Columbia Supreme Court has established that "property settlement agreements occupy a favored position in the law of this state." (*Adams v. Adams*, 1947). The Columbia Legislature embraced this principle. The policy favoring property settlement agreements has been codified in Columbia Family Code section 3850:

"A husband and wife may agree, in writing, to the immediate separation, and may provide in the agreement for the support of either of them and of their children during the separation or upon dissolution of their marriage. The mutual consent of the parties is sufficient consideration for the agreement."

In *Adams*, the Supreme Court stated,

> "When the parties have finally agreed upon the division of their property, the courts are loath to disturb their agreement except for equitable considerations. A property settlement agreement, therefore, that is not tainted by fraud or compulsion or is not in violation of the confidential relationship of the parties is valid and binding on the court."

Property settlement agreements are contracts subject to the general rules of contract interpretation and enforcement. A trial court may set aside a property settlement agreement on traditional contract law. The agreements are governed by the legal principles applicable to contracts generally. These grounds include mistake, unlawfulness of the contract, and prejudice to the public interest.

The trial court also had the power to invalidate the property settlement agreement if it was inequitable. Family law cases are equitable proceedings in which the court must have the ability to exercise discretion to achieve fairness and equity. Equity will assert itself in those situations where right and justice would be defeated but for its intervention. Thus, property settlement agreements may be set aside where the court finds them inequitable even though not induced through fraud or compulsion.

While it frequently occurs in negotiations between a husband and wife for settlement of property matters that one attorney serves both parties, in fairness to both parties concerned, when negotiations for settlement of property matters between a husband and wife are on hand, both parties should at all times be represented by counsel.

It is, of course, much better for all concerned if both sides have independent counsel, but there is no way by which a litigant can be compelled to secure an attorney. Where the attorney for one of the parties is compelled to deal directly with the other litigant he is under a most strict duty to deal with such litigant fairly and objectively, and the agreement will be scrutinized most carefully to be sure that there has been no overreaching. At least the attorney should make sure that each party is fully advised as to his or her legal rights and to the right to independent counsel.

Separation agreements are held to a higher standard of equity than other contracts and may be set aside if manifestly unfair to one spouse because of overreaching by the other, circumstances that the trial court determined existed here. Agreements drafted with only one attorney ostensibly representing both parties are subject to heightened scrutiny.

We find ample basis in this record to sustain the judgment, particularly because the trial court had the advantage of viewing the witnesses and weighing their credibility. Here, the agreement was made under circumstances which at best are described as hurried, stressful and questionable. A major family asset in the possession of wife was ignored. Wife was given the right to buy husband's interest in the marital home containing an income apartment, which husband had purchased prior to the marriage, for a minimal sum. Wife commenced employment with the attorney who ostensibly represented both parties the day following the separation, the reaffirmation of the agreement and the transfer of the property. In sum, there is sufficient evidence to sustain the trial court's findings and conclusions.

The judgment is affirmed.

1)

To: Rena Tishman
From: Applicant
Re: Marriage of Eiffel – Statement of Facts And Argument For Appellant's Opening Brief
Date: February 24, 2005

Below is the two part project you requested – a statement of facts and an argument demonstrating the trial court erred in the Marriage of Eiffel matter. Please let me know should you need further assistance in this matter.

PART A.   STATEMENT OF FACTS

Angela and Paul Eiffel ("Husband and Wife") were married on September 24, 1994. Up until their divorce, Wife had dutifully put Husband through paralegal school while she was still working (despite the fact that this is generally not considered a community property expense) and also made payments on Paul's separate property commercial building which he had inherited. Wife made such payments for the last eight years. As a result of some marital difficulties involving underlying criminal charges and financial debts, the couple agreed to separate on July 13, 2002, and filed a joint petition for marital dissolution. Husband and wife privately and voluntarily each agreed to and signed an agreement dividing their property and payment of debts in an agreement on July 19, 2002. Specifically, Husband voluntarily agreed to refinance and borrow money against real property in his name to pay off the community debts owed by the couple and to fund their separation.

Thereafter, the parties also contacted an attorney, Robert Gant, who had previously represented both Husband and Wife in previous criminal matters in which they were not adverse parties. Mr. Gant drafted a Marital Settlement Agreement ("MSA") on July 19, 2002 despite the fact that the couple had already agreed to and drafted an enforceable contractual agreement between the two [of] them.

The MSA contained the following provisions: 1) $750 of spousal support from Husband to Wife until a new lease is signed by Wife, 2) 50% of new lease income to be paid to Wife, 3) Husband will make up the difference if the new lease accounts for less than $2000 per month, 4) Wife will receive 50% of yearly percentage income from Northland for the lease, 5) the agreement would be in effect for five years or until Wife got back on her feet, 6) Wife would be responsible for $15,000 in legal fees for her defense and Husband would be responsible for his fees in a paternity case, and finally, 7) Wife would receive a copy of new lease after it is signed. Although he was to perform mere perfunctory tasks in his capacity as an attorney, Mr. Gant informed Husband and Wife of the conflict of interest involved by presenting two spouses in this matter, and had them sign a written conflict waiver. (See Exhibit A.)

Despite the fact that these provisions seem to lean in Wife's favor, she allowed Husband to keep a number of community property assets, including art purchased with her community property funds in her account, as well as his car. Wife also made mortgage payments on a commercial building inherited by husband. Attorney Gant fully informed Husband and Wife of a potential conflict in [sic] and did advise them to seek the advice of independent counsel during discussions when 1) they asked him to be an attorney in this matter, 2) when he asked them to sign the MSA, and 3) when he provided a written waiver of conflict form, which specifically mentioned a potential conflict.

PART B.   ARGUMENT

I.   The Court Erred Because The Parties Had Entered A Valid And Binding Marital Agreement Not Tainted By Fraud Or Compulsion And Thus Requires A Peremptory Writ Of Mandate Directing The Trial To Consider Only Whether There Has Been Informed Written Consent.

Under California Rule of Civil Procedure §3-310 regarding "Avoiding the Representation of Adverse Interests," an attorney must make a full written disclosure of an actual or potential conflict and obtain informed written consent before proceeding with the case. The Rule holds that "disclosure" means informing the client or former client of the relevant circumstances and actual and reasonably foreseeable adverse consequences to the client or former client. "Informed written consent" means written agreement by the client to representation following written disclosure. The rule prohibits, without informed written consent, 1) accepting representation where there is a potential conflict, 2) accepting or continuing representation where there is an actual conflict, and 3) representing a client in while representing another at the same time in an adverse matter. Thus, the central issue before this court in the matter at hand is whether parties, Husband and Wife, received full written disclosure.

A.   Despite The Trial Court's Premature Dismissal Of The Agreement At Issue, It Is Common Practice For Attorneys To Represent Husbands And Wives In Drafting Dissolution Agreements, Especially Where Such Agreements Are Not Tainted By Fraud Or Compulsion.

Although the court seems to summarily assume that the case at hand could not have possibly involved informed written consent by the clients, it is common practice for attorneys to represent a husband and wife and other types of joint parties in forming dissolution agreements. For example, in Lessing v. Gibbons, cited by the court in Klemm v. Superior Court, the court approved an attorney acting for both a studio and an actress in concluding negotiations and drawing agreements. The court refers to the common practice of attorneys acting for both parties in drawing and dissolving partnership agreements. Thus, it is common practice for attorneys to represent a husband and wife in drawing up dissolution agreements.

Also as the court in <u>Adams v. Adams</u>, cited by the court in <u>Marriage of Vandenburgh</u>, put it: "When the parties have finally agreed upon the division of their property, the courts are loath to disturb their agreement except for equitable considerations. A property settlement agreement, therefore, that is not tainted by fraud or compulsion or is not in violation of the confidential relationship of the parties is valid and binding on the court." Here, the court has found that the MSA was "in fact the free and voluntary agreement of the parties as of the date it was made and specifically rejects the claim that Husband was forced to consent to its terms as a result of fraud, duress, or undue influence." (See Memorandum of Decision, p. 7.) Although the opponents might argue that the underlying agreement and MSA were not valid because Husband was a paralegal and therefore must have had superior knowledge as to contractual arrangements, this argument will fail because, as noted in the trial transcript, Wife indicated that she understood what she was signing repeatedly and Gant repeatedly asked if she had any questions. (See Transcript p. 14.)

Accordingly, the only issue to consider was whether the parties had received full disclosure of the conflict such that they were fully informed before signing the waiver of conflict form.

II. There Was No Attorney's Role[;] Was Merely That Of a Scrivener Because He Was Merely Typing And Adding Boilerplate Provisions To What Was Merely An Enforceable Contractual Agreement And Thus Requires A Peremptory Writ Of Mandate Directing The Trial To Consider Only Whether There Has Been Informed Consent.

In <u>Blevin v. Mayfield</u>, cited by the author's discussion under CRPC §3-310, it is noted that some tasks by lawyers did not really require legal skill and thus implies that the underlying communications are not subject to the same privilege. Although Appellants do not make the argument that privilege does not apply, it is important to note that Attorney Gant's tasks here were simple and uncomplicated, involving a mere recitation and formalizing of an underlying agreement, and he was merely acting in his named capacity as an attorney to give the document a greater legal effect. In these circumstances, it would seem that the conflict of interests would not be as pressing because the confidentiality interest is not being compromised and the attorney's interests are not tainting the underlying agreement.

Opponents may attempt to argue that no distinction under the Rule is drawn where the lawyer performs perfunctory services and those involving greater complexity, but this is only applied absent unusual circumstances. An unusual circumstance exists here, which is the fact that the husband and wife Angela Eiffel, had already wrote [sic], agreed to, and signed an agreement before the lawyer prepared a later Marital Settlement Agreement. Furthermore, martial dissolution contracts are enforceable and subject to defenses such as mistake, illegality, prejudice to public interests, as well as inequity. (See <u>Marriage of Vandenburgh.</u>) The facts and record established that the parties had already established an enforceable agreement. Moreover, the parties actually signed a waiver of conflict which specifically stated that "Robert Gant's mere typing of an agreement made between the parties...," which indicates all parties and their attorney's knowledge of the attorney's minimal duties in this matter. Considering these unusual circumstances, Appellant submits that the court should reconsider the setting aside of the Marital Settlement Agreement, because Attorney Grant was merely acting as a scrivener.

III.   The Court Erred Because The Eiffel Case Involved A Potential, Not Actual[,] Conflict Because There Was No Point of Difference to Be Litigated As To Husband and Wife's Agreement And The Case Must Be Mandated To The Trial Court To Determine Only If There Was Informed Consent.

In <u>Klemm v. Superior Court</u>, the court deal[t] with the case of a husband and wife who had orally agreed that child support was waived. An attorney– Catherine Bailey, had repres[e]nted the wife during the dissolution hearing. Because the wife was receiving ADFC payments, however, the judge at the family court custody case referred the issue of child support to the Family Support Division, which recommended that the husband actually pay $50 per month in child support. As a friend of husband and wife, Bailey agreed to appear at the hearing on the issue of child support and state that the parties were in agreement on the matter. Later, Baily obtained and filed written consents to joint representation.

The <u>Klemm</u> court determined that this case involved a potential, not actual[,] conflict, despite the fact that Bailey had represented both Husband and Wife and [sic] different points. The court's rationale was that "[t]he parties had settled their differences by agreement. There was no point of difference to be litigated." The only issue of conflict was the county's decision regarding the issue of support, and this was an issue upon which both husband and wife had agree[d]. Thus, once the attorney had obtained written consent of both the husband and the wife, the only remaining issue was whether such consent was procured after knowing, informed, and full disclosure.

Similarly here, Attorney Gant had represented both Husband and Wife in a matter in which they were not adverse. Wife had been charged after threatening a DA's office when they threated [sic] to browbeat her into turning against her Husband. And Husband had a paternity case. Thus, Husband and Wife were not represented by the same attorney in an adverse matter. There was also no point of difference between them as to the current agreement and MSA. Rather, as is indicated in the trial transcript, each agreed to the agreement and simply wanted Attorney Gant to type it up and add boilerplate provisions. The only issue possibly remaining for the court[,] therefore, is to determine whether there has been informed consent based on the prior discussions and waiver of conflict form.

V. **Attorney Fully Advised Parties Of Their Rights And Right to Independent Counsel In The "Waiver Of Conflict" Form And In Prior Discussions[,] Thereby Meeting A Standard Of Heightened Scrutiny[,] And The Only Issue Remaining Is For The Trial Court To Determine the Waiver Was Signed After Informed Consent And Full Disclosure.**

Again, under CRPC §3-310 regarding "Avoiding the Representation of Adverse Interests," "disclosure" means informing the client or former client of the relevant circumstances and actual and reasonably foreseeable adverse consequences to the client or former client. "Informed written consent" means written agreement by the client to representation following written disclosure. Also, in Marriage of Vandenburgh, the court indicated that an attorney drafting a dissolution agreement for both parties is held to a standard of "heightened scrutiny." The attorney must make sure that each part[y] is fully advised of his rights and right to independent counsel.

Here, Attorney Gant actually made sure that the parties actually signed a waiver of conflict which specifically stating [sic] that "Angela Eiffel and Paul E[i]ffel have been advised that Robert Gant's mere typing of an agreement made between the parties may be a potential conflict of interest...". thus foreclosing the possibility that the parties were unaware of the potential conflict. Also, once Husband and Wife asked Attorney Gant to represent them, he refused, stating that each of them had to get their own attorneys. The parties told Mr. Gant that they had no disputes and agreed on everything, and only after which did Gant agree to "merely type" the dissolution agreement. Attorney Gant also insisted that if he were in their shoes he wouldn't sign the agreement or have him as counsel, and the parties still signed and had him as counsel. Thus, the only remaining issue for the court to consider is whether this waiver and the previous discussions was [sic] sufficient.

VI. **Property Settlement Agreements Occupy A Favored Position In Columbia Barring Equitable Considerations And The Settlement Agreement At Issue Was Fair and Equitable, Especially Given Wife's Generous Allowances Of Community Property Assets To Husband, Leaving The Trial Only With The Issue Of Whether There Was Informed Consent And Full Disclosure.**

The Columbia Supreme Court has established that "property settlement agreements occupy a favored position in the law of this state." (See Adams v. Adams). The Legislature has also embraced this principle by codifying Columbia's Family Code section 3850, which provides that husbands and wives may agree to a dissolution agreement based on mutual consent. Barring any claims of unenforceability or conflict of interest or lack of written disclosure, the agreements will be upheld unless they are inequitable.

A. **Respondents Will Fail In Their Argument that The Agreement Was Inequitable Because Wife Paid For Separate Property Mortgage Payments And Agreed To Let Husband Have A Car And Art Purchased With Community Property**

Funds.

The court in <u>Marriage of Vandenburgh</u> setting [sic] aside the separation agreement based on the heightened scrutiny standard of focusing on equitable considerations. The agreement in that case involved the a [sic] dissolution agreement that was "hurried, stressful, and questionable." Specifically, the wife was given the right to buy the husband's interest in the marital home containing an income [a]partment, which husband had purchased prior to the marriage, for a minimal sum. Also, a major family asset in the possession of the wife was ignored. Under such inequitable circumstances, the court determined that the trial court's judgment setting aside the separation agreement should be affirmed.

Here, the MSA contained a provision that Husband would repay the entire loan on the Texas property. Although opponents will argue that this [was] inequitable, it was actually quite generous considering that Wife had dutifully put Husband through paralegal school while she was still working (despite the fact that this is generally not considered a community property expense) and also made payments on Paul's separate property commercial building which he had inherited. This was $460.90 per month. Wife made such payments for the last eight years. Paul also insisted on keeping his car and the avant garde art, all of which had been purchased with Wife's income, which was community property funds.

Accordingly, the case should be issued a peremptory writ of mandate back to the trial court to determine only if there has been informed written consent.

END OF EXAM

2)

FACTS

Appellant Angela Eiffel (Wife) and Appellee Paul Alexandre Eiffel (Husband) dissolved their marriage in 2002. As part of this dissolution, the parties negotiated and executed a detailed Marital Settlement Agreement (MSA).

The parties proceeded through the bulk of the divorce process without the help of counsel. Both parties are competent and intelligent. Paul Eiffel has training as a paralegal, although he does not practice in the field. Angela Eiffel is a competent public administrator in the city planning office. They were therefore able to effectively negotiate the legal system without counsel.

Acting without representation, the parties negotiated the terms of their settlement agreement. However, the parties realized that they were more likely to be able to produce an enforceable, legally binding settlement agreement if they enlisted the help of counsel in the drafting. The parties contacted an attorney, Robert Gant. Gant had represented both parties in the part [sic], in criminal matters that were unrelated to the terms of the settlement agreement. The parties requested that Gant, whom they viewed as their attorney, write up their Marital Settlement Agreement.

As first, Gant flatly refused, stating his concern that this would create a conflict of interest. The parties became concerned that now, in order to realize the enforcement of their deal, they would each need to retain expensive new counsel. To avoid this expense, they attempted to convince Gant to carry out their wishes. Paul Eiffel told Gant emphatically that the parties had agreed on all of the provisions of the ultimate agreement, and that there were no remaining disputes. Based on the parties' persuasion, Gant agreed to "be a draftsman" and to put the parties['] agreement into legally operative form. However, Gant continued to encourage them both to seek independent counsel.

Notwithstanding Gant's advice, both parties chose not to retain independent counsel. At Gant's request, Paul Eiffel "drafted and freely executed" an agreement that would serve as the basis for Gant's full MSA. He then faxed this draft agreement to Gant. Gant used the agreement as the basis for the settlement document, and added boilerplate language to create a legally effective MSA. Where provisions in the faxed agreement were unclear, Gant called the parties and requested clarification.

Throughout the process, Gant declined to give any legal advice to either of the parties. At one point during his telephone conversations with the parties, Paul Eiffel asked Gant for advice about his legal rights. However, Gant responded that giving legal advice would exceed the scope of what he had agreed to do, and he refused to give the requested advice.

After the MSA had been drafted, Gant met with both parties. Before proceeding, Gant requested that both parties read and sign a written waiver that Gant had prepared. The waiver contained the following language:

This will confirm that Angela Eiffel and Paul Alexandre Eiffel have been advised that Robert Gant's mere typing of an agreement made between the parties may be a potential conflict of interest, despite the fact that he was not in an advisory capacity, nor involved in the negotiation of the agreement. Each party knowingly waives any potential conflict of interest in the preparation of the parties' agreement. In addition, each party has been advised to seek independent counsel and advise [sic] with respect to this statement and the agreement.

After reading this form, the parties voluntarily signed it. After obtaining this consent, Gant reviewed with them the MSA that he had typed on the basis of the parties' written agreement. He explained each provision to them in full. Then, each party voluntarily signed the Marital Settlement Agreement.

Following execution of the agreement and the dissolution of the marriage, Appellee [sic] performed her obligations under the settlement agreement in full. However, Appellant's [sic] has not lived up to his obligations under the contract. Specifically, the settlement agreement required that Appellee pay Appellant 50% of the rental income on an out-of-state property. The obligation was to continue until Appellant found a stable job and was capable of self-support. However, the Appellee has made only one, one-time payment of $750 to Appellant. His rental income has been approximately $4400 per month.

Appellee had intended to use this money to finance additional education to obtain a higher paying job. Since the Appellant [sic] has failed to live up to his obligations, Appellee has been unable to obtain this further education.

ARGUMENT

I.   THE COURT'S FINDING THAT THE MARITAL SETTLEMENT AGREEMENT IS UNENFORCEABLE IS INCORRECT AS A MATTER OF LAW, BECAUSE THE COURT MUST GIVE EFFECT TO A SETTLEMENT AGREEMENT UNLESS THE COURT FINDS THAT IT IS THE PRODUCT OF FRAUD OR COMPULSION OR IS MANIFESTLY UNFAIR, AND THIS COURT EXPRESSLY FOUND THAT THE AGREEMENT WAS NOT THE PRODUCT OF SUCH IMPROPRIETY.

Property settlement agreements on dissolution of marriage "occupy a favored position" in the law of Columbia. *Adams v. Adams.* According to the Adams court: "A property settlement agreement . . . that is not tainted by fraud or compulsion or is not in violation of the confidential relationship of the parties is valid and binding on the court." *Id.* Later courts have added as grounds for rejection of a property agreement a finding by the court that the agreement is "manifestly unfair to one spouse because of overreaching by the other." *Marriage of Vandenburgh*.

The trial court ignored this principle of law when it held that the Eiffels' marital settlement agreement was unenforceable. The sole reason for the court's decision was that the parties' attorney had not "adequately" disclosed a potential conflict of interest. The court did not find that the settlement agreement was the product of fraud or compulsion or that it was manifestly unfair.

Indeed, the court expressly found that "the MSA was in fact the free and voluntary agreement of the parties as of the date it was made, and [stated that it] specifically rejects the claim that Husband was forced to consent to its terms as a result of fraud, duress, or undue influence." This finding should have forced the court to find the agreement enforceable as a matter of law.

Instead, the trial court sought to avoid this result by fashioning a new rule of law, under which marital settlement agreements are to be rejected if the court determines that an attorney's disclosure of conflicting interests was less than adequate.

This rule conflicts with Columbia courts' general policy of effecting the voluntary, expressed will of parties to a dissolution as expressed in their marital settlement agreements. Furthermore, this new rule does not serve any overriding public interests. In this case, an informed written consent was obtained, following lengthy discussion between parties and counsel of counsel's role in the matter. Any additional requirement that the court seeks to have imposed would do little to protect parties' interests, over and above what was undertaken in this case.

The court, through its technical rule, has not only failed to promote the purpose of ensuring that settlement agreements are fair and equitable. It has created a situation that is patently *unfair*. In this case, the parties agreed to a discrete set of terms that would govern the dissolution of their marriage. The terms, as in any contract, should be understood as a trade-off between competing interests. However, the court, in finding the agreement unenforceable for a technicality, has denied Appellant the right to receive the benefit of her bargain. She has performed her obligations under the contract, and Appellee has been excused from performing his. This ruling has therefore resulted in an inequity, and should be corrected.

Any concern by the court that the parties were not adequately informed of the risks of the settlement would be better considered, not through the fashioning of an arcane and technical rule regarding disclosures, but through common-sense application of the existing rule that a marital settlement agreement is not valid where it is the product of fraud or duress or where its terms are grossly unfair.

In this case, the court determined that the agreement was not unfair or the product of duress. The facts on which this finding rest presumably include the participation of Attorney Gant in the drafting of the settlement. Therefore, if the court were to properly consider the conduct of the attorney under this jurisdiction's existing precedent, it would be constrained to conclude that the agreement was enforceable.

In sum, the court's expansion of the law in this field should be rejected, and the court's holding that the material settlement agreement is unenforceable should be overturned.

II. THE COURT'S FINDING THAT THE ATTORNEY'S DISCLOSURES WERE INADEQUATE UNDER THE CIRCUMSTANCES IS ERRONEOUS, BECAUSE THE PARTIES HAD RESOLVED THEIR DIFFERENCES BEFORE SEEKING GANT'S ASSISTANCE, GANT WAS ACTING IN A LIMITED CAPACITY AS A DRAFTSMAN, AND GANT HAD EXPRESSLY ADVISED THE PARTIES NOT TO RELY ON HIM FOR LEGAL ADVICE, BUT TO SEEK THEIR OWN, INDEPENDENT COUNSEL.

Even if this Court were to conclude that the rule of law applied by the trial court was proper, it should nevertheless overturn the decision of the trial court for its failure to faithfully apply its rule. The court reasoned that a marital settlement agreement should not be enforceable where the attorney drafting the agreement did not obtain valid, informed consent. However, in this case the attorney did obtain adequate consent. Therefore, failure of consent cannot provide a proper ground for denying enforcement of the parties' settlement agreement.

The trial court's conclusion that the consent obtained in this case was not adequate is erroneous. First, the court mistakenly believed that an attorney can almost never represent two parties to a transaction. This is incorrect. Second, the court seemed to rely on the special status of family law as precluding dual representation. However, this goes against precedent and is not supported by strong policy considerations.

Dual Representation is a Common Practice

The trial court concluded that, as a matter of law, a lawyer may represent two parties to a deal only "in exceptional circumstances." This reading of the law of professional responsibility is erroneous. In *Klemm v. Superior Court* (the very case on which the district court relies for support of its conclusion), the court recognizes that it is a "common practice of attorneys [to] act[] [sic] for both parties in drawing and dissolving partnership agreements, for grantors and grantees, sellers and buyers, lessors and lessees, and lenders and borrowers."

Moreover, this practice of acting on behalf of both sides to a deal is expressly permitted by the Columbia Rules of Professional Conduct. Rule 3-310 provides that attorneys may with the "informed written consent of each client . . . [a]ccept representation of more than one client in a matter in which the interests of the clients potentially conflict." The Rule requires only written consent. It does not require "exceptional circumstances."

Dual Representation Merely Requires Informed Consent, Which Must Be Adequate Under the Circumstances

The requirement of informed written consent is satisfied when the client agrees in writing to the representation, following full written disclosure "of the actual and reasonably foreseeable adverse consequences" of dual representation. Rule 3-310. In this case Attorney Gant provided full disclosure of the relevant circumstances. He informed the parties that they were accepting a grave risk if they entered into a settlement agreement without seeking legal advice as to their respective rights. In addition, Gant informed them that he could not, because of the conflict involved, serve as a advisor to either of them. He agreed only, at the parties' insistence, to serve in the limited capacity of a draftsperson of a legal document based on the parties' independently negotiated agreement, and he fully explained the limitations of his representation. Throughout the process of preparing the document, he refrained from giving the parties any advice whatsoever as to its provisions.

The services performed by Gant were analogous to those found to be proper in *Blevin v. Mayfield*. The court rejected an argument that a deed that had been drafted by a single attorney acting for two parties was invalid. The court stated that "the agreement had already been reached between the two parties and therefore the only service performed by the attorney was that of a scrivener." *Id.* Here, the agreement as to the terms of the marital settlement had already been reached before Gant's participation. This fact is memorialized in the written agreement that Paul Eiffel wrote and both parties signed. Gant simply translated the terms of the pre-existing agreement into the format of a valid marital settlement agreement.

As suggested by the trial court, the adopters of the Columbia Rules of Professional Conduct rejected a per se rule that an attorney acting as scrivener be exempted from the rule regarding disclosure of potential conflicts. However, this conclusion was based on their presumption that "in contemporary practice, it will be unusual for an attorney to fulfill the role of mere scrivener.["] However, the adopters allowed for "unusual circumstances clearly indicating otherwise."

The facts of this case clearly indicate these unusual circumstances. Attorney Gant made every effort to limit his role in the preparation of the settlement agreement to that of scrivener, and to insure that the parties fully understood his function.

The court found that the disclosures were inadequate simply because the attorney did not spell out, in detail, the possible interests of the parties that might be compromised by the agreement. However, this would place a significant burden on attorneys to familiarize themselves with the legal issues in a case for which they intend to provide no legal advice. There would be very little benefit from placing such a burden on attorneys and clients to require extensive research solely for the purpose of securing a waiver allowing the attorney to act in a non-advisory capacity.

Finally, Appellee might dispute that the informed consent is not valid, because the disclosures made by Gant were not "written." As Rule 3-301 provides, the informed written consent must be based on written disclosures. However, the spirit of the rule has clearly been complied with, and Appellee's attempt to enforce this requirement of a writing would not serve to promote the purposes of the rule.

The Court's Suggestion That Family Law is a Special In [sic] Not Supportable.

The court seems to suggest that the context of this case- - - family law - - - merits special requirements. The court quotes language in *Klemm v. Superior Court* to the effect: "Despite spouses' assurances they are in agreement on all issues, all marital cases involve a potential conflict of interests. In our opinion, dual representation is ill-advised, even if arguably permissible under Rule 3-310." This quote is, however, taken out of its context. Indeed, in *Klemm*, the court permitted an attorney to engage in joint representation of two spouses. The court, furthermore, allowed such dual representation where the parties clearly had a serious risk of ending up adverse to each other in future litigation over child support payments, and, furthermore, where there was every indication that the parties were generally confused by the legal process and uncertain whether they should agree to waive their conflict.

Furthermore, the court emphasized that parties should be permitted to make their own waivers, if those waivers appear to be voluntary and knowing. It is not the job of the court to second-guess the wisdom of the parties' decision because, for example, "[w]hile on the face of the matter it may appear foolhardy for the wife to waive child support, other values could very well have been more important to her than such support, such as maintaining a good relationship. . ."

Rather, parties to family-law contracts should be accorded the same sort of freedom of will that parties to other types of contracts enjoy. These parties should be able to choose their attorney based on the considerations that the parties consider important.

In sum, this honorable Court should permit the parties to this case to make decisions on the basis of their own values and to choose to engage the attorney of their choice, where there has been adequate consideration given to this choice. The court should find that the waiver in this case was effective, and that the failure of consent could not possibly operate as a bar to enforcement of the parties' duly negotiated marital settlement agreement.

TUESDAY AFTERNOON
JULY 26, 2005

California
Bar
Examination

Performance Test A
INSTRUCTIONS AND FILE

IN RE WINSTONS

INSTRUCTIONS

1. You will have three hours to complete this session of the examination. This performance test is designed to evaluate your ability to handle a select number of legal authorities in the context of a factual problem involving a client.

2. The problem is set in the fictional States of Columbia and Franklin, two of the United States.

3. You will have two sets of materials with which to work: a File and a Library.

4. The File contains factual materials about your case. The first document is a memorandum containing the instructions for the tasks you are to complete.

5. The Library contains the legal authorities needed to complete the tasks. The case reports may be real, modified, or written solely for the purpose of this performance test. If the cases appear familiar to you, do not assume that they are precisely the same as you have read before. Read each thoroughly, as if it were new to you. You should assume that cases were decided in the jurisdictions and on the dates shown. In citing cases from the Library, you may use abbreviations and omit page citations.

6. Your response must be written in the answer book provided. You should concentrate on the materials provided, but you should also bring to bear on the problem your general knowledge of the law. What you have learned in law school and elsewhere provides the general background for analyzing the problem; the File and Library provide the specific materials with which you must work.

7. Although there are no restrictions on how you apportion your time, you should probably allocate at least 90 minutes to reading and organizing before you begin writing your response.

8. Your response will be graded on its compliance with instructions and on its content, thoroughness, and organization.

IN RE WINSTONS

Columbia Center for Disability Law
Protection and Advocacy System for Columbia
645 Walther Way, Suite 208
Santa Claritan, Columbia 55515

MEMORANDUM

To: Applicant

From: Ginny Klosterman

Date: July 26, 2005

Subject: **In re: Ralph, Margaret and Clint Winston**

The Winstons have asked us to represent them in their attempt to purchase a home in Pinnacle Canyon Estates, a "55-and-older" residential community. Ralph and Margaret Winston have a 23-year-old developmentally disabled son, Clint, who lives with them. When Ralph and Margaret tried to purchase a house in Pinnacle Canyon Estates, they were told that Clint couldn't live there because the residential community has a minimum age of 35 for residents. We have received a letter from the attorney for Pinnacle Canyon Estates Homeowners Association that reiterates and explains its position.

Please write a letter in response that argues persuasively that Pinnacle Canyon Estates Homeowners Association is legally required to waive the age restriction for Clint. In addition to arguing our affirmative position, be sure to address and refute the arguments made in the letter from the attorney for Pinnacle Canyon Estates Homeowners Association.

Transcript of Interview of Ralph and Margaret Winston

Ginny Klosterman (Ginny): Mr. and Mrs. Winston, do you mind if I tape record our interview? It will help me remember what you tell me. I won't do it if you are not comfortable with it.

Margaret Winston (Margaret): No, it is fine with us if you record it.

Ginny: Thanks. Why don't you tell me your full name, your ages, and what is going on that brought you to me?

Mr. Winston (Ralph): My name is Ralph Winston, and I am 59. My wife is Margaret Winston, and she is. . .57?

Margaret: No dear, I'm still only 56. (Laughs.) We are here because we tried to buy a house but were rejected. We have a developmentally disabled son who lives with us, and we think they don't want us to live there because of that.

Ginny: What do you mean, you were rejected?

Margaret: The homeowners association for the community told us that our son couldn't live in the house with us because it is an over-55 only community, and our son is much younger than 55. He has to live with us. He has severe developmental disabilities, and if he didn't live with us he would have to be in some sort of institution, and that is out of the question.

Ginny: What is your son's name?

Ralph: Clint.

Ginny: Can you tell me a bit about your son?

Margaret: He is a wonderful loving person, and we are very proud of him. He was born with serious developmental problems. He functions pretty well, but he can't be safely left alone and can't live without us. He is 23 years old but functions at a level well below that. He has a lot of trouble learning, remembering, and he has some communication difficulty, of course.

Ginny: Ok. What is the name of the community?

Ralph: Pinnacle Canyon Estates.

Ginny: Did you have a particular house in mind?

Margaret: Yes. We saw a listing in the paper for a house for sale by the owner, and when we looked, the house was just perfect. Both Ralph and I are getting a little older, and now that our other children have moved out we don't need all the space just for the three of us. The seller was very nice and very reasonable concerning the price of the house.

Ginny: What was the seller's name?

Margaret: Her name is, I've got it written down here, Pamela Garcia. Pamela wanted to sell because her husband had died and she wants to move to Tucson. So it was a good match. The house has a nice arrangement with a bedroom on one side that would work well for Clint. And it is a very nice community, with a lot of people about Ralph's and my age.

Ginny: When did you find out that the community didn't want you to buy?

Ralph: We had set everything up, and it was a few days before escrow was going to close. At that time, a representative from the Pinnacle Canyon Estates Homeowners Association, Phyllis Lim, told us that our son couldn't live in the home with us because it is a 55-and-over community and he isn't 55 or older. She was very nice, actually. She said they were very sorry, that it had nothing to do with the fact that Clint is developmentally disabled, and that there are in fact a lot of disabled people in the neighborhood. She said something about them having to maintain their situation under the law as housing for a 55-and-over community and that letting anyone under 35 live there is not permitted by something called "the C C and Rs." I didn't know what that meant, and I didn't really believe that had anything to do with it. We thought they just didn't want anyone with disabilities to live there.

Ginny: Yes, it is confusing. The letters C C and R are an abbreviation for covenants, conditions and restrictions. They are very common community requirements for property in a neighborhood and include a bunch of stuff. Some neighborhoods want to be for older residents only and put age requirements in the CC&Rs.

Ralph: Oh, I see. Is it legal for them to do that?

Ginny: That's hard to say. Sometimes 55-and-over communities are allowed in effect to discriminate on the basis of age. But it is not permissible for housing communities to make it hard for people with disabilities to select the housing they want. What did you do when she told you that?

Ralph: Well the seller, Pamela Garcia, got pretty mad and said that was ridiculous, the rules were silly, and where was Clint supposed to live? But we cancelled the closing. She said if we could get the community to agree to let Clint live with us, she will be happy to sell us the house. She also suggested we see a lawyer because she thinks the community should be sued, or something. She was very supportive of us. Of course, she probably wants the sale, but it's not like the price is a great deal for her. So is there anything that can be done?

Ginny: What are your goals at this point? Is it really to find another house somewhere else?

Ralph: We'd like to move into that house if we could. We aren't in an incredible hurry, but we need to move eventually. And I'm kind of worried, because we'd like to live in a community where people are our age, but, if they are all going to do this, we won't be able to do so unless we have Clint institutionalized, and we don't want that and can't afford it.

Ginny: Tell me more about why Clint can't live on his own.

Margaret: He can't prepare meals. He might burn himself on the stove. He needs help with basic housekeeping and hygiene. He can't handle his own finances, things like paying bills and having a checking account. People could easily take advantage of him when it comes to handling money.

Ginny: Does he have a job?

Ralph: He works in a sheltered workshop, you know, where they hire disabled people. But he can't safely use public transportation, so one of us has to drive him there and back.

Ginny: Do you think he would pose difficulties for the other people living in the neighborhood?

Margaret: Oh my goodness, no. Clint is quiet and shy, kind and very gentle. He doesn't really approach strangers and doesn't leave the house without one of us.

Ginny: Has there ever been a problem at any of the places you've lived before?

Margaret: With Clint? No, never.

Ginny: Ok. I think that the appropriate first step is for me to research this a bit more, because I've never run into a situation exactly like yours. But if things are as I think, I can call the Pinnacle Canyon Estates Homeowners Association and request that it waive the 55-and-over age restriction. I've made requests similar to that before for various clients with disabilities, and some homeowner associations are quite flexible about it, while others are not. So they might agree to that. If not, we could go to court to seek a ruling that their refusal to grant your requested waiver violates the Columbia Fair Housing Act. Going to court wouldn't be as extreme as it might sound. Hopefully, we will be able to resolve it with a phone call. Does that sound like a good way to proceed?

Margaret: Yes, that is what we would like you to do, isn't it, Ralph?

Ralph: Yes, I think so. I'd like to work it out if we could, and if we can't, well then let's make Pamela Garcia happy, and sue them. It is worth it to see if we can live there.

Ginny: Ok, then I'll get started with some research and then give them a call.

Ralph: Thank you very much for spending time with us.

End of Interview

COLUMBIA CENTER FOR DISABILITY LAW
Protection and Advocacy System for Columbia
645 Walther Way, Suite 208
Santa Claritan, Columbia 55515

MEMORANDUM

To: File

From: Ginny Klosterman

Date: July 5, 2005

Subject: Phone Call to Pinnacle Canyon Estates Seeking Reasonable Accommodation for Clint Winston

On July 5, 2005 I called Ms. Phyllis Lim ("Lim") of the Pinnacle Canyon Estates Homeowners Association (the "Homeowners Association"). Lim, it turns out, is a real estate lawyer who is the general manager of the Homeowners Association. I told her I was calling on behalf of the Winstons, explained what had happened when the Winstons wanted to purchase the home from Pamela Garcia, and asked Lim if their story was correct. Lim said it was, and that Pinnacle Canyon Estates is a 55-and-older community with a 35-and-older age restriction in the CC&Rs. I then requested that the Homeowners Association waive, for Clint Winston, the CC&R requiring all residents to be over 35. I explained that Ralph and Margaret Winston themselves are both over 55, that their son must live with them because he is developmentally disabled, and that they want to live in a community of people their age but are unwilling to contemplate institutionalization for their son. I also explained that the Columbia Fair Housing Act ("CFHA") prohibits discrimination against people with disabilities, and all we want them to do is waive the age restriction. I suggested that a waiver was also the decent thing to do under the circumstances. To let her know that this wouldn't just go away if they turned down the waiver offer, I alluded to the fact that the Winstons were willing to pursue this and had indicated that the seller, Pamela Garcia, supported them.

Lim said she understood how the Winstons might feel, and that she would ask the Homeowners Association to consider it. But she seemed to almost predict that the Homeowners Association would decline the request. She said the Homeowners Association would follow up with a letter indicating its decision.

Rommett, Fairbrooks, Fromkin, & Zucconi, LLP
Attorneys and Counselors at Law
1332 Via Estrada
Fairview, Columbia, 55521
Telephone: (555)547-4700
Facsimile: (555)547-4705

July 22, 2005

Ginny Klosterman, Esq.
Columbia Center for Disability Law
645 Walther Way, Suite 208
Santa Claritan, Columbia 55515

Reference: Pinnacle Canyon Estates Homeowners Association — Ralph and Margaret Winston, Pamela Garcia Request for Age Waiver

Dear Ms. Klosterman:

Phyllis Lim, the general manager of Pinnacle Canyon Estates Homeowners Association ("Homeowners Association"), has referred to me the request you made on behalf of Mr. and Mrs. Winston for a waiver of the Homeowners Association's age restrictions. They want to purchase the residence of Pamela Garcia and intend to have their disabled son, Clint, reside on the premises with them after they move in.

As you know, Pinnacle Canyon Estates ("PCE") has a general requirement that limits occupancy of residences in the development to "older" persons, meaning those who are aged 55 and above. It is the essence of living in the PCE community that this requirement be observed scrupulously. That is why people chose to live there and is, no doubt, why the Winstons, who are in their late 50s, have offered to purchase the Garcia residence.

As I understand it, Clint Winston is a 23-year-old developmentally disabled person. He requires constant adult supervision and has always lived with his parents. We do not dispute that Clint is disabled within the meaning of the applicable disability laws, and we sympathize completely with Mr. and Mrs. Winston, but, for reasons I will explain here, the Homeowners Association is unable to waive the age requirement.

You have suggested that to refuse to do so would amount to unlawful discrimination against Clint because he is young and disabled. I take issue with your characterization.

First, Clint Winston's disability has nothing at all to do with the Homeowners Association's decision to exclude him from residing in the development. That decision is purely a function of his age. To allow Clint to reside with his parents on the premises would violate PCE's covenants, conditions & restrictions (CC&Rs). Under the CC&Rs, which as you know are contractual in nature, no person under the age of 35 may reside on the premises, even if the principal occupants are over 55. If Clint were at least 35, we would not be having this dispute.

Second, PCE, as a housing development for older persons, is completely exempt from the age discrimination laws. We are legally entitled under the Columbia Fair Housing Act (C.R.S. §41 *et. seq.*) to exclude persons who do not meet our age criteria. Indeed, we are *required* to discriminate in order to continue to qualify for the exemption. We currently meet the criteria set forth in C.R.S. §42, and it is our desire to maintain those qualifications that is a principal reason for our rejection of the Winstons' request for a waiver.

One of the requirements for maintaining eligibility for our exemption is that at least 80% of the units in the development be occupied by persons 55 years of age or older. At the current time, we are right at the 80% level. One of our major concerns is that if we embark on a pattern of waiving the age requirement, we will fall below the 80% breakpoint, as a consequence of which we will lose our age selection exemption.

Third, and it is tied to the commitments we make to the property owners in our CC&Rs concerning the 55-and-older nature of the community, there is the danger that allowing younger persons to reside in the development will disrupt the peace and quietude that the property owners have a contractual right to expect. As a matter of fact, we get an average of two requests a month from current residents for waivers that would allow their teenage and young adult children to move in with them. Sooner or later, the number of teenagers and rowdy young adults would increase traffic and noise pollution to the great detriment of the older residents. The concomitant result would be a diminution in the property values associated with the restrictive nature of the development.

Moreover, granting such waivers would completely change the nature of the PCE community, a consequence that we are not required to risk either under the age laws or the disability laws. The Homeowners Association is not required to waive its statutorily granted ability to preserve the nature of the community. It would not be reasonable to require the Homeowners Association to do so. And to preserve the nature of the community, we must continue to demonstrate our intent to maintain the nature of the PCE community as 55-and-older.

Fourth, death from natural causes and illness is a frequent event among the community's property owners. If that were to happen to the Winstons, what would happen to Clint? Who would care for him? It is a constant concern that the Homeowners Association should not have to shoulder. It would create severe administrative problems, such as, for example, our having to make interim arrangements, tracking down other family members, and the like. The Homeowners Association is not a social services agency and consequently is not equipped to take on these tasks. Under the case law interpreting the disability laws, such an administrative burden obviates the need for entities such as the Homeowners Association to accommodate younger people.

The combination of the administrative burdens, the change in the character of the community, and the probable loss in property values that would result from the granting of frequent waivers creates an undue hardship on the PCE community that it is not required to endure.

As I have said, our concern is *not* that Clint is disabled. We have a number of disabled residents in the development, a circumstance that surprises no one in light of the aged constituency of the community. To the extent that we may have a desire (although we have no affirmative *obligation*) to accommodate the Winstons in their request, it would put us in the untenable position of giving them and Clint *favored* treatment, as opposed to the totally neutral treatment that our age-based policy confers. Rather than being a neutral application of our neutral policy, it would thus be a form of reverse discrimination in *favor* of a disabled person who is not otherwise qualified to be a resident.

I direct your attention to the decision of the courts of our neighboring State of Franklin. In <u>Noble v. Ventosa Ridge Estates</u>, applying a statute identical to the Columbia statute, the Franklin court completely supports our position.

There are no Columbia cases on point. Even the Columbia Court of Appeals' decision in <u>Townley v. Rocking J Residential Community</u>, which arguably comes closest, supports our position that while we *may* have an obligation to make a disability accommodation for *homeowner/residents* who qualify for initial admission under our neutral criteria, we are not required to do so for those who, like Clint, are not qualified for admission as residents.

As a matter of fact, we have never failed to make accommodation for our qualified residents. Over the years, members of the community have spent hundreds of thousands of dollars on access and disability improvements, such as wheelchair ramps, oversized elevators, restroom grab bars, and the like in the community's common areas.

Finally, it goes without saying that there has been a residential housing glut in our greater metropolitan area for the past several years. There are many desirable houses for sale that are not in 55-and-older communities. The Winstons should not have any problem finding housing outside of PCE that will accommodate both them and their son.

Very truly yours,

Emma Zucconi

Emma Zucconi

California
Bar
Examination

Performance Test A
LIBRARY

IN RE WINSTONS

LIBRARY

SELECTED PROVISIONS OF THE COLUMBIA FAIR HOUSING ACT

§41 Definitions

In this article, unless the context otherwise requires:

1. "Disability" means a mental or physical impairment that substantially limits at least one major life activity, a record of such an impairment or being regarded as having such an impairment.

2. "Dwelling" means any building, structure or part of a building or structure that is occupied as, or designed or intended for occupancy as, a residence by one or more families.

3. "Familial status" refers to the status of one or more individuals being younger than the age of eighteen years and domiciled with a parent or another person having legal custody of the minor or minors.

4. "Person" means one or more individuals, corporations, partnerships, associations, legal representatives, mutual companies, trusts, trustees, receivers, and fiduciaries.

§42 Housing for older persons exempted; rules; definition

A. The provisions of this article relating to familial status do not apply to housing for older persons.

B. Housing qualifies as housing for older persons if:

1. At least eighty percent of the units are occupied by at least one person fifty-five years of age or older per unit, and

2. The housing community demonstrates, by publication of and adherence to policies and procedures, an intent by the owner or manager to provide housing for persons fifty-five years of age or older.

§43 Discrimination in sale or rental

A person may not refuse to sell or rent after a bona fide offer has been made, or refuse to negotiate for the sale or rental of or otherwise make unavailable, or deny a dwelling to any person because of race, color, religion, sex, familial status or national origin. A person may not discriminate against any person in the terms, conditions or privileges of sale or rental of a dwelling, or in providing services or facilities in connection with the sale or rental, because of race, color, religion, sex, familial status or national origin.

§44 Discrimination due to disability; definitions

*   *   *

B. A person may not discriminate against any person in the terms, conditions or privileges of sale or rental of a dwelling or in the provision of services or facilities in connection with the dwelling because of a disability of:

    1. That person;

    2. A person residing in or intending to reside in that dwelling after it is so sold, rented or made available;

    3. A person associated with that person.

C. For the purposes of this section, "discrimination" includes:

    1. A refusal to permit, at the expense of the disabled person, reasonable modifications of existing premises occupied or to be occupied by the person if the modifications may be necessary to afford the person full enjoyment of the premises.

    2. A refusal to make reasonable accommodations in rules, policies, practices or services if the accommodations may be necessary to afford the person equal opportunity to use and enjoy a dwelling.

Noble v. Ventosa Ridge Estates
Franklin Court of Appeal (2004)

This case presents a conflict between the Franklin Fair Housing Act's ("Franklin FHA") requirement that people with disabilities be given equal opportunities concerning choice and use of housing and the exemption to the FHA given to communities that qualify as "55 or over." This context appears to be a case of first impression for Franklin courts, and the parties present no case on point from any jurisdiction. The cross-motions for summary judgment concede that there are no material facts in dispute and the issue is the application of the law to those facts. The trial court granted summary judgment for the Defendant and denied summary judgment for the Plaintiffs.

Plaintiffs Mary and Frank Noble are the parents of Doug Noble who, at the time of the events, was a 34-year-old man. Because of Doug's disability, he is unable to live independently and is cared for by his parents. Mr. and Mrs. Noble contracted to purchase from Arnold Peck his home that was for sale in Ventosa Ridge Estates ("VRE"), a development governed by defendant. VRE is a residential community that requires at least one person 55 years of age or older to reside in each unit. VRE's covenants, conditions and restrictions ("CC&Rs") provide that no person under the age of 45 may reside in the community. Accordingly, when the president of the Ventosa Ridge Homeowners Association ("Association") learned of the purchase agreement between the Nobles and Peck, she informed Peck that a person younger than 45 years could not live in the subdivision and that the restriction could not be amended or waived by the Association.

The Nobles filed a housing discrimination action, alleging that the Association had engaged in unlawful housing discrimination against a disabled person in violation of the Franklin FHA by failing to make a reasonable accommodation to allow Doug Noble to live in a VRE home with his parents. The Nobles alleged that the Association should have waived the age restriction as a reasonable accommodation, and that the Association's actions have a disparate impact on persons with disabilities. The Nobles do not allege, for purposes of the motions, that the Association had a discriminatory intent. Nobles contend that the enforcement of the age restriction covenant prevents adults with serious disabilities from living with their parent caregivers in the housing community of their choice, which might force institutionalization of the disabled adult, and which results in a disparate effect on a person with a disability.

The Association denies discrimination based on disability and asserts that its actions were lawful and were intended to enforce the age restriction equally. The Association asserts that the Franklin FHA requirement of a reasonable accommodation does not require it to waive the age requirement, because the Franklin FHA only requires equal treatment to people suffering from a disability and does not require them to grant greater than equal opportunity to use and enjoy a dwelling. The Association also contends that enforcement of the age restriction does not constitute discrimination under the Franklin FHA because it applies to all people under the age of 45 regardless of disability.

Pursuant to the Franklin FHA, a verbatim adoption of the Federal Fair Housing Act, it is unlawful to discriminate in the sale or rental, or to otherwise make unavailable or deny, a dwelling to any buyer or renter because of a disability of (A) that buyer or renter; (B) a person residing in or intending to reside in that dwelling after it is so sold, rented, or made available; or (C) any person associated with that buyer or renter. Discrimination includes "a refusal to make reasonable accommodations in rules, policies, practices, or services, when such accommodations may be necessary to afford such person equal opportunity to use and enjoy a dwelling."

Although the Franklin FHA prohibits housing discrimination on the basis of familial status, qualified "housing for older persons" is exempt from the familial status anti-discrimination provisions in the Franklin FHA. This exemption gives qualified "housing for older persons" (also called "55-or-over") communities the ability to put whatever age restrictions it desires in the CC&Rs without concern that it might be violating the familial status provisions of the FHA. Housing qualifies as "housing for older persons" if

> (i) at least 80 percent of the units are occupied by at least one person who is 55 years of age or older;

(ii) the housing facility or community demonstrates, by publication of, and adherence to, policies and procedures, an intent by the owner or manager to provide housing for persons fifty-five years of age or older.

Accordingly, the parties have competing rights and interests at stake. The age restrictions governing the housing development are a sanctioned form of discrimination. There is a specific exception for communities like the VRE community. In order to qualify for the exception, VRE must establish its intent to maintain housing for occupants 55 and older. VRE must adhere to policies and procedures that demonstrate this intent. In this case, VRE's policy included a provision that no person under the age of 45 shall reside on the property. The Nobles' competing interest is found in the Franklin FHA requirement that providers of housing reasonably accommodate those with disabilities to allow them to enjoy housing on an equal basis with others.

We find that the VRE Homeowners Association's actions do not constitute a failure to reasonably accommodate the needs of a person with a disability. First, the Association is not discriminating against Doug Noble on the basis of his disability, so it does not appear that the Franklin FHA requires it to make a reasonable accommodation. Doug Noble was excluded because of his age rather than because he is a disabled person. The purpose of VRE's age restriction is lawful and does not discriminate based on disability. A significant number of disabled residents reside in VRE, which demonstrates that the Association has not excluded anyone over the age of forty-five on the basis of disability. The Association excluded Doug Noble solely because he did not meet the age requirement, and the Franklin legislature allows communities to maintain age minimums if they follow the requirements, as VRE has done here. There is thus no causal nexus between the Association's invoking of its forty-five and over requirement and Doug Noble's disability.

In addition, the Association is not required to waive its forty-five and over requirement to reasonably accommodate Doug Noble. The goal of a reasonable accommodation is to allow a disabled person to enjoy housing on an equal basis with others, but the requested accommodation here would give Doug Noble greater than "equal opportunity," as it would give him an advantage over all nondisabled people under 45. A duty to accommodate only arises when necessary to afford a disabled person an "equal opportunity" to use and enjoy a dwelling. It is doubtful that any accommodation would be reasonable if it would require abandoning a statutorily granted ability to assert a facially disability-neutral restriction, and, in any event, an accommodation is not reasonable if it requires a fundamental alteration in the nature of a program or imposes undue financial and administrative burdens. To allow a person younger than the age of 45 years to live at VRE would fundamentally alter the nature of its community and jeopardize its status as "housing for older persons" under the Franklin FHA. In addition, allowing an exception for Doug Noble could result in a large number of people under age 45 seeking to live in VRE with their parents and thus create undue administrative burdens. Applying the facially neutral age restriction will not force the Nobles to institutionalize their child and is only a minimal restriction on their housing choices.

Affirmed.

Project HOME vs. City of Catalina

Columbia Court of Appeal (1998)

This is an appeal from the trial court ruling granting summary judgment for Project HOME and denying summary judgment for the City of Catalina ("City"). This case arises under the Columbia Fair Housing Act ("CFHA"). The plaintiff alleges that the defendant City's failure to grant a requested zoning permit for a proposed home for homeless persons constitutes "a refusal to make reasonable accommodations in the rules, policies, practices, or services, when such accommodations may be necessary to afford such person equal opportunity to use and enjoy a dwelling. . . ."

Plaintiff Project HOME is a Columbia nonprofit corporation that provides a continuum of services to homeless persons who are mentally ill and/or recovering substance abusers. The organization operates emergency shelters open to any chronically homeless person in the City and offers treatment at two drug- and alcohol-free transitional homes. Recognizing that many residents of the transitional homes would benefit from more privacy and independence than the two homes afford, Project HOME sought to create a "Single Room Occupancy" ("SRO") facility with small individual rooms and community kitchen facilities that would give the resident a sense of control over his or her environment.

Project HOME acquired a building on Fairmount Avenue to use for its proposed SRO. The property includes a substantial side yard which extends the entire depth of the block, but no rear yard. When Project HOME applied for a zoning and use permit for the Fairmount Avenue property, two civic associations opposed the introduction into the neighborhood of a new residential facility for persons beset with handicaps, and the City denied the zoning and use permit application on the ground that the Fairmount property has no rear yard. Under the Catalina Zoning Code, a commercial building or a residential building housing families must have a rear yard. Project HOME sought a waiver from the back yard requirement on the ground that the ample side yard is an adequate substitute. The City refused.

Project HOME and potential residents seek a declaration that as a matter of law the City's conduct constitutes a violation of 44C(2) of the CFHA, which provides that unlawful discrimination includes failure to make "reasonable accommodations in rules, policies, practices or services . . . necessary to afford [a disabled] person equal opportunity to use and enjoy a dwelling." They argue that the reasonable accommodation they seek, that the back yard requirements are waived because the side yard is adequate, is necessary in order to provide their disabled residents with the housing of their choice. The City seeks a ruling that as a matter of law it need not waive the requirement.

The CFHA is copied from its federal counterpart. In creating the CFHA, the Columbia legislature expressed its intent "that the state undertake vigorous steps to provide equal opportunity in housing . . . extend housing discrimination protection to the disabled, exempt housing for the elderly from the provisions prohibiting discrimination against families with children. . .and obtain substantial equivalency with the federal government's housing discrimination enforcement efforts."

We are mindful of the CFHA's stated policy "to prevent housing discrimination and provide for fair housing throughout Columbia." One of the purposes of the CFHA is to "integrate people with disabilities into the mainstream of the community." The CFHA is a broad mandate to eliminate discrimination against and equalize housing opportunities for disabled individuals. Because it is a broad remedial statute, its provisions are to be generously construed, and any exemptions must be construed narrowly in order to preserve the primary operation of the purposes and policies of the CFHA.

Concerning the reasonable accommodation requirement, we stress the CFHA's imposition of an affirmative duty to reasonably accommodate disabled persons. A facially neutral requirement that affects disabled and non-disabled individuals alike implicates the reasonable accommodation section of the CFHA when it prevents a disabled individual from gaining access to proposed housing. The legislative history of the reasonable accommodation portion of the CFHA indicates that one of the purposes behind the reasonable accommodation provision is to address individual needs and respond to individual circumstances and that the concept of reasonable accommodation has a long history in regulations and case law dealing with discrimination on the basis of a person's disability. A discriminatory rule, policy, practice or service is not defensible simply because that is the manner in which such rule or practice has traditionally been constituted. This section would require that changes be made to such traditional rules or practices if necessary to permit a person with disabilities an equal opportunity to use and enjoy a dwelling.

The City argues that there is no CFHA violation because there is no "causal nexus" between the section of the Zoning Code provision at issue--the rear yard requirement--and the handicaps of the prospective residents. The City contrasts the case at hand with a situation in which a zoning code barred the installation of elevators in three-story buildings. In such a case, a disabled person who sought to install an elevator so that he could live in a three-story building would be able to show a direct causal link between the Zoning Code and a City action that bars him from residing in this dwelling because of his handicap. Although the City acknowledges that "discrimination" is defined in §44C as a refusal to make a reasonable accommodation, it argues that what is unlawful under the CFHA is discrimination "<u>because</u> of disability." §44B (emphasis added).

The City reads the statute too narrowly. The CFHA provision concerning discrimination based on a refusal to make a reasonable accommodation contains an independent definition of "discrimination"--a definition not modified by the phrase "because of a disability" found in §44B. Thus the language of §44C does not suggest that, to establish a CFHA violation on the basis of discrimination against a person with a disability, a plaintiff must show a "causal nexus" between the challenged provision and the disabilities of the prospective residents, and cases that have interpreted §44C provide strong support for the conclusion that no such causal nexus is required.

In addition, according to the legislative history of the CFHA, one method of making housing unavailable to people with disabilities has been the application or enforcement of otherwise neutral rules and regulations on land use in a manner that discriminates against people with disabilities. Such determination often results from false assumptions about the needs of disabled people, as well as unfounded fears of difficulties about the problems their tenancies may pose. These and similar practices are prohibited by the CFHA. The City's argument that the statute only reaches special restrictions that specifically prohibit the sale or rental of a dwelling to disabled individuals is thus without merit. So is the City's argument that prohibiting the SRO facility from operating would have no discriminatory effect on plaintiffs or disabled persons in general because there are other facilities in Columbia.

Enforcement of a restrictive covenant or ordinance can, despite the apparent neutrality of the covenant or ordinance toward people with disabilities, constitute discrimination because of a disability. A reasonable accommodation would have been to waive enforcement of the covenant. Such an accommodation would not impose an undue financial or administrative burden on the private defendants nor would it undermine the basic purpose behind the practice of enforcement, namely, to maintain the residential nature of the neighborhood.

A plaintiff can thus establish a violation of the CFHA by showing that the defendant failed to make reasonable accommodations in rules, policies or practices, including rules, policies or practices that do not themselves discriminate on the basis of disability. If a restriction is an impediment to the disabled person's ability to obtain equal housing opportunity, the disabled person is permitted to invoke the "reasonable accommodation" requirement of the CFHA so long as the accommodation "may be necessary" to afford that person equal opportunity to use and enjoy a dwelling.

In this case, a waiver of the back yard requirement is necessary to afford the plaintiffs the equal opportunity to use and enjoy the Project HOME dwellings envisioned for the property. While an accommodation is not reasonable if it imposes a fundamental alteration or substantial administrative or financial burdens on the accommodating party, the City does not appear seriously to dispute that the requested substitution of side yard for rear yard is reasonable. Substituting side yard for rear yard would impose no financial or administrative burden on the City. Nor does it appear that granting the accommodation requested would require a fundamental alteration of the Zoning Code.

Affirmed.

Townley v. Rocking J Residential Community
Columbia Court of Appeal (2003)

In this case we are asked to decide whether a community permitted by an exemption in the Columbia Fair Housing Act ("CFHA") to exclude persons under the age of 55 violates the CFHA's disability discrimination provisions by refusing to waive its minimum age requirement for an over-55 prospective resident with a disability who requires a live-in caretaker under the age of 55.

According to undisputed facts, plaintiff Art Townley ("Townley"), a 68-year-old man who has a disability that renders him unable to live independently, agreed to purchase from seller Dina Whitmore a home in Rocking J Residential Community ("Rocking J") housing development. Rocking J requires at least one person fifty-five years of age or older to reside in each unit. The Rocking J covenants, conditions and restrictions ("CC&Rs") state that no person under the age of 55 may reside in the community. Townley's live-in caregiver, Frank Johnson ("Johnson"), who has lived with and taken care of Townley for the past five years, is currently 32 years old. When Ms. Whitmore notified the Rocking J Homeowners Association (the "Association") of the purchase and that the buyer would have a 32-year-old live-in caregiver, the Association told Ms. Whitmore and Townley that Townley was welcome as a resident but Johnson would not be permitted to live in any home at Rocking J.

Townley and Ms. Whitmore filed suit to enjoin Rocking J from refusing to permit Townley's live-in caregiver to live in the home. They alleged that Rocking J is required under the CFHA to permit underage caregivers to live with over-55 residents, in order to allow adults with serious disabilities opportunities to live in the housing community of their choice. The trial court granted summary judgment for Rocking J.

Rocking J argues that because Rocking J qualifies as a "55 and over" community under the CFHA, the community is entitled to enforce its CC&R concerning the age requirement. Its position is that if it lets anyone under the age of 55 live in the community, the community will lose its status as exempt "housing for older persons," resulting in a fundamental alteration in the nature of the community. It also argues that permitting the plaintiff buyer to have a 32-year-old living in his home would result in granting to the plaintiff buyer greater than equal opportunity to use and enjoy a dwelling, while the CFHA does not require anything more than equal treatment. It also argues that it does not discriminate against Townley on the basis of disability because it already has many disabled elderly residents living there.

The CFHA's "housing for older persons exemption" does not exempt the defendants from its CFHA-imposed obligation to reasonably accommodate persons with disabilities. Section 41 of the CFHA prohibits discrimination against families with children. At the same time, however, Section 42 of the CFHA explicitly exempts "housing for older persons" from the prohibition against familial status discrimination. In other words, if an over-55 housing community abides by the CFHA's requirements regarding occupancy by persons over the age of 55, such qualifying communities are free to exclude underage persons from the housing community and not be found liable for familial status discrimination. This exemption, however, only protects the housing community from liability for status discrimination. See §42. It does not protect the over-55 community from discrimination claims based upon race, color, national origin, religion, gender or disability.

The Supreme Court of Columbia, adopting United States Supreme Court interpretations of the identical Federal Fair Housing Act, has held that an accommodation is not reasonable (1) if it would require a fundamental alteration in the nature of a program, or (2) if it would impose undue financial or administrative burdens on the defendant. Defendant argues that the waiver would fundamentally alter the nature of the community by jeopardizing its "55 and over status."

Under the "55 and over" housing exemption, an over-55 housing community is exempt from familial status discrimination if: (1) at least eighty percent of the units are occupied by at least one person who is fifty-five years of age or older per unit, and (2) the housing community publishes and adheres to policies and procedures that demonstrate the intent to maintain the community as 55 or over, only. Nothing in the statute requires that all occupants of a unit be over the age of 55 in order to obtain or maintain eligibility for a "55 and over" exemption. The statute specifically requires only "one person who is fifty-five years of age or older. . ." §42 (B)(1). The federal regulations promulgated by The Department of Housing and Urban Development (HUD), which we find useful and persuasive, fully contemplate situations where persons under the age of 55 will reside in over-55 housing communities. Under those regulations, a community will meet the 80% occupancy rule where there are units occupied by persons under 55 who are necessary to provide reasonable accommodation to disabled residents. Thus the HUD regulations implicitly contemplate that an over-55 community does not lose its status as "housing for older persons" if a caretaker under the age of 55 resides with an over-55 resident.

Accordingly, Rocking J is not correct that the community will jeopardize its status as a "55 and over" community if it waives the age requirement for Townley's live-in caregiver. A waiver will not have any impact on the "55 and over" status of the community. Townley's household will still count toward the 80% occupancy requirement, because there will be one person over 55 living in his unit. And the waiver would not indicate that Rocking J had failed to publish and adhere to policies and procedures that demonstrate the intent that Rocking J be housing for older persons and is not inconsistent with the community's intent to remain an over-55 community. A waiver granted in order to comply with a state law that requires reasonable accommodation for a disabled person's need for a live-in caregiver can not be interpreted as an intent to relinquish its status as "housing for older persons." As long as Rocking J's general policies, practices, procedures and services are specifically aimed at providing compatible housing for older persons, the waiver will not jeopardize the community concerning the intent requirement for the exemption.

Nor will the waiver inevitably cause a fundamental change by resulting in a "flood" of people wishing to share a residence with underage individuals. Reasonable accommodations vary depending on the facts of each case, and what is reasonable in a particular circumstance is a fact-intensive, case-specific determination. The CFHA allows Rocking J to consider each request individually and to grant only those requests that are reasonable.

Presumably, only a narrow group of persons would be entitled to the limited exception to the CC&Rs necessitated by disabled individuals' need for an underage live-in caretaker.

Defendant also argues that a waiver is unreasonable because the CFHA requirements that people with disabilities be given equal treatment does not require giving the plaintiff-buyer greater than equal opportunity to use and enjoy a dwelling. Defendant's argument might be persuasive if the definition of "discrimination" under the disability prohibitions of the CFHA were the same as the definitions prohibiting "discrimination" due to an individual's race, color, religion, sex, national origin or familial status. The CFHA prohibition on "discrimination in the sale or rental of housing" has been interpreted to require entities to provide "equal treatment" in their dealing with (for examples) men and women, Hispanics and non-Hispanics, African-Americans and Caucasians. In interpreting this requirement, courts have clearly distinguished "equal treatment" from the affirmative duty to provide a "reasonable accommodation" and an "equal opportunity." Thus the discrimination provisions that require "equal treatment" under this portion of the CFHA have not been interpreted to impose on housing providers a duty of greater than equal treatment to avoid or to rectify discrimination in housing on the basis of an individual's race, color, religion, sex, national origin or familial status. In contrast, the CFHA's provisions defining discrimination due to disability require more of housing providers than to provide equal treatment to disabled and non-disabled persons alike. These CFHA provisions place on housing providers an affirmative duty to, among other things, "reasonably accommodate" a person with a disability if the accommodation may be necessary to afford the person "equal opportunity" to use and enjoy a dwelling, §44C(2). "Equal opportunity" under this portion of the CFHA gives the disabled the right to live in the residence and community of their choice because that right serves to end their exclusion from mainstream society.

Accordingly, although Defendant is correct that the CFHA's general prohibitions concerning housing discrimination do not require an entity to provide anything more than "equal treatment," Defendant is not correct that they have no obligation to give more than "equal treatment," because the CFHA's "reasonable accommodation" requirement concerning housing for people with disabilities by its very nature may impose a duty of more than equal treatment. To reasonably accommodate a disabled person, an individual or group may have to make an affirmative change in an otherwise valid policy. Thus the Rocking J community's CFHA imposed-obligation is more than to provide "equal treatment" for all disabled residents. It is to make necessary alterations in its rules so as to allow Townley "equal opportunity" to live in the residence of his choice.

Similarly, the fact that the Defendant does not generally discriminate against residents with disabilities does not insulate Defendant from its obligation to make a reasonable accommodation to Townley. Defendant's argument that it could not be found to have discriminated against Townley on the basis of disability because it already has many disabled elderly residents living there misses the point. The issue here is not whether the Defendant excludes or discriminates against residents with disabilities in general, but whether it failed to provide a *reasonable accommodation* to a particular individual who needed it in order to live in the Rocking J community. The fact that other disabled persons already live in the community does not relieve the community from its obligation to make reasonable accommodations to permit another disabled individual to live there.

This state has adopted the public policy of assisting the physically and developmentally disabled by promoting their deinstitutionalization and encouraging community integration. The overriding policy of the CFHA, which is to ensure equal opportunity to disabled persons to have adequate opportunities to select the housing of their choice, requires that Rocking J waive the age requirement. Consequently, state policy reflected in the CFHA and other statutes concerning disabled persons requires Rocking J to reasonably accommodate Townley by waiving its age requirement for a live-in caretaker for Townley.

Reversed.

1)

To: Emma Zucconi
Rommett, Fairbrooks, Fromkin & Zucconi, LLP

July 26th, 2005

Columbia Center for Disability Law
Santa Claritan, Columbia

Reference: Pinnacle Canyon Estates Homeowners Association--Request for a Disability Waiver

Dear Ms. Zucconi,

It is with great regret that we received your letter in the matter of the Winstons. The Winstons, naturally, still wish to live in the fine community of Pinnacle Canyon Estates, and the denial of the Homeowners Association of their request for a simple waiver, preventing them from completing the sale of the property from Pamela Garcia, represents, of course, a considerable blow to their aspirations, as they could hardly be expected to place Clint Winston in an institution. While we appreciate the concerns and arguments you have advanced in your letter, we believe that a closer examination of the applicable law will lead you to the same conclusion we have reached: that the denial of the waiver is in violation of the provision of the Columbia Fair Housing Act. We have no desire, of course, to be forced to go into litigation, even though the case is appropriate for summary judgment given the undisputed facts, when reconsideration of the applicable precedents and statutes may lead them to the same conclusion we have reached: that a waiver for Clint is a "reasonable accommodation" under the act.

The Statute

Perhaps, in your excitement over this case, and your obvious concern over maintaining the character of the community, you neglected a few of the finer points of the statute. The Columbia Fair Housing Act (CFHA) is concerned with any sort of discrimination that results in the denial of equal opportunity to enjoy a community, and the age-restrictive nature of Pinnacle Canyon Estates is not a defense to a disability discrimination claim.

Statutory Language

We would like to draw your attention to Section 44 of the CFHA, which bans discrimination on the basis of disability in any of the "terms, conditions or privileges of sale or rental of a dwelling ... because of a disability" either of the person directly purchasing or renting, or because of the disability of a person "residing in or intending to reside in that dwelling." Additionally, "discrimination" is defined as including a "refusal to make accommodations in rules, practices or services" is [sic] the accommodations are "necessary to afford the person equal opportunity to use and enjoy a dwelling." The statute defines a disability as any "mental or physical impairment that substantially limits at least one major life activity" and "dwelling" as "any building ... designed for occupancy." And the "condition" - - the minimum 35 year age requirement - - is equally obvious.

The Statutory Requirements Are Satisfied

While we appreciate your acknowledgment of Clint's disabled status, we would like to make it clear that Clint's disability would not be in dispute in this case: Clint cannot handle basic housekeeping or cooking, cannot handle his own finances, and cannot safely use public transportation – that is, he is restricted in ordinary domestic activities, economic life, and transportation, and these are clearly "major life activities." Similarly, a single-family house at Pinnacle Canyon is clearly "major life activities." Similarly, a single-family house at Pinnacle Canyon is clearly a "dwelling" as it is a building designed for occupancy. Additionally, Clint would, naturally, be a resident in the building, so he falls under 44B2. So the basic provisions are clearly satisfied.

Because Clint is so clearly disabled, a "refusal to make reasonable accommodations in rules," such as the "C C Rs" which the homeowners association refers to, could potentially implicate CFHA - 44C2. As we will explain below, the precedents of *Columbia* [sic] clearly support modification or waiver of age requirements; similarly, the precedents define "equal opportunity" much more broadly than strictly "equal treatment."

Facially Neutral Requirements Can Implicate Disability

Thankfully, we have more cases for guidance than simply *Townley*, which you referenced in your letter. *Project HOME* dealt with reluctance by a government, under pressure from various homeowners' associations, to provide accommodations in their zoning codes from persons with disabilities. The court there was dealing with a facially neutral statute that resulted in a denial of a permit for a facility because it lacked a backyard – a neutral statute that resulted in people with disabilities being denied housing. The court there indicated that any sort of "facially neutral requirement" – such as a minimum age of 35 – that resulted in the "prevent[ion of] a disabled individual from gaining access to proposed housing" would violate the CFHA. The court additionally commented that "traditional" requirements may have to be changed to accommodate those with disabilities.

Enforcement of Facially Neutral Restrictive Covenants Can be Discriminatory

We would certainly hope that the application of this binding precedent to the case would be obvious, it should be clear that under Columbia law, courts have interpreted neutral restrictions that result in individuals with disabilities being denied housing as being discriminatory, and therefore requiring reasonable accommodations. Clint Winston is disabled, and the refusal of the community to waive the requirement can constitute discrimination. The fact that it is a neutral rule applied fairly and broadly is, unfortunately for your clients, not a defense. Of course, while the court in *Project HOME* was dealing directly with zoning, it also explicitly ruled that enforcing a "restrictive covenant or ordinance, can *despite the apparent neutrality of the covenant* ... constitute discrimination because of a disability" as part of its holding (emphasis added).

Equal Opportunity is more than Equal Treatment

As the Court in *Townley* indicated, the requirement of "equal treatment" under CFHA-43 is different from "reasonable accommodation" and "equal opportunity" under s44. The Court in Townley found the "equal opportunity" provisions create an affirmative duty to reasonably accommodate, even when dealing with neutral rules and regulations - - that equal opportunity can incorporate an affirmative duty to waive a general rule in a specific case. In this case, in order to avoid discriminating against an individual with a disability, the CFHA is obliged to make all reasonable accommodations for him.

Waiving an enforcement of a covenant can be reasonable

An individual with a disability, such as Clint Winston, is allowed to invoke the "reasonable accommodation" requirement if the accommodation "may be necessary" to allow that individual full and fair access to housing. The court has expressly found that a "reasonable accommodation would have been to waive enforcement of the covenant;" this is especially true when it would not "impose an undue financial or administrative burden ... nor would it undermine the basic purpose behind the practice of enforcement." Similarly, to "reasonably accommodate a disabled person, an individual or group may have to make an affirmative change in an otherwise valid policy[.]"

The test as outlined in Project HOME indicates what is "reasonable" only in the negative; that is, it defines an unreasonable burden as an undue financial or administrative burden or an accommodation that would undermine the basic purpose behind the practice of enforcement. In this case, we are merely asking that one developmentally disabled individual, so disabled that he is effectively unable to function without adult supervision at all times, be allowed to live with his parents. As he has something of an outside occupation in the workshop, he would not be present during the day, and Margaret and Ralph Winston would be available during the evenings to supervise him and make sure he does not disturb the other residents. Moreover, Clint is "quiet and shy ... [h]e doesn't really approach strangers," meaning that he would be unlikely to disturb the peace of the other residents.

In this instance, the waiver of the age requirement would not lead to a fundamental change, nor would it even lead to minor children residing in the community, but simply one quiet, loving, disabled adult. Specifically, it would not be a financial or administrative burden, because the Winstons would be responsible for caring for Clint, nor would it undermine the basic purpose of enforcing the age restriction, because the Winstons themselves would still meet the age restriction, and Clint is in any event not a minor that the PCE is allowed to discriminate against.

Public Policy Supports the Grant of Accommodations

In drafting the CFHA, Columbia was trying to copy federal law, as well as to "undertake vigorous steps to provide equal opportunity in housing ... extend housing discrimination protection to the disabled, exempt housing for the elderly from the provisions prohibiting discrimination against families with children ..." (with "children" in this context meaning minor children). The legislature, in their inquiry into the problems of people with disabilities, have found that facially neutral rules and regulations resulted in the disabled being denied access to housing. Alas, we fear that what is happening in this case, with the application of Pinnacle Canyon's sensible, neutral rule regarding age being used in such a manner that Clint Winston will not have a place to live, precisely the sort of application of neutral rules to discriminate that the legislature was concerned with.

The legislature also intended to assist the physically and developmentally disabled by promoting their deinstitutionalization and encouraging community integration. Of course, Pinnacle Canyon is essentially trying to force the Winstons to institutionalize their own child, against the goal of encouraging integration, by preventing him from living with the two people who have helped him lead his life happily despite his disability. This goal of integrating the disabled - - of making them welcomed and accepted as part of the community - - is completely thwarted when they are denied their ability to live with their caregivers - - and it was probably this concern that led the legislature to include the aforementioned inclusion of "[disabled people] residing in or intending to reside in that dwelling."

Additionally, while you maintain that *Townley* is only applicable to "homeowner/residents," the statute itself makes no distinctions between people with disabilities, people living with people with disabilities, and people associated with people with disabilities. To assume that courts will make distinction when the legislature did not – and in fact expressly included all three categories, including the one at tissue – strikes me as a rather adventurous litigation strategy. This is especially so when you consider that remedial statutes are to be "generously construed, and any exemptions must be construed narrowly" in order to effectuate the goals of the statute. The goals are clearly to protect individuals with disabilities from discrimination, even discrimination based on neutral statutes.

Conclusion

Pinnacle Canyons [sic] is under a duty not to discriminate against the disabled, even in its applications of neutral rules. Clint is disabled; he is being denied reasonable accommodations, which would not impose a financial burden or change the nature of the community or undermine the purpose of the restriction. The PCE is under an affirmative duty under the law to avoid discriminating even with respect to neutral law, and their position on the waiver issue is resulting in discrimination and a denial of Clint's rights to "equal opportunity" for housing.

Claims of Pinnacle Valley

We hope that you see the logic and justice in the Winstons' request for a simple waiver of the 35-year age minimum for one person. However, we are very much cognizant of some of the concerns and legal issues raised in your letter, and we would like to do our best to alleviate them, to the extent we have failed to do so already.

"Purely a Function of Age"

You indicated in your letter that the decision to deny Clint Winston a waiver was "purely a function of his age." We do not dispute that, and of course believe that you only have the best of intentions, of maintaining the nature of the community as being geared towards "older persons." But as we indicated above, the basis on which you discriminate under the CFHA does not matter; "discrimination" is merely a function of denial of opportunities, and the non-waiver has denied Clint the opportunity to live in that beautiful community. CC&Rs are certainly contractual – but contractual provision must be waived under the CFHA if they result in discrimination against the disabled.

"Completely Exempt from the Age Discrimination Laws"

Your claim that PCE, as a housing development for older persons, is exempt from age discrimination laws is inaccurate, for the reasons described above. However, your letter did indicate a legitimate concern with falling below the "80% breakpoint" and ceasing to be considered as "housing for older persons," and that you are on the 80% level currently. On this subject, I have wonderful news and can completely alleviate your concerns. As the court indicated in *Townley* – and as you indicated in your letter – the 80% requirement only applies to units, not individuals. As the "unit" the Winstons will be purchasing would have not one, but two individuals over 55 living in the unit, a waiver of the age requirement for Clint would have no effect and would maintain Pinnacle Canyon at its current level of 80% of units being inhabited by those over-55. As far as your concern over a "pattern" of waiving the age requirement, Courts have explicitly stated that disability discrimination is a very "fact-specific" process; obliging the Winstons with a waiver in this case would not have the effect of obliging the Homeowners Association to grant them in future cases. It would not "undermine the basic purpose behind the practice of enforcement" of the age restrictions, because the individuals living there would primarily meet them; it is simply an additional accommodation.

We acknowledge that you may be concerned over any sort of "disability" being used as the basis for a waiver; after all, what if disabled individuals under 55 were to try to live in Pinnacle Valley? You may well be obliged to grant accommodations to some of them – but as you point out in your letter, accommodations must be "reasonable." This is a one-off case, and there has been no indication there has been a flood of under-55 disabled individuals seeking to purchase homes (and they would still have to find the money, mind) in Pinnacle Canyon.   But, as indicated above, this is very "fact specific," and accommodations allowing households of those under-55 may well be viewed as "unreasonable by the courts." Even if they are not, if the PCE is already legally obliged under the CFHA, denial of a waiver in this case will not affect their legal duties *viz* other disabled individuals, so the waiver or lack thereof in this case won't affect your clients['] rights.

We, of course, share your concern over current residents who wish to allow teenagers or rowdy young adults to live in your fine community. However, allowing one disabled individual – who cannot drive himself and has difficulty communicating – will not result in a significant increase in "traffic and noise pollution." Clint will not add to traffic, for the simple reason that he cannot drive, and there is no indication anywhere that he is "rowdy" in the least. Of course, your clients may be concerned with the broader principle, but a concern with broad principles in the general case is hardly a viable excuse to discriminate in specific cases. Again, in *Townley*, the court rejected a very similar slippery-slope argument, and it would seem unlikely that the court would accept it here, given the "fact-specific" nature of disability claims. Of course, we very much hope that your clients will somehow see the folly of prolonged litigation on this issue.

Financial and Administrative Burdens

As far as the administrative burdens you are concerned with, you should keep in mind that the courts have warned against the dangers of overestimating the actual administrative burdens individuals with disabilities would pose – the "false assumptions" that people, regretfully, so often make when assessing the costs of disabled individuals. The PCE would only be obliged – if at all, and I am not entirely sure that is the case – to assist with Clint Winston in the event of the death of both Ralph and Margaret Winston. If those sorts of concerns are helping thwart the waiver, we would of course be willing to discuss them with the PCE, and perhaps appoint a trustee or administrator, or prepare an acceptable will to be witnessed by members of the Homeowners Association, to take over in the case that both of the older Winstons perish, so that your Homeowners Association would not be burdened with the tasks of a "social services agency." Additionally, insofar as there are financial burdens, surely prolonged and pointless litigation would pose a more severe one than administrative tasks in the event of the deaths of people who are currently over 15 years below the average U.S. life expectancy.
Overall

I am quite concerned, of course, about your arguments revolving around "reverse discrimination." Unlike the courts in Franklin, Columbia Courts have not found "reverse discrimination" to be a concern in interpreting disability discrimination. While we certainly respect the courts of Franklin, their holdings are not binding on our courts, and our courts have clearly rejected "neutrality" as a basis for evading liability, affirmative duties and responsibilities under the CFHA. In Franklin, "equal treatment" is sufficient to satisfy their version of the FHA; in Columbia, it is not, and the law imposes and affirmative duty to act.

Additionally, we are puzzled by your letter's references to section 42's exemption for "housing for older persons." We fear that you may be misstating the law. Pinnacle Canyon is clearly[,] at the current time, evincing an intent to provide housing to those persons fifty-five years of age or older. However, the exemption for "housing for older persons" only applies to the provisions of the CFHA relating to familial status – and, as indicated in 41's definitions section, "familial status" refers to "individuals younger than the age of eighteen years." Which is to say, the CFHA's discrimination exception speaks to families having minor children, and only allows familial discrimination on that basis. There is no exception for other forms of discrimination on that basis. There is no exception for other forms of discrimination, or indeed for disability discrimination. We would hate for the Homeowners association of a place the Winstons very much intend to live waste their money on litigating an issue based on a simple, and understandable, misreading of the statute.

We of course applaud the accommodations and expenses the PCE have undertaken to make accommodations for your disabled residents. Of course, the general gives way to the specific; accommodations are required in every case where they are appropriate and reasonable – as the court in *Townley* indicated, general non-discrimination does not "insulate [from] obligation[s] to make a reasonable accommodation;" the test is for, as the court indicated, a particular individual and not the disabled in general. However, your client's generosity on accommodations is a great thing, and a significant factor in our client's desire to move there. And as far as a housing glut is concerned, the fact our client's wish to move to the PCE in such a glut, even after being denied a waiver, is indicative of how pleasant a place it is, and of the unique nature of any given piece of property. Moreover, given such a glut, the PCE may wish to consider the consequences of not letting its members sell their property to willing, qualified, and age-appropriate *bona fide* buyers.

Conclusion

The proposed accommodation is not a "fundamental alteration [of the nature of the property or covenant] or substantial administrative or financial burden." As indicated above, many of the concerns you outline in your letter concern a great many things that have little or nothing to do with Clint Winston. Waivers will still be granted on an individual basis, Clint will not significantly impact the community, and we can work around any financial or administrative burdens the PCE is concerned with. We would hate to have to litigate this case, as Columbian law is clear that neutral laws can be considered "discriminatory," that the Winstons fall under the protections given to individuals living with
disabled persons, and that a waiver of a condition of a covenant is clearly a "reasonable accommodation," and such litigation would only result in a waste of resources for a Homeowner's Association that the Winstons fully expect to join shortly.

We are quite cognizant of the emphasis on the legal concerns in this letter. We must, of course, point out that nobody disputes that Clint Winston is a caring, loving individual, or that his parents are excellent caretakers. Nor is it doubtful that a disabled person with limited communication skills, such as Clint, would damage the quiet and placid nature of the community in the same manner as minor children or non-disabled adults would.

      Truly Yours,

The Columbia Center for Disability Law

Answer 2 to Question PT-A

1)

To: Emma Zucconi, attorney for Pinnacle Canyon Estates Homeowners
Association
From: Applicant, Columbia Center for Disability Law
Date: July 26, 2005

Subject: In re: Ralph, Margaret, and Clint Winston

Dear Ms. Zucconi,

I am writing in response to your letter dated July 22, 2005, refusing to grant a waiver to Ralph, Margaret, and Clint Winston from the Pinnacle Canyons [sic] Estates (PCE) covenants, conditions, and restrictions (CC&R). We are disappointed that the PCE Homeowners Association declined to grant the Winstons a waiver from the CC&R provision forbidding persons under the age of 35 from residing on the premises. I write to you now to note that it is our position that the PCE Homeowners Association is legally required to waive the age restriction for Clint in order to comply with § 44C of the Columbia Fair Housing Act (CFHA) preventing discrimination due to disabilities, and to reiterate our request for that waiver.

<u>Under the CFHA, PCE is required to provide "reasonable accommodations in rules, policies, practices or services if the accommodation may be necessary to afford the [disabled] person equal opportunity to use and enjoy a dwelling."</u>

Clint Winston, the 23[-]year[-]old son of Ralph and Margaret, is disabled under the definition used by the CFHA, as he suffers from a mental impairment that "substantially limits at least one major life activity." § 41. Clint functions well below his 23[-]year[-]old level, and has some difficulty learning, remembering and communicating. He is unable to cook for himself or perform his own housekeeping or money management. Thus, he is incapable of living on his own, a major life activity. Furthermore, while he works in a sheltered workshop, he is unable to use public transportation to and from, so he is reliant on Ralph and Margaret to drive him, thus limiting another major life activity, employment.

Clint's parents take care of him, provide assistance with his housekeeping and get him to and from work. Without their assistance, since he cannot live on his own, he would require institutionalization, which his parents absolutely reject. It is their wish that he live with them in the house they attempted to buy in PCE. Section 44C of the CFHA includes in the definition of discrimination against disabled persons the refusal to make "reasonable accommodations in rules" if that accommodation is necessary to afford the disabled person "equal opportunity to use and enjoy a dwelling." Therefore, PCE must provide "reasonable accommodations" so that Clint may enjoy "equal opportunity to use and enjoy a dwelling" with his parents. § 44C. For this reason, the failure to grant a waiver results in discrimination against Clint and his family on the basis of his disability, not on his age as you suggest in your letter we have been arguing.

Equal Opportunity to use and enjoy a dwelling

Columbia courts have interpreted the "equal opportunity to use and enjoy a dwelling" provision to give a right to disabled individuals to live in the residence and community of their choice. Rocking J. The provision was intended to "end their exclusion from mainstream society". Rocking J. For this reason, the mere fact that other housing exists in the community for the Winstons is insufficient to argue that a reasonable accommodation need not be made to allow them equal opportunity to enjoy PCE. Furthermore, § 44B of the CFHA forbids discrimination against any person on the basis not only of the disability of that person, but of "a person residing in or intending to reside in that dwelling" after sale, and of "a person associated with that person." Therefore, since discrimination includes the refusal to make reasonable accommodations, Ralph and Margaret have the same right to those reasonable accommodations as do their son, and it is their intent that he live with them in PCE.

Section 44C covers waivers from rules of otherwise general application

A refusal to make reasonable accommodations in rules to accommodate a disabled person violates § 44C even if that rule is of otherwise general application. The Columbia Court of Appeal held that no "causal nexus" is required between the reasonable accommodation requested and the handicap of the prospective resident. Project Home. The court in Project Home noted that the § 44C contains "an independent definition of 'discrimination'" that is not modified by § 44B's requirement that the discrimination be "because of disability." The Columbia Court of Appeal similarly noted in Rocking J that the CFHA provisions regarding disability discrimination are not governed by the same "equal treatment" construction given to the CFHA provisions governing other types of discrimination (such as race or sex). The court noted that § 44C requires "more of housing providers than to provide equal treatment to disabled and non-disabled persons alike." Rocking J. Therefore, your argument that Clint's disability has nothing to do with application of the age limitation in the CC&R is irrelevant to PCE's legal requirement to provide reasonable accommodation to Clint in the form of a waiver.

While the Franklin Court of Appeal in Noble did find that a similar age restriction in a 55+ community did not need to be waived to accommodate a disabled person, that court used reasoning that has been explicitly rejected by the Columbia Court of Appeal. While the Fair Housing statute in Franklin and Columbia may be identical, the construction made by the courts of the statute have deviated. The Franklin court in Noble argued that the age requirement was not discrimination "based on disability," and found "no causal nexus" between the requirement and Noble's disability, while the Columbia court rejected a requirement for causal nexus in Project Home as I have noted. Similarly, the Franklin court limited Noble's rights to accommodation to situations where necessary to allow a disabled person enjoyment of housing on "an equal basis" with others, while the Columbia court explicitly found a greater requirement in Rocking J. The reasoning of the Franklin court has been rejected by the Columbia courts, and does not justify PCE's refusal to grant Clint a waiver.

<u>PCE's accommodation of other disabled residents does not rebut their discrimination in this case.</u>

You argued that PCE has never failed to make accommodation for your qualified residents. This is an admirable position for PCE to take, and shows an attention to the needs of disabled residents that we hoped would be extended to Clint. However, the lack of discrimination against other residents does not affect your legal responsibility to reasonably accommodate Clint. Rocking J. The purpose of the CFHA was in part to address individual needs and circumstances. Project Home. The obligation of the community to make these reasonable accommodations extends to each and every disabled individual who requires it.

<u>The reasoning of Rocking J is not limited to individuals who have already qualified for residence[.]</u>

Furthermore, your argument that Rocking J is limited to homeowners/residents who qualify for admission under the neutral criterial is not supported by either the statute in question or the case. While Rocking J does indeed concern a disabled man over 55 and his request for a waiver for his assistant who did not meet the age requirement, the reasoning in no way limits the case to this scenario, but addresses generally the waiver of the age requirement as a reasonable accommodation to a disabled person. Furthermore, as noted previously, the protections of § 44 extend not only to the disabled person himself, but to persons associated with him, and to cases where the disabled person will be living in the residence after sale, and thus will extend to the Winstons here.

<u>The waiver being asked for here is a "reasonable accommodation" as 1) it will not result in the fundamental alteration in the nature of a program and (2) it will not impose undue financial or administrative burdens on defendant[.]</u>

The Supreme Court of Columbia has held that an accommodation is not reasonable if it (1) requires a fundamental alteration in the nature of a program, or (2) imposes undue financial or administrative burdens on the defendant. Rocking J. The waiver of the age limitation in the CC &R requested by the Winstons meets neither of these criteria and thus is a reasonable accommodation that PCE is legally obligated to make.

<u>Fundamental alteration in the nature of the program</u>

In your letter, you suggest that this waiver will result in a fundamental alteration in the PCE community for a number of reasons; however, none of these reasons are entirely accurate.

First, you argue that the grant of the waiver will result in the loss of the exemption under § 42 because PCE must maintain 80% unit occupancy by person 55+. However, the language of the waiver provision only requires that 80% of the units are occupied by at least one person 55 or older. Here, both Ralph and Margaret are over 55; therefore, they will be part of the 80% requirement you need regardless of whether Clint lives with them. Rocking J.

Second, you argue that PCE will run the risk of losing its exemption from the familial status provisions because PCE is required by § 42 to publish and adhere to policies and procedures demonstrating "an intent by the owner or manager to provide housing for persons fifty-five years of age or older." However, as the Columbia Court of Appeal noted in Rocking J, a waiver granted "in order to comply with state law" by reasonably accommodating the needs of a disabled person does not demonstrate any change in an intent to provide housing for the elderly.

Third, PCE will not be subject to a fundamental change based on changes in the community resulting from a flood of applications. You note that you receive two requests a month for waivers. However, granting Clint's waiver, as required by law, will not require you to grant the waivers of non-disabled persons. This is a waiver based on Clint's disability, not his age, and each waiver will still remain a "fact-intensive, case-specific' determination. Rocking J. Therefore, your concerns that frequent granting of waivers will result in a change in the suitability of the community for your elderly residents, and a decrease in property values, are unwarranted as this waiver would not require you to remove the age provision entirely.

Undue financial and administrative burdens

In your letter, you also suggest that this waiver will present undue financial and administrative burdens for PCE, and is therefor an unreasonable accommodation. However, the waiver will not present the burdens you describe. First, PCE already makes accommodations to its common areas to provide for its other disabled residents, this showing that PCE is able, and admirably, willing, to so accommodate its residents. Second, you suggest that the potential of the Ralph and Margaret predeceasing Clint presents the danger of administrative costs in caring for Clint after their deaths. This concern relates to "unfounded fears of difficulties about the problems their [the disabled persons] tenancies may pose." Project Home. It is exactly these types of concerns that resulted in the housing discrimination against disabled persons that the CFHA' s provision against disability discrimination were enacted to prevent. PCE has other disabled residents that have not apparently provided this type of administrative burden. Furthermore, as an elderly housing community, [it] is likely often formed to make interim arrangements and track down family members. The concern that Clint's disability in and of itself presents an administrative burden is not a sufficient or acceptable rationale to avoid the application of Columbia law preventing discrimination against the disabled in housing.

Finally, Ralph and Margaret are in their late fifties, and will likely be available to take care of Clint for many years. On the event of their deaths, the Winstons had other children that will likely be available to caretake for Clint. The Winstons, as Clint's caretakers and like parents everywhere, have the responsibility of arranging for his needs now and after their death. PCE, as a housing association, bears no greater administrative burden from their residency than they do for other residents.

For these reasons, we ask that you reconsider the decision to refuse a waiver of the age limitation in the PCE CC&Rs for the Winstons. PCE is legally required to waive the age provision, even though it is a provision of general applicability, in order to make a reasonable accommodation for Clint. Furthermore, the waiver does not present the danger of a fundamental alteration to the nature of PCE, nor does it present a risk of undue financial and administrative burdens and thus is a reasonable accommodation. Clint is a quiet, gentle man who has never posed a difficulty at any of the places he's previously lived, and the Winstons are ready and willing to pursue this matter in court if that becomes necessary. We hope that it does not come to that.

Respectfully,

Applicant

APPENDIX B

PASS SAMPLE ANSWERS TO SELECTED PERFORMANCE TEST QUESTIONS

Table of Contents

PASS SAMPLE ANSWER to July 2001 Performance Test B – *People v. Wils*

Introduction to Appellant's Opening Brief in the matter of the People v. Wils

Appellant Thomas Wils brings this appeal following conviction in the Columbia Superior Court on counts of robbery and burglary. A careful review of the trial court record reveals, among other points, the material facts set forth below. Based on these facts, and on the legal argument that follows, Mr. Wils contends that the jury was erroneously instructed on a number of key questions that resulted in the miscarriage of justice for which Mr. Wils is now unfortunately paying most dearly. Accordingly, Mr. Wils urges this Court to reverse the judgment against him on both counts.

Statement of Facts for Appellant's Opening Brief

Mr. Thomas Wils fled his native Ruritania to seek political asylum in this country, and was welcomed into the home of Arno and Vivian Pir. The Pirs were also natives of Ruritania and were active in local political efforts to obtain freedom for their homeland. The Pirs, who had no children, entered into an informal agreement with Mr. Wils, whereby they provided him free room and board in exchange for some unspecified number of odd jobs he would do around their home. In addition, from time to time, Vivian Pir gave Mr. Wils some additional small amounts of spending money.

There appears to have been no time frame set for the informal living arrangement that was first established when Mr. Wils initially moved in with the Pirs, though both Vivian and Arno Pir claimed that they hoped and expected Mr. Wils would eventually either obtain some gainful employment and/or go to college.

At some point, Mr. Wils was asked to perform more extensive work for the Pirs, namely a remodeling of their garage into a sort of guesthouse. And all concur that at some point in and around this time, Vivian Pir promised to give Mr. Wils a used automobile owned by the Pirs, the Triumph Spitfire that is central to the alleged burglary and alleged robbery. What is unclear from and in fact disputed in the trial record, is the exact financial arrangement for this garage work, and whether or not delivery of the car was tied in to completion of the garage work. According to the testimony of Mr. Wils, and, quite significantly, according to that of Arno Pir as well, Vivian Pir had agreed give Mr. Wils the car for the work done in the garage. Accordingly, Mr. Wils believed that he had the right to claim ownership of the Spitfire car after he had completed the garage job. And, as discussed below, Mr. Wils promised to give Mr. Wils the car and ownership papers in July of 1999.

Vivian Pir, however, testified that she agreed to give Wils the Spitfire car, not in exchange for work, but as transportation if he went to college. Therefore, by her account, he had no right to the car because he had never gone to college. An additional fact testified to in the lower court, bearing on the car dispute, is that Mr. Wils was unable to drive due to blackouts he suffered after having been severely beaten by Ruritanian police. Because of this, Mr. Wils would never have been able to use the car as transportation anyway, and therefore understood the car was being offered as payment, and that Mr. Wils would then be able to sell it in exchange for cash that he was owed.

The car in question was central to a dispute between the Pirs and Mr. Wils in the spring of 1999, after which Mr. Wils was thrown out of the Pirs' home. Mr. Wils subsequently sought work and places to live in the homes of other Ruritanians, but was refused by many of them, according to his accounts, because of negative things Vivian Pir said about him in the community. Eventually reduced to living on the streets and begging for food, Mr. Wils once again turned to Arno Pir, this time in a request on July 3, 1999 that the Pirs turn over to Mr. Wils the Triumph Spitfire. Arno Pir told Mr. Wils that Vivian Pir had or probably had the car's ownership papers in her purse, and that Arno Pir would deliver the car and ownership documents to Mr. Wils on or around July 20, 1999.

On July 5, 1999, Mr. Wils went to the Pir house to get the car himself. Mr. Wils entered the Pir's home, while neither Vivian nor Arno Pir was present, and waited for Vivian to return. Mrs. Pirs returned some time later to find Mr. Wils eating some food from the Pirs' refrigerator. Exactly what happened next, when Vivian Pir found Thomas Wils in her kitchen, is disputed. According to Vivian Pir, Thomas Wils started toward her in a threatening manner, and she grabbed a broom to defend herself. By Thomas Wils' account, however, it was Mrs. Pir who first acted aggressively toward him, shouting at him and threatening to call the police. What happened next is also unclear. There was some physical contact between the two, as Mr. Wils attempted to gain access to documents he believed to be inside Vivian Pir's purse. She claims that Mr. Wils punched her, while he contends that he merely pushed her aside to reach the purse.

After looking inside Mrs. Pir's purse for the title papers to the automobile, papers which Arno Pir himself had said would likely be in his wife's purse, and not finding those papers, Thomas Wils took some credit cards, a cell phone, and a mirror. He pawned the phone and mirror (for about $15) and charged about $4,000 worth of expenses on the cards–a sum of money he testified that he viewed as equivalent to the value of the Spitfire that he believed was his. On July 31, Mr. Wils was arrested on those charges, which now form the subject of this appeal.

<u>Argument</u>

I. <u>The trial court's error of refusing to instruct the jury that a bona fide belief in a claim of right to property would negate the larcenous intent element of burglary resulted in a miscarriage of justice, as such evidence existed that would have exculpated the defendant had jurors been properly instructed.</u>

"Every person who, without consent, enters any house apartment or other building with intent to commit larceny is guilty of burglary," Columbia Penal Code Section 459. And larceny is defined under the Columbia Penal Code as "the taking of personal property of another, without his consent, *with the intent to steal*," Columbia Penal Code Section 454, emphasis added.

This intent to deprive element has been defined by the Columbia courts as an intent to permanently deprive *(Brown)*; the intent to merely deprive temporarily will not suffice. Further, Columbia courts have long held that if the defendant holds a bona fide belief that his taking is based on a claim of right to the property, that belief negates the intent to permanently deprive, the requisite larcenous intent element of a burglary offense *(Alvarado)*.

It is undisputed that Mr. Wils entered the Pirs' home without their consent. However, ample evidence was presented at trial that Mr. Wils did not enter their home with intent to steal anything, but rather to claim a car he believed he had the right to as payment for services he rendered to the Pirs in remodeling their garage. He further believed that Vivian Pir had promised him the car as said payment, and that Arno Pir had told him that he would find ownership papers to the car in Mrs. Pir's purse.

Because larceny is a requisite and necessary element of burglary, had the jury been properly instructed about the effect of a genuine claim of right on the larcenous intent element, and had they found the testimony of Thomas Wils and Arno Pir to be credible evidence that Mr. Wils in fact held such a genuine belief in his right to the Triumph Spitfire, then the jury would have found the defendant Thomas Wils innocent of the burglary offense, for which he is now paying such a dear price.

In *Alvarado*, cited above, the Columbia court found that the defendant's actions did not demonstrate a bona fide claim of right. Here, however, in the case of Thomas Wils, there is ample evidence that would likely have led jurors to find a claim of right. In *Alvarado*, there was doubt that the defendant truly intended to retrieve property to which she believed that she was entitled. Rather, it seemed in the *Alvarado* factual situation, the taking was more of a retribution and effort to general compensation. By contrast, in the case at bar, not only did the defendant himself testify that he went to the Pirs' home to obtain the car he was promised, but he went looking for title to that same car in the exact spot Mr. Pir told him he would find the title documents: Mrs. Pir's purse. This was not a general foraging through the home of the Pirs, but a particularized quest to retrieve property Mr. Wils believed was his. And, had the trial court properly instructed the jury, there is a substantial likelihood that they would have found evidence of his true intent and, thus, found him not guilty of the alleged burglary.

II. The trial court's error of refusing to instruct the jury that a bona fide belief in a claim of right to property would negate the larcenous intent element of robbery resulted in a miscarriage of justice.

As stated in *People v. Cutler*, "[t]he taking of property is not larceny in the absence of an intent to steal, i.e. an intent to deprive its owner of it permanently." In *Cutler*, as in the case at bar, the defendant went to the alleged victim's house, not with the intent to rob, but intending only to recover money (in *Cutler*, and property in Wils' case), money/property that was due and owing. The argument, that the defendant honestly believed he was entitled to the money he took, was the sole basis of the *Cutler* defense. And the *Cutler* court held that the trial court's failure to allow jurors to consider that defense was a miscarriage of justice, which *required reversal* under the Columbia Constitution, because it "removed completely from the consideration of the jury a material issue raised by substantial evidence." The same is true here in the pending case: Evidence was presented by both the defense and the prosecution that Mr. Wils came to the Pirs' home seeking items that he believed he had the right to and that he believed would be located in Mrs. Pir's purse. Therefore, had the jury been properly instructed, there is a great likelihood that they would have exonerated Mr. Wils of the larceny charge. Accordingly, as was held by the court in *Cutler*, the trial court's failure to so properly instruct the jury now requires a reversal of the robbery conviction.

III. The trial court's error of refusing to instruct the jury sua sponte on trespass as a lesser included offense of burglary resulted in a miscarriage of justice.

Under *Alvarado*, it is clear that trespass is a lesser-included offense of burglary. Trespass includes the elements of unconsented entry into a building, but does not include the additional element requisite for burglary, that of larcenous intent. As also stated in *Alvarado*, a "trial court must instruct the jury sua sponte on a lesser-included offense . . . if there is substantial evidence that, if accepted, would absolve the defendant from guilt of the greater offense but not the lesser." In other words, the trial court in *People v. Wils* was required to, and failed to, instruct the jury on the lesser-included offense of trespass, because, as is clear from the trial court record, there is substantial evidence of an unconsented entry into the Pirs' home (the trespass), but also of substantial evidence that would negate the misconception that Mr. Wils entered said home with intent to steal (requisite for the alleged burglary), evidence that proves instead that Mr. Wils entered that building only with the intent to reclaim property he believed to be his own. Had the trial court properly instructed the jury on the lesser-included offense of trespass, therefore, as it was required to have done, there is a substantial likelihood that Mr. Wils would only have been convicted on that much less serious offense and not of the offense of burglary, for which he is now unjustly being punished.

Conclusion

For the foregoing reasons, and based on the facts of record and the three aforementioned legal grounds, Appellant, Mr. Thomas Wils, respectfully requests that his appeal be granted and that his convictions on the charges of burglary and robbery correspondingly be reversed.

PASS SAMPLE ANSWER to February 2002 Performance Test A – *Estate of Keefe*

Memorandum

To: Gretchen Pronko
From: Applicant
Re: Documents requested in matter of Estate of Keefe

Attached please find declarations for the four witnesses whose testimony, it appears from the file, may be useful to supporting our client. In addition, please find the drafts you requested of Sections III and IV of our Memorandum of Points and Authorities in Opposition to Grant Keefe's Motion for Summary Judgment.

Declarations

Declaration of Mason Finch

I, Mason Finch, declare as follows:

1. I am the plaintiff in the currently pending action.

2. I am 38 years old, and am a single father of a 16 year-old daughter, Megan Finch.

3. I have been in practice as a marriage and family counselor in Columbia for the past 12 years.

4. I met Sandra Keefe, the decedent, in 1990, the same year I opened my own private practice.

5. Sandra Keefe and her sister, Mabel Keefe, owned a commercial building, which I managed for them in exchange for rent reduction on office space for my practice.

6. The office rental was originally $500, and I paid them $250 after the 50% discount, for which in return I provided approximately six hours per month of building management services.

7. At the time, my hourly rate was $40, though it gradually increased to $85 by 1994. Thus, at the $85 rate, I was providing the Keefe sisters with approximately $440 of my time in exchange for the $250 discount.

8. During this period, my daughter and I became close socially, as family friends, with Sandra and Mabel Keefe.

9. In 1994, Mabel Keefe suffered a stroke, and Sandra Keefe asked if I would reduce my counseling hours in order to provide caretaking services for Mabel (in the mornings) and for Sandra and Mabel (in the evenings), which reduction I agreed to out of affection for the Keefe

sisters, to further the communal bond that had been forged between our two families, and in exchange for their offer to allow Megan and me to live rent-free in an apartment-type unit attached to their home. Sandra also wanted me to use the office space rent-free for those hours I was still counseling.

10. Because of my having reduced counseling hours to care for Mabel and Sandra, the monthly revenue from my counseling practice was reduced by about $1000. In addition, I also had to reduce the amount of time I was able to devote to building and maintaining my practice (i.e. I had much less time for networking, professional development, and the like.).

11. I was also obliged to forego a then-present opportunity for a tuition waiver and graduate stipend in a Ph.D. program at the University of Columbia, the cost of which would be prohibitive to me were I to attempt to enroll today. Without that additional degree, I had hit a ceiling in terms of the value of my services, in contrast with colleagues such as Ralph Sanchez (whose education, experience, and pay rate mirrored my own up until that time), who enjoyed substantial increases in salary after completing the same Ph.D. program I delayed pursuing in order to care for Mabel and Sandra Keefe.

12. After Mabel died, Megan and I moved into the main house, at Sandra's request. Also at Sandra's request, I increased the amount of time I cared for Sandra, reducing my counseling practice to only three hours per week so that I could do such things for Sandra as cooking, shopping, cleaning, and miscellaneous errands, taking Sandra to doctors' appointment and the like.

13. I performed such caretaking services for Sandra for approximately five years until her death.

14. Until near the very end, Sandra was most lucid and clear thinking. She continually thanked me and assured me that I would be free to live in her house for the rest of my life, and that I would be given income from the office building rentals also for my entire lifetime, for the great service and sacrifices I performed for her.

15. Motivated by this thankfulness she felt for me and the sacrifices I made, and by sincere affection for myself and my daughter, Sandra Keefe told me she would write into her will that I could live in her home rent-free for however long I wanted for the rest of my life, and would make sure in her will that I would have the rental income from the office building for my lifetime.

16. Also motivated by this appreciation and by familial-like sincere affection for myself and my daughter Megan, Sandra Keefe contributed some $50,000 over five years toward Megan's college education. She knew that I had sacrificed my earning potential for her and wanted to make sure that I could take care of Megan properly and that I would be provided for.

17. Megan and I continued to live in the Keefe home as Sandra had wished for 2.5 years following Sandra's death, and only just recently did I learn of Grant Keefe's intent to evict us from his aunt's home when I received such notice from a real estate broker.

Declaration of Mildred Fowler

I, Mildred Fowler, declare as follows:

1. I served as a housekeeper in the Keefe home, cleaning house for Mabel and Sandra Keefe for some 20 years.

2. I knew Sandra Keefe well, after working for her for all those years, and she frequently shared with me details of her family and personal life.

3. Mabel and Sandra told me about Mr. Finch, that they had given him space in their office building in exchange for the helpful work he was doing for them, and I regularly heard them both speak well of him.

4. Mr. Finch and his daughter moved into the Keefe home after Mabel had a stroke, and Sandra told me how much Mr. Finch helped her and how dependent she had become on his assistance. Among other nice things she had said about him, she said she "didn't know what she'd do without him."

5. Sandra Keefe told me repeatedly that she was so thankful for Mr. Finch's help that she intended to make a will that would allow Mr. Finch and Megan to continue living in her home for his lifetime, so long as he wanted, and that she wanted to do so to help him and Megan and to thank him for having taken such good care of her.

Declaration of Ralph Sanchez

I, Ralph Sanchez, declare as follows:

1. I know Mason Finch professionally and consider him a colleague.

2. I have known Mason Finch since college, where we both attended undergraduate and advanced courses together.

3. Mason Finch and I both received the same undergraduate and master's degrees from the University.

4. After completing those initial degree programs, we both entered private practice and, from what I understood, Mr. Finch and I had parallel billing rates and earnings.

5. My earnings dipped nearly 50% during the couple of years I went back to the University, but after completing the Ph.D. program and receiving my doctoral degree in 1995, my earning scale increased substantially.

6. I now earn approximately $78,000 annually.

(*Note*: Applicants could have, but did not have to, draft a declaration of Tori Phillips as well.)

Section III—Statement of Disputed Facts

Statement	Citation to Evidence
1. Sandra Keefe orally promised to allow Mr. Finch to live in her home for the rest of his life for free.	Declaration of Mason Finch at parg. 14
2. Sandra Keefe orally promised that Mr. Finch would be given rental income from the proceeds of the apartment building she owned, for his lifetime.	Declaration of Mason Finch at parg. 14 Declaration of Mildred Fowler at parg. 5
3. Sandra Keefe promised to confirm both of the promises made in paragraphs two and three above, in writing, in her will.	Declaration of Mason Finch at parg. 15
4. Sandra Keefe felt that she had not yet thanked Mr. Finch enough for all that he had sacrificed and for all the care and support he had given both her sister and herself, and Sandra Keefe wanted to see him further compensated by making sure that she provided for Mr. Finch and his daughter after she died.	Declaration of Mason Finch at pargs. 14, 15 Declaration of Mildred Fowler at parg. 5
5. Grant Keefe did not spend substantial amounts of time with his aunt, only about six hours a week, and only in the months before she died.	Declaration of Grant Keefe at parg.4

Section IV—Argument

A. <u>Because evidence exists which proves that the decedent made an oral contract to make a will, and because that evidence is disputed by the Defendant, the Plaintiff's claim based on that oral contract is valid and ripe for litigation on the merits, and Defendant's attempt to resolve the claim based on summary judgment is improper.</u>

Defendant allegedly reviewed the papers and effects of the decedent, and claims that he found no signed writing evidencing the promises made by Sandra Keefe to Mason Finch. (Declaration of Grant Keefe at parg. 3). This does not mean, however, that no such promises were made.

Plaintiff presents credible evidence in the forms of sworn declarations from himself and from Mildred Fowler, the trusted housekeeper who served the Keefe sisters for 20 years, that Sandra Keefe promised Mason Finch a life estate in her home and in the rental proceeds from the office building she owned. (See Statement of Disputed Facts, hereinafter "DF," at pargs. 1, 2, and 3.) The Plaintiff's claim that such promises were made to him is further supported by the extensive evidence of detrimental reliance—that Plaintiff made great professional sacrifices in order to care for Mabel and Sandra Keefe because he was relying on Sandra's express oral promises to take care of his financial needs. (DF at parg. 4.)

Because the existence of those promises is disputed and because those promises are material to the claim based on oral contract, there exist triable issues of fact because of which the motion for summary judgment should be denied.

B. <u>The plaintiff's claim based on an oral contract does not fail simply by not being in writing, as it falls within one or more of the recognized exceptions to the Statute of Frauds, namely part performance or estoppel and/or unjust enrichment.</u>

Part Performance/Estoppel

Although the type of contract at issue in this action normally must be in writing (under Probate Code Section 150), Columbia courts have recognized that in some situations sufficient facts may be presented so as to take certain oral contracts out of the strict requirements of the statute of frauds (*Riganti*). *Riganti* recognizes this 'part performance exception' in those situations: 1) where the value of services is not clearly estimable and where the parties did not intend to measure them with ordinary pecuniary remuneration and 2) where, after the performance of said services, the plaintiff could not be restored to his pre-service situation.

These *Riganti* factors are met in the situation of Plaintiff, Mr. Finch, who provided extensive daily care for the Keefes, preparing meals, shopping, cooking, and even moving into the Keefe home in order to simply be available to Mabel and Sandra Keefe. (DF at parg. 4) There is no ordinary standard for measuring such broad services and it would be difficult, if not impossible, to place a fixed value on them, as Mr. Finch's actions were so extensive. Mr. Finch was compensated, in small part, by rent-free work and living space, but because this could not begin to compensate adequately for the great time, effort, and sacrifices he made, the clear inference is that these exchanges were not meant to compensate Mr. Finch fully, rather that he was meant to be compensated by the agreement to provide a life estate in the Keefe home and office rental proceeds. (DF at parg. 4)

As to the second *Riganti* element, it is clear that Mr. Finch so sacrificed his career to care for the Keefes that there is no way to restore him to his pre-service earning potential. (Finch Declaration at pargs. 10 and 11.) Thus, to now refuse to uphold that oral contract upon which Mr. Finch detrimentally relied, would result in an unconscionable injury (*Kennedy*).

Unjust Enrichment

In addition to the part performance/estoppel grounds set forth above, it would also serve to <u>unjustly enrich</u> the Defendant should the contract be barred simply by virtue of its oral nature, and thus equity here compels its enforcement (*Riganti*, *Kennedy*). Though the Defendant claims to have spent a lot of time with Sandra Keefe, he spent but six hours a week, and that only toward the end of her life, whereas the Plaintiff lived with her and cared for her some five years. To reward the Defendant simply because he is the legal heir, and disregard the multitude of facts that point to the Plaintiff's sacrifices and just reliance upon the oral promises, is inequitable and unjustly enriches the Defendant.

<u>C. The Plaintiff's claim, based on an oral contract, is not barred by the statute of limitations, as it was brought within the four-year period, applicable here to actions for quasi-specific performance.</u>

Plaintiff's claim here is for quasi-specific performance; he seeks a declaration of constructive trust over certain real property in order to accomplish the just results of the decedent's oral agreement to leave property rights to him by will. Per *Riganti*, such an action accrues on the death of the person who breached the agreement (here, Sandra Keefe, by failing to actually write the will). The action is governed by a four-year, rather than the two-year, statute of limitations that ordinarily applies to oral contracts *(Riganti)*. Because Plaintiff commenced this action in January of 2002, his claim is well within that four-year period (Sandra Keefe having died in August of 1999), and thus should not be barred by the statute of limitations.

Finally, even if this Court does not agree that the four-year statute of limitations should govern this action, under <u>equitable principles of laches,</u> it would seem unjust to allow the Defendant to come forth at this late stage, after some 2.5 years of allowing Mr. Finch to continue to reside in the Keefe home, and now contend that Mr. Finch does not have the right to even litigate his claim that he should be allowed the life estate in the Keefe home that he was promised and upon which he relied.

Conclusion

For the foregoing reasons and based on the disputed facts set forth above, there are genuine issues of material facts that are ripe for trial Accordingly, Plaintiff respectfully requests that the Defendant's Motion for Summary Judgment be denied.

The two requested memos are set forth below.

MEMORANDUM #1
To: Matt Mato
From: Applicant
Re: The Government's Case in a Possible Criminal Prosecution of Mr. Cruz

Below, please find my assessment of your requests to:

1. Identify the elements of a criminal violation of Section 515.201 of the Trading with the Enemies Act (hereinafter "TWEA"),

2. Indicate the evidence the government now possesses to establish each element, and

3. Determine whether the government may constitutionally use the presumption in the TWEA in a related criminal prosecution of Cruz, should the government in fact bring these charges against him.

1. Elements of a Criminal Violation of Section 515.201 of the TWEA

The TWEA, whose primary purpose according to *U.S. v. Macko* "is to stop the flow of hard currency from the U.S. to Cuba," has both civil and criminal penalties. In order to find a *criminal violation* of Section 515.201 of the TWEA, the government must prove, beyond a reasonable doubt, each of the following elements:

- that the defendant is a person subject to U.S. jurisdiction (e.g., a U.S. citizen or resident),
- who willfully (this mens rea element is met by voluntarily breaching a known duty)
- transfers, withdraws, or exports money, property, or evidence of indebtedness, or evidences of ownership of property, with respect to transactions that involve money or property in which Cuba or any Cuban national has an interest. (In plain English, this third element, the actus reus element of the criminal violation, essentially means to spend money in Cuba, or to buy anything from or sell anything to Cuba or a Cuban national.)

2. The Government's Evidence

I have looked through the information you included in the File, and set forth below the main items of evidence the government now possesses with respect to each of the three main elements of TWEA Section 515.201.

a. Subject to U.S. Jurisdiction

U.S. citizens and residents are subject to the jurisdiction of the United States with respect to the TWEA. It appears from the Customs Report in the File that Alejandro Cruz holds a U.S. passport and that he was born in Falls Church, Columbia, one of the United States. Assuming this information is accurate, the government has sufficient evidence to prove that Cruz is a U.S. citizen and therefore subject to United States jurisdiction, satisfying the first and easiest-to-prove element of Section 515.201 of the TWEA beyond a reasonable doubt.

b. Acted with Willful Intent

The second element, that Cruz's *intent* to *willfully* transfer money to and property from Cuba and/or Cuban nationals, is one of which the government has only circumstantial evidence. Before assessing the evidence the government possesses with respect to this intent element, we need to understand first exactly what the government has to prove to show Cruz's willfulness. *Frade*, an 11th Circuit case from 1985, which also deals with the Cuban trade embargo, is instructive. Though the defendants in *Frade* were charged under a different section of the TWEA, the *Frade* Court notes that the term "willfully" for a criminal violation such as the one in Section 515.201, "connotes a *voluntary breach* of a *known duty*" (emphasis added). Therefore, the precise question we need to focus on here is what evidence does the government now have that Cruz knew of the embargo and voluntarily violated it. The answer appears to be that the government has at least some evidence of Cruz's willful intent, based on the following:

— According to the official customs report, Cruz at one point "volunteered that he had bought the Cuban-origin commodities in Jamaica, so he did not believe that they 'were a problem with the embargo.'" Such an admission, if it were introduced against Cruz, at a minimum reveals that *he knew there was an embargo*. Cruz told you much more about his knowledge of the Cuban embargo than he told the customs officer, but this was in the course of a confidential lawyer-client setting, and is not information the government has access to. (See Memo #2 below on your ethical duties.)

— The customs report found the rum and cigars inside dirty laundry that was stuffed inside an old camera case. It may be inferred from Cruz's having packed them in such a manner that he was hiding them, and that therefore he knew it was illegal to have bought them. Evidence of Cruz's knowledge is further substantiated by the facts (also taken from the customs report) that Cruz did not declare the rum and cigars, affirmatively denied having any alcohol or tobacco products when asked, and then later said that he had bought them in a duty-free store in Jamaica, stating that he therefore did not believe they "were a problem with the Cuba embargo." After that, Cruz changed his story yet again and tried to claim that he had gotten them in Cuba, but as gifts.

Cruz's secrecy may well be sufficient evidence to prove knowledge and therefore voluntary breach of the Cuban embargo, as this was precisely what the *Macko* court held. In *Macko*, an 11th Circuit case decided in 1999 that the fact that Mr. Macko, like Cruz, initially lied to customs officers about having traveled to Cuba was enough to prove the intent element of Section 515.201. Cruz's hiding his travel to Cuba here may be proven by the fact that he paid cash for his ticket (which can be established circumstantially by his admission that he was in Cuba, he possessed credit card receipts for the Jamaica leg, and he lacked such receipts for the Cuba leg), and by his having removed the luggage tags from Cuba (assuming the customs official recalls and can testify that there were no Cuban tags on the luggage that they searched).

There is also evidence, from the customs report, that Cruz was nervous. If the evidence of Cruz's perceived "secrecy" is equally open to being interpreted as simply evidence of nervousness (perhaps over not knowing whether it violated the embargo to receive gifts in Cuba), then perhaps the government will not be able to demonstrate the requisite willfulness beyond a reasonable doubt. See *Frade*, where the defendants' fears and concerns over general awareness that they might be violating the embargo were not sufficient to prove willfulness. Cruz's situation, however, appears much more analogous to the secrecy evidenced by the defendant in *Macko*, and based on this authority and the evidence cited above, the government likely will be able to establish willfulness.

c. Transferred Money and/or Property to or from Cuba or Cuban Nationals

In your meeting, Cruz told you he spent approximately $2,000 for hotel, meals ,and transportation, including airfare. He has no receipts for these expenditures and did not say anything about them to the Customs Officer. Therefore, in order to show that he made these transfers of money, the government will have to find other evidence of these, and they may not be able to without Cruz's assistance (or via the presumption, discussed further below). And, as detailed further in Memo #2 below, regarding ethical considerations, Cruz does not have to assist the government in convicting him; he is innocent until they prove him guilty.

As to the rum, cigars, and other small items, though, the government will try to use these to prove that Cruz spent money on Cuban-origin commodities. In the customs report, it is stated that Cruz at first said he bought the items in Jamaica. If believed by the trier of fact, this would nonetheless be a violation, as the purchase does not have to be *in Cuba*; proof of a sale to or purchase from a Cuban national will suffice to establish this element. Later, in the customs report, it says that Cruz volunteered that he had misspoken when he said he purchased the items in Jamaica, and that, in fact, he had gotten them in Cuba, but as *gifts*, not through purchases.

defendant to present evidence, the instruction violated the defendant's due process rights by allowing the government to circumvent its job of fully proving the intent element.

In Cruz's case, if the prosecution is allowed to use the presumption, he may well be found guilty of having engaged in monetary transactions in Cuba without the government's producing any evidence at all that he spent a dime in Cuba, but just by proving that he was in Cuba—with the only path to innocence being for *Cruz to prove he did not* engage in such transactions. Just as in *Sandstrom*, this appears to unconstitutionally shift the burden of proof (see also *Winship*, cited in *Sandstrom*).

The government may try to argue that the TWEA presumption is lawful based upon Fifth Circuit authority in *Bustos* that a prima facie showing of deportability may be made by the alien's failure to refute statements made by the government, but *Bustos* is readily distinguishable from both the case at bar and *Sandstrom*, cited above. As *Bustos* makes clear, deportation hearings are *purely civil proceedings*, and the alien is not guaranteed all the constitutional rights of a criminal defendant—as Cruz would be. In addition, though the government bears the ultimate burden of proof in the deportation hearing, the burden is merely of proof by clear and convincing evidence, not the highest standard—beyond a reasonable doubt—required in criminal cases.

For these reasons, it appears that should the government try to use the presumption to convict Cruz of violating TWEA Section 515.201, we would have a strong argument opposing the use of that presumption.

MEMORANDUM #2

To: Matt Mato
From: Applicant
Re: Cruz—Privileged, Attorney Work Product

Below please find my assessment of the ethical considerations you have to take into account in drafting the reply letter to the OFAC on Mr. Cruz's behalf.

As you undertake to draft your response to the OFAC, you must be mindful of several ethical considerations, balancing your duties of candor with your duties of confidentiality.

Turning to the Columbia Rules of Professional Responsibility, as counsel to someone who faces possible criminal prosecution (here Cruz), "[Y]ou *may* decline to aid in the investigation of the case" (Rule 3.21, emphasis added), but you *may not* knowingly make false statements of material facts (Rule 4.1, emphasis added). Nor, by extension, may you affirm the false statements of another (comment to Rule 4.1). Thus, in drafting the reply letter to the OFAC, you may not write anything that you know to be false, but you do not have to volunteer any information either. (Note that even something like your referring to the customs report might

This, if provable, might help Cruz, but Cruz will not be able to establish these as gifts (and you cannot support his doing so), short of Cruz convincing you that he had lied in your confidential meeting when he told you he bought the items on the black market and he in fact comes up with some sort of proof that these were gifts.

3. Use of the Statutory Presumption in a Criminal Prosecution

The last area you have asked me to address in this memo is the constitutionality of the government's use of the presumption in Section 515.201 of the TWEA.

The TWEA section, under which Cruz may be charged, essentially prohibits unauthorized travel-related expenditures in Cuba. It includes a provision that someone like Cruz, who is subject to U.S. jurisdiction and who has traveled to Cuba (Cruz, a U.S. citizen, admitted to having been in Cuba, see Customs Report), *shall be presumed* to have engaged in such travel-related expenses. The accused may rebut the presumption by either proving that neither he nor anyone on his behalf engaged in such prohibited transactions, or that his trip was fully hosted by someone not subject to U.S. jurisdiction.

Even if Cruz wanted to make such rebuttal assertions, based on what he told you, they would be false statements. He was not traveling under a license; he spent some $2000 on hotel, meals, and transportation, clearly violating the actus reus element of the crime; and his trip was not fully hosted. While you as Cruz's lawyer do not have to assist the government in convicting your own client, you *may not* assist Cruz in making false statements to the government, which seems to be the case here were Cruz to try to rebut the presumption. (More on your ethical responsibilities below.)

The only plausible defense here, therefore, with respect to the presumption, is to argue that *in a criminal case* such as this, because the effect of the presumption is to fully shift the burden of persuasion, it violates Cruz's 5th and 14th Amendment rights and is therefore unconstitutional. (*Note*: TWEA Section 515.201 contains both civil and criminal penalties, and the presumption may be valid in conjunction with a civil action, but, we would argue, not in a criminal action.)

In *Sandstrom*, the Supreme Court held that jury instructions given by the Montana state court, that "the law presumes that a person intends the ordinary consequences of his voluntary acts," were unconstitutional. In that case, the defendant in a criminal prosecution admitted to having killed the victim, but claimed he did not do so purposely or knowingly. The prosecution, however, argued that it had sufficient evidence to prove a "deliberate homicide," with the jury's inference based on the presumption instruction above. The Supreme Court reversed the lower court, though, holding that because intent is a material element of the offense, the prosecution must affirmatively prove that intent beyond a reasonable doubt, and that because the jury instruction could be interpreted as either conclusive or as requiring a burden shift that forced the itself be a misrepresentation, since among other things, Cruz told the customs official that the cigars were gifts and told you that he purchased them on the black market.)

You are also under an obligation, generally under <u>Rule 4.1</u>, to refrain from knowingly failing to disclose material facts such as those the OFAC requested that Cruz provide in this case. There is an exception to <u>Rule 4.1</u>, however, under which you may ethically refrain from disclosing such facts here—the exception for *confidential information,* where the criminal action that may result from the failure to disclose is not likely to result in imminent death or substantial bodily harm. This exception seems to fit Cruz's situation precisely: 1) Cruz told you the details about his trip and travel-related expenses in a confidential meeting with you as his attorney, therefore in a privileged setting and 2) though Cruz's failure to provide the information requested may result in criminal violations of the TWEA, not revealing these facts will not result in a crime likely to cause injury or death.

You are, however, under no duty to assist the OFAC in building their case against Cruz. Under <u>Rule 3.21</u>, while you may not defend a baseless or frivolous position, you may defend Cruz by requiring that the government prove each and every element of the violation beyond a reasonable doubt. Knowing though, as stated above, that you may not make false statements, it seems that your best choice here is to respond succinctly and politely to the OFAC that your client respectfully declines the offer to furnish information.

The reason for this conclusion is that any information you could now offer, on any of the three rebuttal grounds, would either be an affirmation of a false statement or truthful information that might well assist the government in convicting Cruz—neither of which is acceptable. Cruz told you outright that 1) his travel was not licensed, 2) he spent money on travel-related expenses in Cuba, and 3) his trip was not fully hosted. If he now tries to say his trip was licensed or fully hosted, or deny that he spent money in Cuba, he would be lying and you would be affirming his false statements. If he admits to the truth about these three points, he is essentially pleading guilty.

(Note: you might want to research plea bargain deals that other similarly situated travelers have struck with the OFAC and explore with Cruz the possibility of negotiating a deal. This, of course, would be Cruz's choice, but given what he did tell you, this might be the best course of action in the long run. He appears to be an upstanding citizen, one who gave to the United States through service in the Peace Corps; this is a first violation; and he was only spending money on himself, not selling to others as was the defendant in *Macko*. Let me know if would like my assistance in researching this possibility further.)

Conclusion

In conclusion, without any further admissions or information from Cruz, there is a question as to whether the prosecution will prevail in proving beyond a reasonable doubt that Cruz bought Cuban-origin commodities or had other Cuban travel-related expenses—unless they are able to use the presumption. (See discussion in my first memo above as to how we would contest their use of that presumption.) You may not advance any false statements, but you must maintain the confidences of your client. Here, that client, Mr. Cruz, is innocent until the prosecution proves him guilty, and you are therefore on solid ethical grounds in refusing to assist the OFAC in their investigation of Cruz's possible criminal activities and in requiring that they prove Cruz guilty of each element of the offense in order to convict him.

To: Rena Tishman
From: Bar Applicant
Re: Marriage of Eiffel
Date: Feb. 24, 2005

Please find, below, the Draft Statement of Facts and Argument for the Appellant's Opening Brief that you requested assistance in preparing on behalf of our client Angela Killian.

Select Sections of Appellant's Opening Brief

Statement of facts:

1. In July 2002, Husband, Paul Eiffel, and Wife, Angela Killian, whose married name was "Angela Eiffel," (hereinafter referred to jointly as "the parties"), agreed to separate and agreed as to how to divide their property and pay their debts at that same time.
2. After fully deciding how they wanted to divide their property and debts, the parties contacted Mr. Gant.
3. Mr. Gant advised both parties to seek independent counsel. Both urged him not to require them to do so for largely financial reasons and because they had already come to an agreement that merely needed to be formalized.
4. Mr. Gant advised both Angela and Paul Eiffel that his capacity was merely that of draftsman, to write up what they had already agreed to.
5. The parties' agreement was signed after due consideration and admonitions from Mr. Gant, and there was ample time for reflection following the drafting of the agreement before it took final form. This was not drawn up hastily.
6. Mr. Gant read and explained to the parties the meaning of a fully adequate waiver of conflict of interest, which waivers and disclosures both parties voluntarily signed, confirming their knowledge of the waivers and their desire to conclude the MSA, despite any potential or future conflicts of interest.
7. Mr. Gant had the parties re-read every word of the MSA before formalizing the document, he explained what the terms meant, and he sought and received continual assurances that both parties knew and agreed to those terms.
8. The trial court concluded that Mr. Gant was not motivated to obtain payment of monies owing in prior unrelated matters, that Mr. Gant was not trying to protect himself, and Mr. Gant was not guilty of overreaching.
9. The trial court found that the MSA was entered into freely and voluntarily on the date it was made, and specifically rejected claims that the husband may have been forced to consent to any of those terms that he himself drafted.

Argument

Introduction

There is only one issue before this Court, and that is the enforceability of the September 2002 MSA (hereinafter "the Eiffel MSA"). As to this issue, for the reasons presented herein below, Appellant respectfully contends that the Trial Court erred and urges this Court to now find that the Eiffel MSA is indeed fully enforceable.

The trial court erred in finding that the MSA was subject to attack and not enforceable because, given Mr. Gant's full and adequate disclosures of all the facts and circumstances necessary for both parties to make fully informed decisions and their written consent thereto, and the fact that there were no actual conflicts at the time the MSA was formalized, Mr. Gant could and did properly proceed with dual representation of both parties in the drafting of the Eiffel MSA.

While there are many instances in which it would be plainly improper for one lawyer to represent two parties, the Courts of Columbia have recognized that a situation such as that of drafting the Eiffel's MSA was just such an instance where dual representation was indeed proper. Specifically, in *Klemm*, the Court held that, where a conflict, if any, were only potential, and where written consents were knowing and informed after full disclosures by counsel - just as Mr. Gant did here - then the attorney may appear in court on behalf of both parties on issues about which they agree. And if, as *Klemm* holds, this is allowed in the litigation context, where there is far greater risk for dispute, then surely the attorney should be permitted to do so in a transactional context, especially in cases such as the instant one where the lawyer is merely formalizing an agreement of the parties.

Like the parties in *Klemm*, the Eiffels had no actual disagreements at the time the MSA was executed. And, while it is recognized that marital property settlements always have the possibility of *potential* conflicts (*Klemm* citing law journal), this was valid because there were no *actual* conflicts and because Mr. Gant duly warned of those potential conflicts (in fact did so repeatedly), advised both parties to seek independent counsel, and only formalized the agreement the parties had already decided upon after full disclosures and securing their complete, written informed consent.

Mr. Gant disclosed the potential adverse aspects of the representation several times. First, he refused the representation altogether. Then, after being urged to do so as a favor to both parties (to save them additional attorney fees), he reluctantly agreed and consented to only act as the draftsman, and only after both were advised and re-advised that they should seek independent counsel. When a question arose as to certain properties in Texas, Mr. Gant yet again told Paul Eiffel that there were potential conflicts and that he should seek separate counsel.

Mr. Eiffel's latter-day complaints of what he might or might not have agreed to, had he known more, ring hollow today and should not prevent this agreement from being enforced, as Mr.

Eiffel himself agrees there were no actual conflicts at the time the MSA was drafted and signed. He also agrees that he was repeatedly warned of the possibilities for potential conflicts, told more than once to seek independent counsel and refused, and agreed to be bound by the MSA all the same. Invalidating this agreement now would be creating new obligations on lawyers to paternalistically refuse all dual representation, on the speculative grounds of potential conflicts alone - a standard that would clearly go far beyond the holding in *Klemm*, by which this Court is bound.

Even under the necessary heightened scrutiny standard, this is just the type of unusual and uncomplicated case where it is appropriate for a lawyer to perform, as Mr. Gant did here, the perfunctory services of "scrivener." The parties' repeatedly offered assurances that they were in actual agreement, they reviewed and agreed that they understood and wanted to be bound by all the terms, and they voluntarily asked the lawyer to perform draftsman services for their own convenience and benefit.

In *Vandenburgh*, a Columbia Court affirmed the decision in the lower court setting aside a marital agreement that was prepared by one lawyer. That case is distinguishable from the Eiffel's case on several grounds and should not in any way control here. One, the *Vandenburgh* agreement was drawn up and agreed to in haste. The Eiffel MSA was anything but hasty. The parties discussed the terms, wrote up those terms themselves, then reviewed each term, provision-by-provision, with counsel before signing - a slow, careful and deliberate process. Also distinguishable is the key fact that Paul Eiffel himself (an educated man who completed paralegal studies), who is now seeking to invalidate the agreement, was the one who first wrote, and then typed, the draft agreement the parties took to Mr. Gant to formalize. By contrast, in *Vandenburgh*, it was counsel who first drafted the agreement.

Note, too, that the Eiffels had few assets and debts and had thought carefully over what they agreed to. And, this was not a case that involved great "complexity or moment" but, rather, was analogous to the earlier cases where courts upheld lawyers' drawing up agreements that parties had reached themselves. (*See* discussions re: Rule 3-310, Library at 1-2.) In fact, the discussion of that Ethical Rule 3-31 clearly cites as an example an "uncontested marital dissolution," where, for the sake of convenience and economy (as here), the parties preferred a single counsel (Library at 2). In this instance, the Comments require, just as Mr. Gant did here, "disclosing the potential adverse aspects of the multiple representation and seeking more than once informed written consent."
That is exactly what happened. The parties so agreed and, in fact, they had begged Mr. Gant to take on this task of drawing up the terms they had already agreed to, so as to save each of them the expense of hiring a lawyer. Even after Mr. Gant refused, they repeatedly beseeched him, especially Mr. Eiffel. They then read the agreement, provision by provision, and continued to refuse Mr. Gant's suggestions that there might be potential conflicts and that they should seek independent counsel. There were no actual disagreements or conflicts, they both assured Mr. Gant. And they then both freely signed written waivers of the full disclosure and informed consent before signing the agreement itself. The trial court specifically found that Mr. Eiffel's

signatures were voluntary and not in any way coerced. The trial court also specifically found that Mr. Gant was not in any way motivated by fees that were due him from previous representations. Thus, it would be fundamentally unjust to now hold Mr. Gant in error for having simply helped out two fully informed parties seeking merely to memorialize their full and complete agreement.

Conclusion

Because of the full and adequate disclosures and written informed consent and the unique nature of this case, and because the parties repeatedly expressed their full agreement and desire to have Mr. Gant draw up the agreement they themselves concluded, Appellant urges that this Court enforce and uphold that agreement.

To: Ginny Klosterman
From: Bar Applicant
Re: In re: Ralph, Margaret and Clint Winston
Date: July 26, 2005

Please find, below, the draft letter you requested to the Pinnacle Canyon Estates Homeowners Association. Please let me know if you need anything further with regard to the Winston family and the home they wish to purchase in Pinnacle Canyon.

Columbia Center for Disability Law
645 Walther Way, Suite 208
Santa Claritan, Columbia 55515

Ms. Emma Zucconi, Esq.
Rommet, Fairbrooks, Fromkin, & Zucconi, LLP
1332 Via Estrada
Fairview, Columbia 55521

Re: Pinnacle Canyon Estates Homeowners Association, Age waiver request from Pamela Garcia for Ralph and Margaret Winston

Dear Ms. Zucconi:

Thank you for your letter of July 22, 2005, regarding the Winstons and their desire to purchase a home in the Pinnacle Canyon Estates ("Pinnacle").

As you know, one of your residents, Pamela Garcia, had agreed to sell her property in Pinnacle to the Winstons and the sale was in fact pending when the actions of the Pinnacle Homeowners Association thwarted that sale. In your letter, you attempt to justify this action and claim the Association was within its rights to disrupt this sale. However, this was, in fact, a violation of law; the Association is required to make reasonable accommodations for disabled people and thus far has failed to do so.

The position you set forth attempts to cast the Association's refusal to waive the age requirement for the Winstons' son Clint, not as discriminatory, based on disability, but solely based upon age.

First, many of your arguments simply do not hold water and, given many of your own admissions, appear to be thinly veiled discrimination. Regardless of the intent, however, for the reasons set forth below, the Association's actions here resulted in impermissible discrimination. I, therefore, renew the request that, as counsel for the Association, you direct the Association to immediately waive the age requirement for Clint and allow Ms. Garcia's sale of the Pinnacle residence to the Winstons to go forward as scheduled.

THE ASSOCIATION'S FAILURE TO ALLOW CLINT TO LIVE WITH HIS PARENTS AT PINNACLE IS NOT, AS YOU CONTEND, PURELY A FUNCTION OF AGE BUT IS DISCRIMINATORY BY PINNACLE'S OWN ADMISSIONS ON CLINT BEING A DISABLED PERSON.

The reasons you have given for refusing to waive the age requirement appear pretextual, and, given all the facts, the Association should let the Winstons buy the Pinnacle home and let Clint live in that home with his parents.

1. The waiver would not adversely affect Pinnacle's status as elder housing.

The Association qualifies as a housing development for older persons. As such, you say Pinnacle is entitled to exclude people who do not meet your age requirement. In order to qualify for and maintain your eligibility, however, all you must do is maintain 80 percent of the units with at least one person age 55 and older. Mr. and Mrs. Winston are both older than 55 and, thus, your eligibility would not be adversely affected by allowing Clint to live in one of the Pinnacle homes.

2. Pinnacle's age requirements are not reasonably related to its status as elder housing.

Your inclusion of an age-35 minimum for other (nonprincipal) residents is not tied to the status as a qualified housing for older persons but, rather, by your own admission as a means for keeping out "teenagers and rowdy young adults ... [and the] traffic and noise pollution" you presume they would bring. Clint is a quiet fellow. Clint is 23 years old, not a teenager, and not "rowdy" in the slightest.

And making an accommodation for Clint will hardly cause the floodgates to pour in tons of noisy teenagers, as appears to be your true concern. The Association would not be setting precedent for allowing anyone under age 35 in, but only those who qualify as disabled and need to live with family who qualify as principals (over 55).

Likewise your continual reliance on wishing to maintain the nature of a "community as 55-and-older" is itself undermined by your allowing anyone under 55 in at all. Setting a limit at 35 is arbitrary. (*See* discussion of *Noble, infra*.)

3. Pinnacle's claim that Clint poses certain administrative problems, that he might become a ward

of Pinnacle, is a nonsensical fear, and reveals the Association's true, underlying and impermissible discrimination.

Yet another factor that shows that the Association's underlying discrimination is based upon disability rather than age is the alleged concern about "administrative problems" of potentially having to care for Clint should both Winstons pass away. This appears to be not-so-thinly-veiled discrimination because you likely face, far more plausibly, such problems from the many residents who live alone or where there are two or more over-55 residents. The Winstons are not likely to both die from natural causes simultaneously leaving Clint alone, and surely knowing of his disabilities, they have provided for guardians to step up should they both die simultaneously, no matter where they live. Clint also has other siblings who could be contacted to immediately come help.

If, in fact, these administrative problems are a real concern of the Association's, then the Association should not let anyone in who does not have a guardian and estate plan in place. This, however, is not the American way. In our country, people provide for their own arrangements, estate plans, elder care and guardianships arrangements. Rarely, if ever, would such a concern fall on a housing development (other than possibly to contact the police, who would then contact next of kin). Again, this is a spurious argument and really appears to reveal a blatant bias against Clint because he is disabled.

COLUMBIA LAW REQUIRES THE PINNACLE ASSOCIATION TO MAKE REASONABLE ACCOMODATIONS FOR DISABLED PEOPLE, AND A WAIVER OF THE AGE REQUIREMENT HERE IS PRECISELY SUCH A REASONABLE ACCOMODATION.

First, let me confirm: (1) that the Association does not deny that Clint has a "disability" per Columbia Fair Housing Act ("CFHA") Section 41; (2) that the Winstons are both over 55; and (3) that they had entered into a contract to purchase one Pinnacle estate home from the owner, Ms. Garcia, but that, after Ms. Garcia made a bona fide offer and the Winstons accepted it, the sale was cancelled. These actions constitute both a violation of CFHA Section 43 (discrimination in sale) and Section 44 (discrimination due to disability, detailed further below).

A plain reading of CFHA Section 44 holds that discrimination includes a "refusal to make reasonable accommodations in rules, policies, practices or services if the accommodations may be necessary to afford the person equal opportunity to use and enjoy a dwelling." The Pinnacle Association's failure to waive the age requirement for the Winston's adult disabled child is precisely such a refusal to make reasonable accommodations and denies Clint the equal opportunity to use and enjoy the home of his parents' choosing. This is the mandate of fair housing laws, and where private contracts (such as Pinnacle's Covenants, Conditions and Restrictions here) conflict with applicable state or federal law, it is the former that must be revised and not the latter. The legislature enacted fair housing laws for policy concerns that individuals and private groups cannot circumvent contractually.

In addition to the statutory authority, applicable case law mandates the age waiver. The Association's reliance on *Noble* is misplaced, both because it is out of state and, thus, nonbinding precedent and because it is factually distinguishable. The plaintiffs in *Noble* did not allege discriminatory intent; perhaps there was no evidence of such intent. Here, however, as discussed above, there is ample evidence of not-so-thinly-veiled discrimination based not merely on age but on disability.

Further in *Noble*, the minimum age was 45 - much closer to a 55-and-older community - perhaps designed to accommodate some of the 55 and older who have spouses 10 years younger. The Pinnacle Association's age limit of 35 for nonprincipal residents is a full 20 years from the so-called "community nature" of 55 and older, and appears arbitrary at best, designed by the Association's admissions only as a way of keeping out "noisy" and "rowdy" folks. Many 35 year olds (and older) are single, some dating and/or otherwise active, stay out late, and make noise, while many 20 years olds are quiet. (Clint is quiet.) Thus, to set a limit at 35 appears to bear no rational connection to an "elder" communal sort of life.

The more relevant legal authorities (in addition to the binding and straightforward statutory authority cited above, the CFHA) are two Columbia cases: *Project HOME* and *Townley* (which you reference incorrectly as not requiring these reasonable accommodations.) *Project HOME* reminds us that a main purpose of the CFHA is to "integrate people with disabilities into the mainstream of the community" and the court reminds us all that the CFHA must be *construed broadly*. *Project HOME* states that to treat disabled and nondisabled people alike (here, per the Association, excluding *all* people over 35, disabled and nondisabled) *is* discriminatory "when it prevents a disabled individual from gaining access to the proposed housing." (*Project HOME*, Library at 8.)

In fact, in the *Project HOME* case, the Columbia court (binding as you know in our situation) specially states that "one method of making housing unavailable to people with disabilities has been the application or enforcement of *otherwise neutral rules*." (Emphasis added.) This is precisely what the Association is doing by imposing the arbitrary 35-year-old age requirement here, in a so-called neutral manner to disabled and nondisabled individuals. To avoid discriminating against Clint, the Association must vary from this policy and make an affirmation exception to accommodate.

The *Project HOME* Court goes on to say that often such discriminatory decisions are based on unfounded fears about disabled people. The Association's admissions about its potential "administrative" responsibilities should both of Clint's parents die, as shown above, amounts to precisely that kind of unfounded prejudice, which the CFHA accommodation provisions were designed to combat.

Lastly, your contention that *Townley* does not control here is also erroneous. It does. *Townley* makes clear several key points, in addition to mandating, on facts nearly identical to those of the Winstons' situation, that a 55-and-older housing community waive its age requirement to allow for the reasonable accommodation of a disabled resident. *Townley* concludes both that: (1)

"reasonable accommodations" are not generic but rather must be decided on a case-by-case basis, and (2) the fact that other disabled people live in the community does not relieve the community of the obligation to make accommodations for another disabled person.

Thus, Pinnacle's continued assertion that it has made accommodations for other disabled people has no bearing on its obligation to make room for one more, Clint Winston. And the fact that in *Townley,* the disabled person was the resident and the younger person a caretaker is irrelevant to its mandate to allow a younger person in (waiving the age requirement) as a reasonable accommodation to a disabled person, because, like in *Townley*, the community will maintain its status as long as at least one person over 55 will be living in the unit. This would be true in the Winstons' situation as well. Likewise in the case at hand, there will be no financial or other burdens on the Association to make this accommodation, as the Winstons will take care of all of Clint's needs. It is merely a form-over-substance age waiver and one that is clearly mandated by Columbia law.

In conclusion, because reasonable accommodations are required under Columbia statutory and case law and because granting the requested waiver here will pose no financial or other hardships on the Association, I am, therefore, once again formally requesting that you direct the Association to immediately waive the age requirement for Clint Winston and allow the Winstons to purchase the Pinnacle residence of their choice, and thereby avoid any unnecessary costs of further litigation to your clients.

Sincerely yours,

Bar Applicant

APPENDIX C
PASS Summary of Past California Performance Tests

(7/83) PT-A. *Carleton v. Mid-Central Shipping*: Substantive law: Torts

Tasks: Draft a memorandum of law (analytical), thinking through legal theories available to the plaintiff, who was injured while allegedly trespassing on defendant's property. Memo included a section anticipating factual or proof problems client would likely encounter in pursuing the litigation. Applicants also had to complete a set of multiple-choice questions. (*Note*: The July 1983 and February 1984 Performance Tests contained multiple-choice questions, but thereafter the Committee stopped including multiple-choice questions in the performance test portion of the Bar.)

(7/83) PT-B. *Lee v. Western Steel*: Substantive law: Civil Procedure

Tasks: Draft one memorandum of points and authorities that argues that the defendants should be denied certification as a class. Draft a second memorandum of points and authorities that argues that another party who seeks to intervene in the action should not be allowed to do so. Applicants also had to complete a set of multiple-choice questions.

(2/84) PT-A. *Powell v. Columbia*: Substantive law: Constitutional Law and Torts

Tasks: Answer multiple-choice questions and draft an appellate brief that seeks reversal of a summary judgment.

(2/84) PT-B. *Potter v. Transco*: Substantive law: Torts

Tasks: Answer multiple-choice questions. Draft an analytical memorandum of law regarding the defendant's position about liability and determining whether or not to make a motion to dismiss the plaintiff's complaint or to answer the complaint.

(7/84) PT-A. *Abner v. Chemco*: Substantive law: Corporations

Task: Draft a memorandum of law that addresses procedural issues in a derivative suit and addresses the merits of claims that the board of directors breached their duties to the corporation.

(7/84) PT-B. *Klare v. Journal of Human Experience*: Substantive law: Contracts

Tasks: Draft an internal memorandum that analyzes negotiation and settlement strategies and possibilities, and authority supporting remedies of damages and/or specific performance. Draft an offer to settlement in letter form to opposing counsel.

(2/85) PT-A. *State v. Reed*: Substantive law: Criminal Law and Criminal Procedure

Tasks: Draft a memorandum to an investigator hired by your office to gather additional evidence with respect to criminal charges against your client of statutory rape and drug-related offenses. Draft a second memorandum of law regarding legal research issues.

(2/85) PT-B. *Reynolds v. ACME*: Substantive law: Evidence
Tasks: Draft memorandum of points and authorities regarding expert testimony. Draft internal memorandum of law regarding admissibility of certain evidence at trial.

(7/85) PT-A. *In Re Marriage of Halberte*: Substantive law: Community Property
Task: Draft a detailed letter to your client, a husband who is anticipating a divorce action, that analyzes a myriad of legal, ethical, and strategic issues.

(7/85) PT-B. *Hale v. Delbert*: Substantive law: Torts
Task: Draft an internal memorandum and a discovery plan for use in obtaining information to support the plaintiff's claim in an action for legal malpractice.

(2/86) PT-A. *In Re Estate of Stern*: Substantive law: Wills
Tasks: Draft an analytical memorandum regarding factual and legal issues with respect to the effect of a prenuptial agreement. Draft a second internal memorandum about what to investigate in deposition of widow. Draft a third memorandum on ethical issues with respect to law firm handling both prenuptial agreement and probate of the related estate, commenting as well on guidelines for the firm's future client representation.

(2/86) PT-B. *"Look-alikes" Legislation*: Substantive law: Constitutional Law
Tasks: Redraft proposed legislation in order to satisfy a number of legal requirements and political objectives. Draft a second memorandum to persuade representative to support passage of the redrafted legislation.

(7/86) PT-A. *In Re Computech*: Substantive law: Contracts
Task: Analyze and revise a contract for purchase on behalf of your client in order to meet your client's many business needs and goals, and to satisfy applicable legal requirements.

(7/86) PT-B. *In Re Cook*: Substantive law: Trusts
Tasks: Draft a plan to interview client regarding potential estate planning. Analyze and critique trust documents prepared by junior lawyer in your firm to comply with relevant legal and ethical rules.

(2/87) PT-A. *In Re Sharon Davis*: Substantive law: Disabilities Regulations
Task: Draft a memorandum counseling the client, a dyslexic woman who has been dismissed from dental school, about her legal rights, remedies, and non-legal options that may be available to resolve her problems.

(2/87) PT-B. *State v. Burke*: Substantive law: Criminal Law
Tasks: Draft a memorandum to determine whether or not there currently exists enough credible evidence to bring charges against the defendant (a union organizer) on two counts: assault with

a deadly weapon and trespass. Draft a second memorandum that outlines possible additional evidence that may be developed to support the prosecution.

(7/87) PT-A. *Hill v. Hill*: Substantive law: Torts

Tasks: Draft a memorandum that analyzes the possible defenses that might be raised in response to a defamation lawsuit against your clients. Critique an existing Answer to the Complaint. Also, write a letter to your client informing client about issues likely to be raised in an upcoming deposition, information the opposing party will likely seek to obtain, and conflicting factual information.

(7/87) PT-B. *Honabach v. Mark Schools, Inc.*: Substantive law: Real Property/Remedies

Task: Draft a brief in support of a motion for summary judgment in a suit seeking to stop the operation of a group home for mentally retarded people on grounds that the home violates applicable restrictive covenant.

(2/88) PT-A. *In re Alison Adams*: Substantive law: Real Property and Contracts

Task: Draft a memo that analyzes client's situation with respect to the potential sale of property client owns, including discussion of client's goals and alternative ways to resolve her dispute. For each alternative, applicant was to assess the outcomes and impact of each on the client's needs and desires, as well as to detail any additional evidence that may be necessary to fully evaluate those alternative options.

(2/88) PT-B. *In re Gold*: Substantive law: Veterans' Benefits, Administrative Law

Task: Write a memorandum that sets forth procedures culled from regulations in Library for hearings appealing decisions about veteran's benefits; analyze potential problems for your client that may arise because of the procedures used in disability benefits claims hearings. Write a second memorandum that determines the highest disability rating that you can plausibly justify the client be awarded, identifying contradictory evidence and assessing the types of additional evidence that may be sought to prove your client merits a particular disability rating.

(7/88) PT-A. *Bart's Kingdom of Toys v. Soto Toy Wholesalers*: Substantive law: Contracts

Task: Draft a memo that analyzes whether the parties have an enforceable contract and, if so, what are its terms and what are the legal consequences of accepting or rejecting certain goods. Analyze the situation as if the contract were not enforceable as well, i.e. whether there would nonetheless be a pending offer. Assess your client's options and make recommendations to your client with respect to goods that have already been delivered.

(7/88) PT-B. *Estate of Crenshaw*: Substantive law: Wills

Task: Draft the closing argument to the jury on behalf of the proponent's of the decedent's will in a will contest case against the decedent's children. Your argument presents the affirmative evidence in your client's favor and also rebuts your adversary's charges that the will was procured by undue influence.

(2/89) PT-A. *Flinders v. Gum Springs, etc.* Substantive law: Criminal Law and Procedure
Tasks: Draft a brief in support of a motion to exclude statement made by your client to the police subsequent to arrest. Prepare factual statement for client's declaration. Statement supports client's motion for summary judgment in pending civil action regarding ownership of lost money. Draft brief in support of summary judgment against adversary who present competing claims to the money your client found.

(2/89) PT-B. *Trent Clinic*: Substantive law: Constitutional Law
Task: Draft a position paper advancing your client's (a fertility clinic) interests in proposed legislation regarding surrogate parents.

(7/89) PT-A. *Application of The National Gazette, Inc.*: Substantive law: Corporations
Tasks: Draft a statement on behalf of your corporate client who is seeking to persuade Canadian officials that it will comply with particular Canadian legislation in its bid to purchase a Canadian publishing company. Also, draft a memorandum suggesting responses to a minority stockholder opposed to the Canadian purchase.

(7/89) PT-B. *Stolier v. Wallach.*: Substantive law: Family Law and Evidence
Task: Draft a memorandum regarding the evidence necessary to prove that your client (a grandmother) should be granted visitation rights with her granddaughter, and how and where to go about gathering such evidence.

(2/90) PT-A. *Calhoun County Public Schools v. Richards*: Substantive law: Administrative and Education Law
Task: Draft a plan for witness examination (of multiple potential witnesses) to establish violations by schools with respect to a special education student.

(2/90) PT-B. *In Re Matthews*: Substantive law: Community Property
Tasks: Draft a memorandum for a lawyer in your firm who is handling a divorce mediation. Include division of assets issues and ethical issues. Also draft a letter to the couple seeking a divorce, advising them on litigation vs. mediation and related issues with respect to how they can best achieve their articulated goals.

(7/90) PT-A. *Anaesthesia Affiliates, P.C.*: Substantive law: Contracts
Tasks: Draft an outline that identifies rules for doctors with respect to non-compete and con-interference provisions of contract. Draft an analytical memorandum detailing information that should be obtained in witness interviews (including discussion of relevance of information sought). In a third memo, discuss the ethical issues that may arise with respect to the interviews and suggest ways of resolving those issues.

(7/90) PT-B. *Hilary v. Whittington and Rollins*: Substantive law: Property and Contracts
Task: Draft a letter to the client, advising her with respect to an offer of settlement she has received from the defendant real estate broker.

(2/91) PT-A. *U.S. v. Ramirez*: Substantive law: Immigration
Tasks: Draft a brief in support of a motion requesting judicial recommendation against deportation. Draft a second internal memo on legal actions possible should the client's motion be denied.

(2/91) PT-B. *In re Amanda Deale*: Substantive law: Professional Responsibility
Task: Draft an internal memo that identifies and resolves past, present, and potential future ethical issues involved in the representation of the client. (*Note*: This is an excellent PT to do as practice for a review of essential PR issues such as conflicts of interest, confidentiality, and subornation of perjury.)

(7/91) PT-A. *In Re Lori S.*: Substantive law: Evidence/Statutory Interpretation
Task: Draft a brief to the court, advancing the Child Protective Services Agency's contention that certain files are confidential.

(7/91) PT-B. *Nancy O'Brian/Mototech*: Substantive law: Civil Procedure
Tasks: Draft a brief that contends that the trial court does not have jurisdiction over sanctions motion. Draft an internal fact-gathering memo for a lawyer in your firm who is preparing to interview the client with respect to sanctions motion.

(2/92) PT-A. *In Re Columbia State University*: Substantive law: Constitutional Law
Tasks: Draft a memo for in-house counsel to university client re draft legislation on speech restrictions. Draft also a letter to persuade legislator that the proposed law is necessary.

(2/92) PT-B. *Martin v. Samuels*: Substantive law: Family Law
Tasks: Draft an internal memo about evidence to be presented at trial in child custody case and re possible settlement.

(7/92) PT-A. *E.L. v. Bloomfield Adoption Agency*
Task: Draft letter to client giving legal opinion as to client's obligations with respect to adoption policies and procedures.

(7/92) PT-B. *Bates and Jones v. Peterson Developers*
Task: Draft a letter to advocate on behalf of clients that an administrative agency should investigate housing discrimination complaints.

(2/93) PT-A. *In Re Berger*: Substantive law: Contracts

Tasks: Draft a memo to investigator, setting out (in plain English) those legal rules applicable to rescinding of a land sale contract. Draft a second document, also for the investigator, setting out the factual evidence that proves each of the legal elements described in your first memo.

(2/93) PT-B. *Centerville Housing Authority v. Richardson*: Substantive law: Administrative Law

Tasks: Draft a position paper, similar to a closing argument, to be delivered orally at an adminstrative hearing. Also draft five affidavits for witnesses supporting the client's version of events at the administrative hearing.

(7/93) PT-A. *Dodson v. Canadian Equipment Company*: Substantive law: Evidence/Civil Procedure

Tasks: Draft a cross-examination plan of the main defense witness in a car accident case (applicants represent plaintiff). Draft a memorandum of law that analyzes a choice of law question with respect to the admissibility of certain evidence.

(7/93 PT-B. *Xenophanes v. Dr. George Vectrove et al. and Xenophanes v. Warden et al.*: Substantive law: Constitutional Law

Tasks: Draft a brief in summary of summary judgment motion for prisoner's Section 1983 action against doctor and state hospital, alleging First Amendment freedom of religion violations. Also draft a closing argument to (advisory) jury with respect to client's Eighth Amendment (cruel and unusual punishment) allegations.

(2/94) PT-A. *State v. Dubin*: Substantive law: Criminal Law

Tasks: Draft a brief to trial court supporting the conviction of the defendant on numerous charges. Also draft the best possible closing argument the defendant might offer, to assist the prosecutor in preparing her argument.

(2/94) PT-B. *Peterson Properties*: Substantive law: Real Property and Torts

Task: Draft a letter to client, the landlord, advising of his rights, remedies, and obligations with respect to demands from one of his tenants.

(7/94) PT-A. *In re Richard D. Martinek*: Substantive law: Professional Responsibility

Tasks: Draft a letter to client, giving legal opinion as to client's professional obligations with respect to representation in a legal matter (client is a civil rights lawyer). Draft a second internal memo that details the facts to be investigated in order to support the client's being awarded attorney's fees that he seeks.

(7/94) PT-B. *Farmpride, Inc. v. J.P. Kay, et al.*: Substantive law: Torts/Remedies

Task: Draft a pre-litigation counseling letter to prepare for counseling client on how the client should proceed with choices to be made in potential future litigation.

(2/95) PT-A. _Zwier v. Sea Quest (Cayman) Limited, et al._: Substantive law: Civil Procedure
Tasks: Draft a memo regarding factors court will use to determine client's motion to dismiss, identifying facts that support position and additional evidence that may be gathered. Draft the affidavits of two witnesses to support the client's motion.

(2/95) PT-B. _Peabody v. Middletown_: Substantive law: Constitutional Law
Tasks: Draft a "theory of the case" memorandum to demonstrate how law and facts prove client's asserted Fourth Amendment. Also draft an affidavit for client (plaintiff) that would provide evidence supporting client's version of events.

(7/95) PT-A. _In re Design Software, Inc._: Substantive law: Contracts and Choice of Law
Tasks: Draft an internal memo that analyzes whether international or UCC law will apply to contractual conflict between the parties. Draft a letter to the client regarding questions client has about specific contract provisions, and setting forth the options available for the client to best protect its interests and meet its business needs.

(7/95) PT-B. _State v. King_: Substantive law: Evidence
Task: Draft an analytical memo to assist the prosecutor with possible evidentiary problems and possible methods of curing or resolving those problems.

(2/96) PT-A. _People v. Lloyd and Miguel_: Substantive law: Criminal Procedure and Professional Responsibility
Task: Draft an internal memorandum for the prosecutor's office, analyzing past, present, and future ethical obligations with respect to an ongoing criminal investigation.

(2/96) PT-B. _Micas v. Eisen_: Substantive law: Evidence and Torts
Task: Draft a brief in support of client's motion to dismiss, and draft proposed jury instructions favoring the client, the defendant in a personal injury action.

(7/96) PT-A. _Farber v. Arlen Electronics, Inc._: Substantive law: Evidence and Age
          Discrimination Law
Tasks: Draft a brief that opposes plaintiff's motion in limine, arguing why evidence in question should be admitted and how that evidence bars the plaintiff's claim. Also draft select portions of the anticipated opening statement, should case proceed to trial.

(7/96) PT-B. _Kramer v. Wolfolk_: Substantive law: Torts
Tasks: Draft a brief that opposes the defendant's motion for summary judgment in a personal injury lawsuit. Draft an internal memorandum of law that analyzes the client's likelihood of prevailing at trial.

(2/97) PT-A. _In re: Denise Walsh_: Substantive law: Administrative Law and Family Law

Task: Draft a brief in support of child support request and changes in policies and practices of the Department of Human Services, to be submitted to ALJ (administrative law judge).

(2/97) PT-B. *DSI, Inc.*: Substantive law: Sports Law
Task: Draft a memo analyzing client's representation of women athletes, assessing whether the client's activities fall within certain regulatory legislation, and other rights, responsibilities, and remedies available to the client (sports agency).

(7/97) PT-A. *In re: Christopher Small*: Substantive law: Professional Responsibility and
　　　　　Family Law
Tasks: Draft a memo re responsibilities of guardian ad litem (who is also the senior partner) for child and draft a case plan that outlines the steps to be taken in representing that child in a dispute between the foster parent and the Department of Social Services.

(7/97) PT-B. *The Merida Discovery Group v. Consortium of Maritime Insurers*: Substantive
　　　　　Law: Admiralty Law
Tasks: Draft a brief as part of an arbitration settlement, setting forth the client's position that it is entitled as finder to ownership of valuables recovered from shipwreck. Draft a settlement proposal that includes detailed justification of the reasonableness of proposed settlement figures.

(2/98) PT-A. *Altaville Police Department*: Substantive law: Labor Law
Tasks: Draft a memo that analyzes employer police department's obligations with respect to certain overtime and union-related issues. Also draft a memo to assist the City Attorney in meeting with the police chief re union activities.

(2/98) PT-B. *F & R v. Michael Klarce, et al.*: Substantive law: Environmental Law
Tasks: Draft a memo to senior partner who is special master in environmental ("Superfund") case, analyzing legal obligations, especially of the defendant. Also prepare a settlement proposal to assist partner to persuade parties that it is in their best interests to settle, proposing a settlement that takes into account fairness and the respective parties' needs and resources.

(7/98) PT-A. *State v. Arthur*: Substantive law: Criminal Procedure
Task: Draft a brief in support of a motion to suppress evidence in a criminal case that arose during the defendant's search at a prison while visiting his inmate brother.

(7/98) PT-B. *Cranfield Downtown Improvement Association*: Substantive law: Constitutional
　　　　　Law
Tasks: Draft a memo that analyzes whether client event being held on public and private property constitutes state action. Also draft an opinion letter to the client re First Amendment limitations, legality of proposed handling of the event, and options available to the client.

<u>(2 /99)</u> PT-A. *BudgeTel v. Ameman*: Substantive law: Torts

Tasks: Draft an internal memo that addresses issues of whether parents are liable for son's computer hacking. Include analysis of theories of liability available to plaintiff phone company and potential defenses, and discussion of how damages claims may potentially be reduced.

<u>(2 /99)</u> PT-B. *People v. Mata*: Substantive law: Criminal Law

Tasks: Draft a trial preparation worksheet that prepares to defend a criminal defendant in misdemeanor battery action. Detailed format included setting out charges and elements of those charges, summary of witness testimony for each element of prima facie case, elements of potential affirmative defenses, summaries of potential defense witnesses, cross-examination, and theory of the case.

<u>(7/99)</u> PT-A. *In re: Stan Richardson*: Substantive law: Professional Responsibility

Task: Draft an internal memo to assist client, a lawyer, in understanding his ethical obligations with respect to pending disciplinary matter relating to past representation of two clients.

<u>(7/99)</u> PT-B. *Westside Community Corporation*: Substantive law: Real Property

Tasks: Draft a memo that analyzes a sale/lease agreement to determine whether it violates the rule against perpetuities and to determine the potential effect of new legislation on certain provisions. Also draft a second memo that discusses proposed alternatives to the client's current plan, incorporating thoughts and suggestions from various Board Members (of client corporation).

<u>(2/00)</u> PT-A. *Carlsbad Pizza Co.*: Substantive law: Partnerships and Family Law

Tasks: Draft an internal memo that explores the client's partnership agreement—specifically what he will receive if he withdraws from the company. Also analyze the interest his wife would receive upon dissolution and advise the client on how to best accomplish his business and personal goals.

<u>(2/00)</u> PT-B. *In re: Sunrise Galleria Mall Curfew*: Substantive law: Constitutional Law

Tasks: Draft an alternative proposal for acceptable language to achieve client (mall's) goals with respect to curfew-related issues. Also draft a letter to the client's general counsel, explaining how the mall's current curfew is unconstitutional, how the new proposal suggested *is* constitutional, and how new alternative proposal meets the client's goals.

<u>(7/00)</u> PT-A. *Berov v. Nadchev*: Substantive law: Labor Law

Task: Draft an internal memo that analyzes whether the plaintiff is covered by minimum wage and overtime provisions of the Fair Labor Standards Act (FLSA), what the plaintiff must prove to assert claimed violation(s), and what defenses are likely to be asserted. In the memo, applicants must analyze provisions of the Act, determine under which portions the plaintiff is likely to recover, and identify additional evidence to be obtained to help prove the plaintiff's claims, where relevant.

<u>(7/02)</u> PT-A. *In re: Thomas Outdoor Advertising*: Substantive law: Constitutional Law
Tasks: Draft a memo that analyzes the constitutionality of a proposed ordinance. Identify and evaluate arguments the senior partner could make on behalf of the client (a private business owner) to the City Attorney, showing that the ordinance in question is unconstitutional. Second, identify ways to modify the ordinance so as to meet the client's and the city's respective needs and concerns and still be constitutional. (Applicants were not to redraft the ordinance itself, but merely to propose and explain suggested modifications.)

<u>(7/02)</u> PT-B. *U.S. v. Alejandro Cruz*: Substantive law: Criminal Law and Procedure, Ethics
Tasks: Draft internal memoranda that identify elements of federal criminal statute and set forth that evidence the government now possesses to prove each of those elements. Also analyze the constitutionality of a burden-shifting provision of the statute. Draft a second memo explaining partner's ethical obligations with respect to the government's request for further information from the client, given that the lawyer obtained significant information from the client in confidence.

<u>(2/03)</u> PT-A. *Morales et al. v. Parsons*: Substantive law: Torts
Task: Draft memo to senior partner presenting persuasive arguments that farm worker plaintiffs and their families assert to prevail in action against landowner assert theories of premises liability and negligence per se.

<u>(2/03)</u> PT-B. *Reese v. Kennel Kare, Inc.*: Substantive law: Civil Procedure/Evidence
Task: Draft memo analyzing pretrial discovery obligations, with particular emphasis on privilege and waiver issues in connection with document production requests.

<u>(7/03)</u> PT-A. *In re: Marriage of Nittardi*: Substantive law: Family Law
Task: Draft opinion letter advising with respect to a divorced parent's rights to move a child out of state. (Applicants were directed to write in a manner that would be clear and understandable to client, a lay person.)

<u>(7/03)</u> PT-B. *In re: Ryan Cox*: Substantive law: Contracts
Task: Draft memo focused on counseling client on numerous issues in a land sale contract. Particular emphasis was to be given to potential remedies if the contract is ultimately enforceable or not.

<u>(2/04)</u> PT-A. *In re: Snow King Mountain Resort*: Substantive law: Torts
Tasks: First draft a persuasive letter to client's insurance company arguing that client falls under certain statutory protection that would reduce their insurance rates. Second, draft memo to client advising how resort should be operated to most likely fall under umbrella of recreational use statute's protection.

(7/00) PT-B. *RTC Partnership*: Substantive law: Professional Responsibility

Task: Draft memos analyzing whether representation of numerous partnerships with overlapping interests and memberships, particularly with respect to certain property acquisitions, creates any actual or potential ethical issues (particularly conflicts of interest), and what action(s) should be taken in light of those issues.

(2/01) PT-A. *Sierra Corp.*: Substantive law: Labor Law

Task: Draft a pre-counseling letter to help CEO of Sierra Corp. company understand its legal obligations in light of union activities, including relevant identification and discussion of corporate goals, NLRB definitions re collective bargaining provisions and scope of coverage, and courses of action available to the company in light of possible union action.

(2/01 PT-B. *State v. Sizemore*: Substantive law: Criminal Law

Task: Draft a closing argument on behalf of prosecution in attempted murder trial of Defendant Sizemore.

(7/01) PT-A. *In re: J.S.*: Substantive law: Public Health Law

Tasks: Draft a memo that sets forth the persuasive arguments that the client (public health department) may advance to involuntarily commit a homeless patient to County Hospital for TB treatment. Set out as well those legal authorities that support commitment, and explain the procedural requirements with which the department must comply. Finally, explore creative alternative solutions for ensuring that the patient gets treatment if the department is unable to commit him.

(7/01) PT-B. *People v. Wils*: Substantive law: Criminal Law

Task: Draft a statement of fact and argument portion of Appellant's opening brief, arguing that the lower court erred in convicting the defendant of robbery and burglary.

(2/02) PT-A. *Estate of Keefe*: Substantive law: Contracts and Civil Procedure

Tasks: Draft declarations for three to four witnesses whose versions of events (when contrasted with those of the defendant) show that there are disputed issues of fact. Next, draft two parts of the plaintiff's (client's) opposition to the defendant's motion for summary judgment, the statement of disputed facts, and the argument portions of brief.

(2/02) PT-B. *Adair v. Oldfield*: Substantive law: Torts

Task: Draft an internal memo that evaluates the likelihood of the client's successfully defending a personal injury lawsuit brought by the plaintiff as a result of a rock-climbing injury, on an express assumption of the risk (waiver) doctrine and/or an implied assumption of the risk theory. Memo is to include discussion of evidentiary concerns, namely what defense expert will be able to testify about.

(2/04) PT-B. *In re: Progressive Builders, Inc.*: Substantive law: Contracts and Arbitration Law
Task: Draft pre-counseling letter to client (lay person and owner of construction company) in anticipation of negotiating home building contract. Applicants were to give special attention to arbitration provisions.

(7/04) PT-A. *Donovan v. Bargain Mart, Inc.*: Substantive law: Consumer Protection
Task: Draft memo identifying claims client may have against a retail store regarding potential check scam. Applicants had to identify elements supporting plaintiffs claims, and both known facts and facts to be discovered to prove those elements.

(7/04) PT-B. *Jaynes v. Palm Gardens Group*: Substantive law: Torts
Task: Draft responsive brief on behalf of plaintiff client opposing defendant's motion to dismiss her claims stemming from injuries she suffered in parking garage of apartment complex owned by defendant.

(2/05) PT-A. *Sandra Castro v. Tom Miller*: Substantive law: Torts
Task : Draft letter on behalf of defendant to opposing counsel for the plaintiff proposing settlement figure (following incident in which defendant's car struck plaintiff while riding on a bicycle) and presenting arguments in support of that figure.

(2/05) PT-B. *Marriage of Eiffel*: Substantive law: Professional Responsibility
Task: Draft statement of facts and argument section of appellant's opening brief in case involving potential ethical issues with respect to lawyer's role in drafting and the enforceability of a marital settlement agreement.

(7/05) PT-A. *In re: Winstons*: Substantive law: Fair Housing Act
Task: Draft letter to Homeowner's Association arguing that they are legally obligated to waive age requirements so that client may move into the community with their disabled son.

(7/05) PT-B. *Property Clerk v. Grinnell*: Substantive law: 8th Amendment and Forfeiture Laws
Task: Draft brief supporting forfeiture action on behalf of City Attorney's seizing of vehicle driven by defendant when he was arrested for driving under the influence.

(2/06) PT-A. *Hensen v. Build A Burger*: Substantive law: Professional Responsibility
Task : Draft brief arguing that law firm violated no ethical rules in certain contacts it had (that defendant alleges were improper ex parte contacts) with two employees of the defendant.

(2/06) PT-B. *Estate of Small*: Substantive law: Wills
Task: Draft statement of facts and argument portions of mediation brief supporting client's position that she should take as an omitted spouse under her deceased husband's will.

<u>(7/06)</u> PT-A. *SavAll Drugstores, Inc. v. Phister Pharmaceuticals Corp.* Substantive law: Evidence

Task: Draft fact statement and argument portions of persuasive brief supporting client's position that defendant is obligated to produce certain electronically stored data.

<u>(7/06)</u> PT-B. *Breene and Frost*: Substantive law: Professional Responsibility

Task: Draft opinion letter to assist senior partner in counseling client (a patent lawyer) as to options available to him to enforce and recover the full amount he believes he is due in a fee-splitting agreement with another lawyer.